IP Telephony Self-Study

Cisco IP Telephony
Flash Cards and
Exam Practice Pack

Kevin Wallace, CCIE No. 7945

IP Telephony Self-Study

Cisco IP Telephony Flash Cards and Exam Practice Pack

Kevin Wallace

Copyright© 2005 Cisco Systems, Inc.

Published by:
Cisco Press
800 East 96th Street
Indianapolis, IN 46240 USA

All rights reserved. No part of this book may be reproduced or transmitted in any form or by any means, electronic or mechanical, including photocopying, recording, or by any information storage and retrieval system, without written permission from the publisher, except for the inclusion of brief quotations in a review.

Printed in the United States of America   1 2 3 4 5 6 7 8 9 0

Library of Congress Cataloging-in-Publication Number: 2004105556

ISBN: 1-58720-128-3

First Printing   October 2004

Trademark Acknowledgments

All terms mentioned in this book that are known to be trademarks or service marks have been appropriately capitalized. Cisco Press or Cisco Systems, Inc. cannot attest to the accuracy of this information. Use of a term in this book should not be regarded as affecting the validity of any trademark or service mark.

Warning and Disclaimer

This book is designed to provide information about the Cisco IP Telephony Certification Exams. Every effort has been made to make this book as complete and as accurate as possible, but no warranty or fitness is implied.

The information is provided on an "as is" basis. The author, Cisco Press, and Cisco Systems, Inc., shall have neither liability nor responsibility to any person or entity with respect to any loss or damages arising from the information contained in this book or from the use of the discs or programs that may accompany it.

The opinions expressed in this book belong to the author and are not necessarily those of Cisco Systems, Inc.

Corporate and Government Sales

Cisco Press offers excellent discounts on this book when ordered in quantity for bulk purchases or special sales.

For more information please contact:
U.S. Corporate and Government Sales 1-800-382-3419
corpsales@pearsontechgroup.com

For sales outside the U.S. please contact:
International Sales international@pearsoned.com

Feedback Information

At Cisco Press, our goal is to create in-depth technical books of the highest quality and value. Each book is crafted with care and precision, undergoing rigorous development that involves the unique expertise of members from the professional technical community.

Readers' feedback is a natural continuation of this process. If you have any comments regarding how we could improve the quality of this book, or otherwise alter it to better suit your needs, you can contact us through e-mail at feedback@ciscopress.com. Please make sure to include the book title and ISBN in your message.

We greatly appreciate your assistance.

Credits

Publisher	John Wait
Editor-in-Chief	John Kane
Executive Editor	Brett Bartow
Acquisitions Editor	Michelle Grandin
Cisco Representative	Anthony Wolfenden
Cisco Press Program Manager	Nannette M. Noble
Production Manager	Patrick Kanouse
Senior Editor	San Dee Phillips
Copy Editor	John Edwards
Technical Editors	Jeremy Cioara, Jose Martinez, Paul Giralt
Media Developer	Brandon Penticuff and Boson Software
Editorial Assistant	Tammi Barnett
Cover Designer	Louisa Adair
Interior Designer and Compositor	Mark Shirar
Proofreader	Karen A. Gill

CISCO SYSTEMS

Corporate Headquarters
Cisco Systems, Inc.
170 West Tasman Drive
San Jose, CA 95134-1706
USA
www.cisco.com
Tel: 408 526-4000
    800 553-NETS (6387)
Fax: 408 526-4100

European Headquarters
Cisco Systems International BV
Haarlerbergpark
Haarlerbergweg 13-19
1101 CH Amsterdam
The Netherlands
www-europe.cisco.com
Tel: 31 0 20 357 1000
Fax: 31 0 20 357 1100

Americas Headquarters
Cisco Systems, Inc.
170 West Tasman Drive
San Jose, CA 95134-1706
USA
www.cisco.com
Tel: 408 526-7660
Fax: 408 527-0883

Asia Pacific Headquarters
Cisco Systems, Inc.
Capital Tower
168 Robinson Road
#22-01 to #29-01
Singapore 068912
www.cisco.com
Tel: +65 6317 7777
Fax: +65 6317 7799

Cisco Systems has more than 200 offices in the following countries and regions. Addresses, phone numbers, and fax numbers are listed on the
Cisco.com Web site at www.cisco.com/go/offices.

Argentina • Australia • Austria • Belgium • Brazil • Bulgaria • Canada • Chile • China PRC • Colombia • Costa Rica • Croatia • Czech Republic
Denmark • Dubai, UAE • Finland • France • Germany • Greece • Hong Kong SAR • Hungary • India • Indonesia • Ireland • Israel • Italy
Japan • Korea • Luxembourg • Malaysia • Mexico • The Netherlands • New Zealand • Norway • Peru • Philippines • Poland • Portugal
Puerto Rico • Romania • Russia • Saudi Arabia • Scotland • Singapore • Slovakia • Slovenia • South Africa • Spain • Sweden
Switzerland • Taiwan • Thailand • Turkey • Ukraine • United Kingdom • United States • Venezuela • Vietnam • Zimbabwe

Copyright © 2003 Cisco Systems, Inc. All rights reserved. CCIP, CCSP, the Cisco Arrow logo, the Cisco *Powered* Network mark, the Cisco Systems Verified logo, Cisco Unity, Follow Me Browsing, FormShare, iQ Net Readiness Scorecard, Networking Academy, and ScriptShare are trademarks of Cisco Systems, Inc.; Changing the Way We Work, Live, Play, and Learn, The Fastest Way to Increase Your Internet Quotient, and iQuick Study are service marks of Cisco Systems, Inc.; and Aironet, ASIST, BPX, Catalyst, CCDA, CCDP, CCIE, CCNA, CCNP, Cisco, the Cisco Certified Internetwork Expert logo, Cisco IOS, the Cisco IOS logo, Cisco Press, Cisco Systems, Cisco Systems Capital, the Cisco Systems logo, Empowering the Internet Generation, Enterprise/Solver, EtherChannel, EtherSwitch, Fast Step, GigaStack, Internet Quotient, IOS, IP/TV, iQ Expertise, the iQ logo, LightStream, MGX, MICA, the Networkers logo, Network Registrar, *Packet*, PIX, Post-Routing, Pre-Routing, RateMUX, Registrar, SlideCast, SMARTnet, StrataView Plus, Stratm, SwitchProbe, TeleRouter, TransPath, and VCO are registered trademarks of Cisco Systems, Inc. and/or its affiliates in the U.S. and certain other countries.

All other trademarks mentioned in this document or Web site are the property of their respective owners. The use of the word partner does not imply a partnership relationship between Cisco and any other company. (0303R)

Printed in the USA

About the Author

Kevin Wallace, CCIE No. 7945, CCSI, CCNP, CCDP, MCSE 4, CNE 4/5, is a full-time instructor for KnowledgeNet, a pioneer of next-generation e-learning. With 15 years of Cisco internetworking experience, Kevin has been a network design specialist for The Walt Disney World Resort and a network manager for Eastern Kentucky University. Kevin holds a bachelor of science degree in electrical engineering from the University of Kentucky. Among Kevin's other publication credits are the *CCDA/CCDP Flash Cards and Exam Practice Pack* and the *CCIE Routing and Switching Flash Cards and Exam Practice Pack,* both coauthored with Anthony Sequeria and available from Cisco Press. In addition, Kevin authored the Cisco Enterprise Voice over Data Design (EVoDD) 3.3 course and has written for the Cisco *Packet* magazine. Kevin also holds the IP Telephony Design Specialist and IP Telephony Support Specialist CQS certifications.

About the Technical Reviewers

Jeremy D. Cioara, CCIE, MCSE 4/2000, CNE 4/5, is a trainer at KnowledgeNet, a Cisco Learning Partner providing career Cisco certification training. In addition to training in all major certification programs (Cisco, Microsoft, and Novell) for more than seven years, he has authored many books, including *Cisco IP Telephony (CIPT) 3.3 Curriculum* and *Cisco IP Telephony Troubleshooting (IPTT) 3.3 Curriculum,* and he attained the three Cisco IP Telephony Specialist certifications. Outside of training, Jeremy has consulted for companies such as Qwest, MicroAge, Terminal Processing Systems, and IKON.

Paul Giralt, CCIE R&S, CCIE Voice No. 4793, is an escalation engineer at the Cisco Systems Technical Assistance Center in Research Triangle Park, NC. He has been troubleshooting complex IP telephony networks since the release of CallManager 3.0. Paul has troubleshot problems in some of the largest Cisco IP Telephony deployments and has provided training for TAC teams around the globe. He holds a bachelor of science degree in computer engineering from the University of Miami and is the author of *Troubleshooting Cisco IP Telephony.*

Jose Martinez, CCIE No. 1690, is an escalation engineer at the Cisco Systems Technical Assistance Center in Research Triangle Park, NC. Since 1995, he has worked in the TAC, supporting multiple technologies, including IBM protocols, L2 and L3 switches, and most recently, IP telephony. As an escalation engineer, Jose has been involved in numerous network deployments. He has troubleshot problems involving critical situations in customer's networks and has provided training to other Cisco engineers, partners, and customers.

Dedication

This book is dedicated to my late father, Lowell Wallace. He worked for the local telephone company (GTE) for more than 30 years. My passion for telephony is merely a reflection of his.

Acknowledgments

My family's unending support made this book possible. Vivian, my lovely bride of ten years, is always by my side cheering me on to the next level. My oldest daughter Stacie wants to be an artist when she grows up. Who knows, maybe she can illustrate a book with me in a few years, although she likes drawing horses more than routers right now. My youngest daughter Sabrina was thoroughly embarrassed by my acknowledgment of her in my last book. After she read her name, she said, "Dad. It's embarrassing. Now everyone in the whole world is going to know who I am." Well, Sabrina, I've done it again, and I'm proud for the whole world to know you're mine.

The instructor team at KnowledgeNet, lead by Tom Warrick, fosters an environment of continual growth. What a privilege it is to work with you. Michelle Grandin and the whole team at Cisco Press, you are a class act. And as always, I acknowledge my Heavenly Father for His blessings on my life.

Table of Contents

Foreword

Cisco IP Telephony Flash Cards and Exam Practice Pack is a late-stage practice tool that provides you with a variety of proven exam-preparation methods, including physical and electronic flash cards, study- and practice-mode assessment tests, and review-oriented quick reference sheets. Together, these elements help you assess your knowledge of IP Telephony concepts and focus your practice on those areas where you need the most help. This book was developed in cooperation with the Cisco Internet Learning Solutions Group. Cisco Press books are the only self-study books authorized by Cisco Systems for Cisco IP Telephony exam preparation.

Cisco and Cisco Press present this material in a text-based format to provide another learning vehicle for our customers and the broader user community in general. Although a publication does not duplicate the instructor-led or e-learning environment, we acknowledge that not everyone responds in the same way to the same delivery mechanism. It is our intent that presenting this material through a Cisco Press publication will enhance the transfer of knowledge to a broad audience of networking professionals.

Cisco Press will present existing and future practice test products through these Flash Cards and Exam Practice Packs to help achieve the Cisco Internet Learning Solutions Group's principal objectives: to educate the Cisco community of networking professionals and to enable that community to build and maintain reliable, scalable networks. The Cisco Career Certifications and classes that support these certifications are directed at meeting these objectives through a disciplined approach to progressive learning. To succeed on the Cisco Career Certifications exams, in your daily job as a Cisco certified professional, we recommend a blended learning solution that combines instructor-led, e-learning, and self- study training with hands-on experience. Cisco Systems has created an authorized Cisco Learning Partner program to provide you with the most highly qualified instruction and invaluable hands-on experience in lab and simulation environments. To learn more about Cisco Learning Partner programs available in your area, please go to www.cisco.com/go/authorizedtraining.

The books Cisco Press creates, in partnership with Cisco Systems, meet the same standards for content quality demanded of the courses and certifications. Our intent is that you will find this and subsequent Cisco Press certification and training publications of value as you build your networking knowledge base.

Thomas M. Kelly
Vice President, Internet Learning Solutions Group
Cisco Systems, Inc.
September 2004

Introduction

Since the Cisco Systems, Inc. career certification programs were announced in 1998, they have been the most sought-after and prestigious certifications in the networking industry. Among the Cisco career certifications are the focused certifications, designed to demonstrate competency in specific areas of technology. The pinnacle of the four IP telephony focused certifications is the IP Telephony Support Specialist. In addition to possessing the coveted CCNP certification, the IP Telephony Support Specialist also requires successful completion of the CVOICE, CIPT, and QOS exams.

Notorious as being some of the most difficult certifications in the networking industry, Cisco exams can cause much stress to the ill-prepared. Unlike other certification exams, the Cisco exams require that students truly understand the material instead of just memorizing answers. This pack has been designed to help you assess whether you are prepared to pass the IP Telephony Support Specialist exams. This pack contains flash cards that assist in memorization, quick reference sheets that provide condensed exam information, and a powerful exam engine to help you determine whether you are prepared for the actual exams.

The Purpose of Flash Cards

For years, flash cards have been recognized as a quick and effective study aid. They have been used to complement classroom training and significantly boost memory retention. The flash cards in this pack serve as a final preparation tool for the CVOICE, CIPT, and QOS exams.

These flash cards work best when used in conjunction with official study aids for the CVOICE, CIPT, and QOS exams. Table I-1 presents the required exams and recommended study for IP Telephony Specialization. Note that these cards and quick reference sheets can be used in conjunction with any other CVOICE, CIPT, and QOS exam preparation book or course of study. They might also be useful to you as a quick desk or field reference guide.

Table I-1 Exams and Courses Required to Achieve the IP Telephony Support Specialist Focused Certification*

Exam Number	Name	Course Most Closely Matching Exam Requirements
642-432	CVOICE exam	Cisco Voice over IP (CVOICE)
642-443	CIPT exam	Cisco IP Telephony (CIPT)
642-642	QOS exam	Implementing Cisco Quality of Service (QOS)

*NOTE: CCNP certification is a prerequisite.

Who These Flash Cards Are For

These flash cards are designed for network administrators, network designers, and any professional or student looking to advance his or her career through achieving the Cisco IP Telephony Support Specialist focused certification.

How to Use These Flash Cards

Review one section at a time, reading each flash card until you can answer it correctly on your own. When you can correctly answer every card in a given section, move on to the next.

These flash cards are a condensed form of study and review. Don't rush to move through each section. The amount of time you spend reviewing the cards directly affects how long you'll be able to retain the information needed to pass the test. A couple of days before your exam, review each section as a final refresher.

Although these flash cards are designed to be used as a final-stage study aid (30 days before the exam), they also can be used in the following situations:

- **Prestudy evaluation**—Before charting out your course of study, read one or two questions at the beginning and end of every section to gauge your competence in the specific areas.

- **Reinforcement of key topics**—After you complete your study in each area, read through the answer cards (on the left side of the pages) to identify key topics and reinforce concepts.

- **Identifying areas for last-minute review**—In the days before an exam, review the study cards and carefully note your areas of weakness. Concentrate your remaining study time on these areas.

- **Poststudy quiz**—By flipping through this book at random and viewing the questions on the right side of the pages, you can randomize your self-quiz to be sure you're prepared in all areas.

- **Desk reference or field guide to core concepts (quick reference sheets section only)**—Networking professionals, sales representatives, and help-desk technicians alike can benefit from a handy, simple-to-navigate book that outlines the major topics aligned with networking principles and the Cisco IP Telephony Support Specialist focused certification.

Quick Reference Sheets

At the back of this book, you will find nearly 100 pages of quick reference sheets. These sheets serve as both a study guide for the CVOICE, CIPT, QOS exams and as a companion reference to the text. For readers who seek the IP Telephony Support Specialist focused certification, these quick reference sheets are well suited to reinforce the concepts learned in the text rather than as a sole source of information. For readers who have either already obtained IP Telephony Support Specialist focused certification or simply need a basic overview, these sheets can serve as a standalone reference. A complete set of the notes can also be printed from the enclosed CD-ROM.

What Is Included on the CD-ROM

The CD-ROM includes copies of the 450 flash cards and quick reference sheets presented in the physical set. Also included is an electronic version of the flash cards that runs on all Windows and Palm platforms. The CD-ROM allows you to shuffle the flash cards so that you can randomize your study. The CD-ROM also includes a powerful 550-question practice test engine designed to simulate each of the CVOICE, CIPT, and QOS exams. The practice test engine will help you become familiar with the format of the exams and reinforce the knowledge needed to pass them.

Special Features

You might notice that some flash cards on the CD-ROM provide pointers to the quick reference sheets included on PDF, to provide you with an additional mode of reviewing. Additional CD-ROM features include the following:

- Palm Pilot format so that you can study for the CVOICE, CIPT, and QOS exams on your Palm
- The ability to shuffle the flash cards and the option to review custom sets that focus your study on difficult terms, basic concepts, or a "final exam"

PART I QOS

QOS Section 1
QoS Overview

Many of today's networks support voice, video, and data traffic flowing side by side over the same physical medium. When congestion occurs on the network (perhaps because of a temporary lack of available bandwidth), some traffic types (for example, voice) might react more adversely than other traffic types (for example, FTP). Fortunately, Cisco offers a plethora of quality of service (QoS) solutions that allow a designer to proactively create policies for various applications. For example, you might want to give video conference traffic 512 kbps of bandwidth, and you might want those packets treated with higher priority than Telnet traffic. QoS features that are available on our Cisco devices support the creation of just such a policy.

The flash cards in this section review the need for QoS and challenge your knowledge of the three basic steps to configure QoS solutions. Finally, these flash cards assess your understanding of the various methods for deploying QoS features in an enterprise network.

Question 1

List the three main converged network quality issues, in the absence of QoS.

Question 2

When two devices are communicating across multiple network links, what determines the effective bandwidth (that is, the available bandwidth) between those devices?

Question 3

Describe the purpose of queuing.

Question 1 Answer

Without QoS, today's converged networks (that is, networks that carry voice, video, and data) can suffer from one or more of the following issues:

- **Delay**—Delay is the time that is required for a packet to travel from its source to its destination.
- **Jitter**—Jitter is the uneven arrival of packets.
- **Drops**—Packet drops occur, for example, when a link is congested and a buffer overflows.

Question 2 Answer

As a packet travels from its source to its destination, its effective bandwidth is the bandwidth of the slowest link along that path. As an analogy, consider water flowing through a series of pipes with varying diameters. The water's flow rate through those pipes is limited to the water's flow rate through the pipe that has the smallest diameter.

Question 3 Answer

Queuing determines in what order packets are emptied from an interface's output queue. Queuing can send higher-priority traffic ahead of lower-priority traffic and make specific amounts of bandwidth available for those traffic types. Therefore, queuing can reduce delay, jitter, and packet drops for specific traffic types.

Question 4

Describe the advantage of using compression technologies on slow-speed links.

Question 5

List the three basic steps to QoS configuration. (Note that this question is not referring to the three-step modular QoS CLI (MQC) process.)

Question 6

List four approaches for QoS deployment in a network.

Question 4 Answer

By compressing a packet's header or payload, fewer bits are sent across the link. This effectively provides more bandwidth.

Question 5 Answer

The three basic steps to QoS configuration are the following:

Step 1   Determine the network performance requirements for various traffic types.

Step 2   Arrange the traffic in specific categories.

Step 3   Document your QoS policy, and make it available to your users.

Question 6 Answer

The four approaches to QoS deployment follow:

- Command-Line Interface (CLI)
- Modular QoS CLI (MQC)
- AutoQoS
- QoS Policy Manager (QPM)

Note that Cisco recommends QPM for large enterprise environments, because QPM works in conjunction with CiscoWorks to centralize QoS configuration. Policies that are created with QPM can be pushed out to routers throughout an enterprise, thus reducing the potential for misconfiguration.

Question 7

What types of Cisco networking devices support the AutoQoS feature?

Question 8

As a design best practice, what should be the maximum one-way delay for voice traffic?

Question 9

Name an advantage of MQC over CLI as the two relate to QoS deployment.

Question 7 Answer

Many Cisco routers and switches support the AutoQoS feature, which automates the process of QoS configuration. AutoQoS is designed to prioritize the treatment of VoIP packets. The features that are enabled by AutoQoS, however, differ between switches and routers.

Question 8 Answer

Based on the G.114 recommendation, the one-way delay for voice packets should be no more than 150 ms.

Question 9 Answer

The Modular QoS CLI (MQC) allows a global policy to be configured. You then can apply that global policy to multiple interfaces on a router. Conversely, the CLI approach to QoS configuration requires specific QoS settings to be configured on an interface-by-interface basis. Therefore, MQC is more scalable than CLI, and configuration errors are less likely to occur.

Question 10

As a design best practice, what should be the maximum jitter (in milliseconds) for interactive video traffic?

Question 10 Answer

For both voice and interactive video traffic, the maximum jitter experienced should be no more than 30 ms.

QOS Section 2
QoS Components

All Cisco QoS tools fall in one of three categories. The flash cards in this section review the characteristics of those categories. However, the primary category that I focus on is Differentiated Services (DiffServ). These flash cards verify your understanding of how the DiffServ model differentiates between flows through packet marking.

Focusing on the DiffServ model, you need to understand the benefits that are offered by various categories of QoS tools (for example, congestion-management tools). Finally, these flash cards challenge you to identify specific QoS tools in these DiffServ categories.

Question 1

Identify the three broad categories of QoS tools.

Question 2

RSVP falls under which category of QoS tools?

Question 3

What byte in an IPv4 packet header can you use for IP Precedence or Differentiated Services Code Point (DSCP) markings?

Question 1 Answer

All of the Cisco QoS tools fall in one of the following categories:

- Best-Effort
- Integrated Services (IntServ)
- Differentiated Services (DiffServ)

Note that the Best-Effort category does not truly perform QoS packet manipulation. Rather, Best-Effort uses the first-in first-out (FIFO) queuing strategy, in which packets are emptied from a queue in the same order that they entered it. FIFO is the default behavior on high-speed interfaces (that is, interfaces that run at speeds of 2.048 Mbps or greater).

Question 2 Answer

RSVP (Resource Reservation Protocol) is considered to be an Integrated Services (IntServ) QoS tool because it uses signaling to request network resources for applications. RSVP does not rely on packet marking, as DiffServ approaches do.

Question 3 Answer

You can use the type of service (ToS) byte in an IPv4 packet header for QoS markings at Layer 3. Specifically, the IP Precedence marking uses the 3 leftmost bits in the ToS byte, whereas DSCP uses the 6 leftmost bits in that ToS byte.

Question 4

How many levels of priority can be specified using DSCP?

Question 5

Which of the following per-hop behaviors (PHBs) have the highest drop preference?

- AF11
- AF12
- AF22
- AF43

Question 6

Which QoS tool does the Cisco IOS use to prevent a queue from ever filling to capacity?

Question 4 Answer

DSCP uses the 6 leftmost bits in an IPv4 header's ToS byte. These 6 bits have 64 possible binary combinations. Therefore, DSCP can specify up to 64 levels of priority, in the range of 0 through 63.

Question 5 Answer

Of the PHBs listed, the AF12 value has the highest drop preference. The Assured Forwarding (AF) PHBs are divided into four classes. Lower classes have higher drop preferences. For example, all AF1 PHBs have a higher drop preference than any AF2 PHBs. Within a class, there are three PHB values (indicated by the last digit in the PHB). A 1 indicates the lowest drop preference, a 2 indicates a medium drop preference, and a 3 indicates the highest drop preference. Therefore, within the AF1 class, AF13 has a higher drop preference than AF12, which has a higher drop preference than AF11.

Question 6 Answer

Cisco IOS can use Weighted Random Early Detection (WRED) to prevent an interface's output queue from ever filling to capacity by discarding traffic more aggressively as the queue begins to fill. Dropping decisions are made based on the traffic's priority markings.

Question 7

You can use both policing and shaping tools to limit bandwidth that is available to specific traffic. Discuss how policing and shaping differ.

Question 8

How many levels of priority can you specify using IP Precedence?

Question 9

Which type of PHB is completely backward compatible with IP Precedence?

Question 7 Answer

Policing typically limits traffic rates by dropping excess traffic. However, shaping limits traffic rates by delaying excess traffic (that is, by buffering the excess traffic). Policing, unlike shaping, can also mark packets. In addition, you can apply policing either in the inbound or outbound direction on an interface, whereas you can apply only shaping in the outbound direction.

Question 8 Answer

IP Precedence uses the 3 leftmost bits in an IPv4 header's ToS byte. These 3 bits have eight possible binary combinations. Therefore, IP Precedence can specify up to eight levels of priority, in the range of 0 through 7. However, Cisco recommends that values 6 and 7 never be used, because they are reserved for network use.

Question 9 Answer

The Class Selector (CS) PHBs are backward compatible with IP Precedence values, because just like IP Precedence, Class Selector PHBs have 0s in the 4th, 5th, and 6th bits of the ToS byte.

Question 10

List two approaches to link efficiency.

Question 11

Describe how LFI contributes to link efficiency.

Question 12

List the four categories of PHBs, as defined by the Internet Engineering Task Force (IETF).

Question 10 Answer

Link efficiency mechanisms make the most of the limited bandwidth that is available on a relatively slower-speed interface. Two common approaches are header compression (for example, Real-Time Transport Protocol [RTP] header compression or Transport Control Protocol [TCP] header compression) and Link Fragmentation and Interleaving (LFI).

Question 11 Answer

LFI addresses the issue of *serialization delay*, which is the amount of time required for a packet to exit an interface. A large data packet, for example, on a slower-speed link could create excessive delay for a voice packet because of the time required for the data packet to exit the interface. LFI fragments the large packets and interleaves the smaller packets among the fragments, reducing the serialization delay that the smaller packets experience.

Question 12 Answer

The IETF defines the following four categories of PHBs:

- **Default**—Traffic that needs only best-effort treatment can be marked with the Default PHB, which has a decimal value of 0.

- **Expedited Forwarding (EF)**—This category has a DSCP value of 46 and is used for latency-sensitive applications such as voice or video.

- **Assured Forwarding (AF)**—This is the broadest category of PHBs, in which up to 12 values can be assigned to various traffic classes.

- **Class Selector (CS)**—This category provides backward compatibility with IP Precedence markings.

Question 13

You mark a mission-critical application with a DSCP value of AF43. Without enabling any other QoS mechanisms on the network, how does the network treat the packet that you marked?

Question 14

Define *tail drop*.

Question 13 Answer

Marking alone does not change how the network treats a packet. Other tools (for example, queuing tools) can, however, reference those markings and make decisions based on them.

Question 14 Answer

Tail drop occurs when an interface's output queue fills to capacity, and newly arriving packets are discarded because no room exists in the buffer (that is, in the queue). The dropping of these newly arriving packets is called *tail drop*.

QOS Section 3
Basic QoS Configuration

Other than using the QoS Policy Manager (QPM), which relies on
CiscoWorks, the primary ways to configure QoS features on Cisco routers
are the Modular Quality of Service Command-Line Interface (MQC) and
AutoQoS. The flash cards in this section review the characteristics of these
approaches.

A primary focus of these flash cards is syntax. After you master the syntax
for the three steps of MQC, you can leverage MQC to configure a wide
variety of QoS mechanisms. The AutoQoS feature has varying syntax,
which is platform specific. You also are challenged to recall which specific
QoS features are enabled by AutoQoS on a specific platform.

Question 1

List the three steps for configuring MQC.

Question 2

What is the default class-map behavior when multiple match statements are configured under a single class-map?

Question 3

Which command would you use to apply a policy-map named VOICE in the outbound direction on an interface?

Question 1 Answer

The MQC is a process for configuring multiple QoS mechanisms. The three basic steps to MQC are as follows:

Step 1 Classify traffic by creating class-maps.

Step 2 Create a policy-map to specify how the router treats packets in the various class-maps.

Step 3 Apply the policy-map to an interface with the **service-policy** command.

Question 2 Answer

When a class-map contains more than one **match** statement, by default, for a packet to be classified by the class-map, it must meet the criteria of all the configured **match** statements. This default behavior is called match-all. Optionally, a class-map can be configured as match-any, which classifies a packet under a class-map if a single match criterion is met.

Question 3 Answer

To apply a policy-map to an interface, which is the third step of the MQC, use the following command:

```
Router(config-if)#service-policy {input | output} policy-map-name
```

In this example, the command would be as follows:

```
Router(config-if)#service-policy output VOICE
```

Question 4

Which command would you use to view policy-map statistics for packets that are crossing a specific interface?

Question 5

Identify the command that enables you to view the traffic that is matched by all the class-maps on a router.

Question 6

Which command enables you to view the policy that is applied to the classes within a policy-map?

Question 4 Answer

In addition to showing how traffic is classified and what policies are applied to those traffic classes, the following command displays traffic statistics:

```
show policy-map interface interface-identifier [input | output]
```

This command indicates that packets are being classified on a particular interface.

Question 5 Answer

The command **show class-map** lists the match criteria that all class-maps on the router use. Optionally, you can specify the specific class-map that you want to interrogate.

Question 6 Answer

The command **show policy-map** [*policy-map-name*] shows the specific policies (for example, bandwidth allocations or policing limits) that are applied to classes of traffic within a class-map.

Question 7

If you do not match specific traffic with a class-map, in what predefined class-map is the traffic placed?

Question 8

How many class-maps can you associate with a single policy-map?

Question 9

Identify at least three router platforms that support the AutoQoS feature.

Question 7 Answer

Traffic that you do not explicitly match with a class-map is placed in the **class-default** class-map. This class-map is created by default and cannot be deleted. It contains a single **match** statement that matches **any** traffic. In a policy-map, the **class-default** class-map is placed automatically at the bottom of the class-maps that you configure. Therefore, the **class-default** class-map only classifies traffic that you did not otherwise classify.

Question 8 Answer

You can associate up to 256 class-maps with a single policy-map. However, for queuing configurations such as Class-Based Weighted Fair Queuing (CB-WFQ) and Low Latency Queuing (LLQ), you can use only 64 class-maps. These numbers include the **class-default** class-map, which is preconfigured and cannot be deleted.

Question 9 Answer

The following router platforms support the AutoQoS feature, which automatically configures a router with QoS policies that are targeted toward the optimization of VoIP traffic:

- 1700 Series
- 2600 Series
- 3600 Series
- 3700 Series
- 7200 Series

Question 10

Identify at least three Catalyst switch platforms that support the AutoQoS feature.

Question 11

Which command would you enter on a router's serial interface, configured for PPP encapsulation, to enable the AutoQoS feature to classify VoIP using Network-Based Application Recognition (NBAR)?

Question 12

List at least two prerequisites for configuring AutoQoS on a router interface.

Question 10 Answer

The following Catalyst switch platforms support the AutoQoS feature:

- 2950(EI)
- 3550
- 4500
- 6500

It is critical to note that only the Enhanced Image (EI) version of the Catalyst 2950 supports the AutoQoS feature.

Question 11 Answer

The syntax for configuring AutoQoS on a router interface is as follows:

```
auto qos voip [trust] [fr-atm]
```

The **trust** option tells AutoQoS to classify voice packets based on Differentiated Services Code Point (DSCP) values instead of NBAR. The **fr-atm** option enables the AutoQoS feature for Frame Relay–to–ATM links and is issued from the Data Link Connection Identifier (DLCI) configuration mode. Therefore, in this example, the interface-configuration-mode command that should be entered is as follows:

```
auto qos voip
```

Question 12 Answer

The following are prerequisites for configuring AutoQoS on a router interface:

- No QoS policy currently attached to interface
- Bandwidth configured on the interface
- IP address configured on the interface
- Interface not administratively shut down
- CEF required if the **trust** keyword is not used

Question 13

On what platform would you use the set qos autoqos command to enable AutoQoS globally?

Question 14

When you are configuring AutoQoS, under what circumstance would Cisco Discovery Protocol (CDP) version 2 be required on a Catalyst 6500 port?

Question 15

Which type of congestion-management feature does AutoQoS configure on an IOS-based Catalyst switch?

Question 13 Answer

You can enable AutoQoS on a Catalyst 6500 running in Hybrid mode with the command **set qos autoqos**. After enabling AutoQoS globally, you next enable AutoQoS for a specific port or ports with the following command:

```
set port qos autoqos <mod/port> trust [cos | dscp]
```

Question 14 Answer

When you are configuring AutoQoS on a Catalyst 6500, you must enable CDP version 2 for the port in order for it to detect its connection to a Cisco IP Phone.

Question 15 Answer

On a router platform, the AutoQoS feature configures LLQ as the congestion-management feature. However, on an IOS-based Catalyst platform, AutoQoS configures the Weighted Round Robin (WRR) congestion-management mechanism.

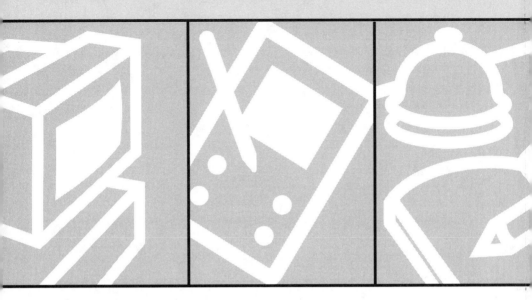

QOS Section 4
Traffic Classification and Marking

As traffic begins its journey through the network, the first QoS mechanism that typically is applied is classification. When traffic is classified, it is categorized based on one or more characteristics, such as the interface on which it entered the router or by matching an access list. After traffic is classified, you can mark it so that other devices in the network (for example, switches and routers) can reference those markings and make decisions (for example, dropping or forwarding decisions) based on those markings.

These flash cards challenge you to recall various approaches to classification and marking, including syntax. Classification and marking over a Border Gateway Protocol (BGP) network and over a Virtual Private Network (VPN) are considered also. Finally, these flash cards address classification and marking on the LAN, using Catalyst switches. Specifically, the features and syntax of the Catalyst 2950 switch are addressed.

Question 1

What range of values can be used for a class of service (CoS) marking?

Question 2

The IEEE 802.1p standard defines what type of marking?

Question 3

In a Frame Relay network, what bit can you set in a frame to indicate to the service provider that the frame can be discarded during periods of congestion?

Question 1 Answer

A class of service marking is a Layer 2 marking that is used over a trunk connection (that is, either an IEEE 802.1Q or Inter-Switch Link [ISL] trunk) to identify the priority of a frame. Three bits are used for the CoS marking. Therefore, eight possible CoS values exist, in the range of 0 to 7. As a design best practice, Cisco recommends not using CoS values of 6 or 7 because they are reserved for network use.

Question 2 Answer

An IEEE 802.1Q trunk can use 3 bits in one of its tag-control bytes for a CoS marking. An ISL trunk uses 3 bits in the ISL header for CoS markings. However, the IEEE 802.1p standard refers to CoS markings over an IEEE 802.1Q trunk.

Question 3 Answer

You can mark the Discard Eligible (DE) bit within a Frame Relay frame to indicate to the service provider which frames it can drop during periods of congestion.

Question 4

In an Asynchronous Transfer Mode (ATM) network, what bit can you set in a cell to indicate to the service provider that a cell can be discarded during periods of congestion?

Question 5

Define a trust boundary.

Question 6

List at least three criteria that you can use to match traffic as part of a class-map.

Question 4 Answer

You can mark the Cell Loss Priority (CLP) bit within an ATM cell to indicate to the service provider which cells it can drop during periods of congestion.

Question 5 Answer

A *trust boundary* is the point in the network that does not trust incoming markings. Cisco recommends that a trust boundary be placed near the source. An example of a device that would form a trust boundary is a wiring-closet switch that does not trust incoming markings from attached devices.

Question 6 Answer

In class-map configuration mode, you can use **match** statements to classify traffic based on one or more of the following criteria:

- Access control lists (ACLs)
- Existing markings (for example, CoS, IP Precedence, or DSCP)
- QoS group (a locally significant grouping of packets)
- Protocol (using Network-Based Application Recognition [NBAR])
- Traffic that matches another class-map
- Incoming interface
- Media Access Control (MAC) address (source or destination)
- Range of UDP port numbers

Question 7

What single match statement in class-map configuration mode matches traffic that has a CoS value of 1, 2, or 3?

Question 8

In policy-map-class configuration mode, what command can you use to mark traffic with a Differentiated Services Code Point (DSCP) value of AF11?

Question 9

What show command can you issue to view all the class-based marking policies on a router?

Question 7 Answer

In class-map configuration mode, the **match cos** command matches up to four CoS values, with the values separated with a space. In this case, the command to match CoS values of 1, 2, or 3 is **match cos 1 2 3**.

Question 8 Answer

With current versions of the IOS, you can use either of the following commands to mark traffic with a DSCP value of AF11:

```
set ip dscp af11
set dscp af11
```

Note that prior to IOS 12.2(13T) only the **set ip dscp af11** command was valid.

Question 9 Answer

Class-based marking parameters are configured within a policy-map. Therefore, you can view these parameters with the **show policy-map** command.

Question 10

How is NBAR's classification ability more granular than an extended access list?

Question 11

Which type of file can a router reference to extend NBAR's ability to recognize traffic types?

Question 12

Which interface configuration-mode command enables NBAR protocol discovery?

Question 10 Answer

NBAR can look beyond Layer 3 or Layer 4 information. In fact, it can examine Layer 7 information, such as URL strings. NBAR is also useful for classifying **stateful** protocols, which can change port numbers.

Question 11 Answer

A Packet Description Language Module (PDLM) is a file that the IOS can reference to extend NBAR's ability to recognize traffic types. For example, the kazaa2.pdlm file could be installed in a router's flash and be referenced with the **ip nbar pdlm flash://kazaa2.pdlm** command to allow a router to recognize KaZaa version 2 traffic.

Question 12 Answer

In addition to NBAR's ability to classify traffic, it also can be used to gather statistics about traffic that is flowing across an interface. This feature is called *NBAR protocol discovery*. As an example, NBAR protocol discovery can identify the five "top talkers" on an interface (that is, the five applications that are consuming the most bandwidth on an interface). The NBAR protocol discovery feature is enabled with the interface configuration-mode command **ip nbar protocol-discovery**.

Question 13

Which command can you use to view NBAR's protocol discovery statistics?

Question 14

In class-map configuration mode, what match statement invokes the NBAR feature?

Question 15

Which command points a router's configuration to a PDLM file?

Question 13 Answer

NBAR protocol discovery can gather traffic statistics for an interface, such as the top talkers for that interface. To view these statistics, use the **show ip nbar protocol-discovery** command.

Question 14 Answer

NBAR is being used whenever the **match protocol** *protocol* command is used in class-map configuration mode. NBAR offers an advantage over other classification mechanisms, because it can look beyond Layer 3 or Layer 4 information, all the way up to Layer 7.

Question 15 Answer

A PDLM can extend a router's ability to recognize applications. In global configuration mode, you can point to a PDLM file with the **ip pdlm** *pdlm-file* command. For example, if you copy the edonkey.pdlm file to the router's flash, you can point to it with the **ip nbar pdlm flash://** **edonkey.pdlm** command.

Question 16

Which match command can match the content of a URL string?

Question 17

Explain the challenge of applying QoS mechanisms to tunneled packets.

Question 18

Which command enables the tunnel pre-classification feature?

Question 16 Answer

NBAR can match traffic based on Layer 7 URL content. The format of the command, in class-map configuration mode, is as follows:

```
match protocol http url url-string
```

For example, to match web pages that have the word *cisco* in a URL, perhaps as part of a graphics image name on the page, you could use the following command:

```
match protocol http url "*cisco*"
```

Question 17 Answer

A tunnel encapsulates packets inside tunnel packets. Tunneling is used commonly in VPN deployments. The challenge of applying QoS mechanisms to tunneled packets is that all packets have the same level of priority, because classification is based on the tunnel header, not on the original packet header.

Question 18 Answer

Cisco's tunnel pre-classification feature can overcome the issue of applying QoS mechanisms to tunneled packets by classifying packets before they are encapsulated in a tunnel. The **qos pre-classify** command enables the pre-classification feature. Note that the configuration mode from which you issue the **pre-classify** command varies based on the type of tunnel that you are dealing with. For example, you can give the command in interface-configuration mode for a Generic Routing Encapsulation (GRE) tunnel, but if you are configuring an IPSec tunnel, the command would be issued from crypto-map configuration mode.

Question 19

Identify the purpose of QoS Policy Propagation through BGP (QPPB).

Question 20

List at least two advantages of applying QoS features at the edge of the network.

Question 21

If a frame enters a Catalyst 2950 switch port that is "untrusted," which CoS value does the frame assume?

Question 19 Answer

QPPB can encode QoS information by assigning Border Gateway Protocol (BGP) attributes such as an autonomous system number, a community string, or an IP prefix. For example, instead of setting the IP Precedence marking inside every packet, you could send the traffic with a certain community string. Then, after the far-end router received the traffic, it could mark the traffic with an IP Precedence value that is based on the traffic's community string.

Question 20 Answer

Cisco recommends that you set a trust boundary and begin applying QoS features as close to the source as possible (that is, at the edge of the network). Applying QoS features at the edge of the network (for example, in a wiring closet) offers several benefits, including the following:

- Provides immediate traffic classification
- Reduces congestion within the remainder of the network
- Eases the processor burden on the distribution or core routers

Question 21 Answer

Traffic that enters an untrusted Catalyst 2950 port takes on the port's CoS value. Ports can be configured, however, to trust the CoS or DSCP value of a packet, or even to trust the CoS value of a packet only if it originated from a Cisco IP Phone.

Question 22

How many queues does a Catalyst 2950 have?

Question 23

Why does the Catalyst 2950 assign an internal DSCP value to all incoming traffic?

Question 24

Which command is used to configure the trust state of a Catalyst 2950 port?

Question 22 Answer

A Catalyst 2950 has four queues, and by default, it places traffic into the queues based on the traffic's CoS values. For example, traffic that enters the switch with a CoS value of 0 is placed in queue 1, whereas traffic that enters the switch with a CoS value of 5 is placed in queue 3.

Question 23 Answer

A Catalyst 2950 assigns an internal DSCP value to all incoming traffic for internal QoS processing. Interestingly, these internal DSCP values are assigned to all traffic, including non-IP traffic.

Question 24 Answer

The following command tells a Catalyst 2950 port what to trust:

```
Switch(config-if)#mls qos trust [cos [pass-through dscp] | device cisco-phone | dscp]
```

The **pass-through dscp** option does not modify the DSCP values. (That is, it does not remark them based on CoS values.)

Question 25

Which command assigns a default CoS value to a Catalyst 2950 port?

Question 26

Which command configures CoS-to-DSCP mappings on a Catalyst 2950 switch?

Question 27

Which type of access lists can you use on a Catalyst 2950 to classify traffic?

Question 25 Answer

The following command assigns a default CoS value for a port:

```
Switch(config-if)#mls qos cos {default-cos | override}
```

The **override** option applies the default CoS value to a frame, even though a frame might already have a CoS marking.

Question 26 Answer

A Catalyst 2950 has default CoS-to-DSCP mappings. However, those mappings can be manipulated with the following command:

```
Switch(config)#mls qos map cos-dscp dscpvalue1 dscpvalue2 ...
dscpvalue8
```

Consider the following example:

```
Switch(config)#mls qos map cos-dscp 0 16 24 32 34 40 48 56
```

In this example, the eight DSCP values that were entered correspond to CoS values 0 through 7.

Question 27 Answer

The Catalyst 2950 supports standard and extended IP access lists and Layer 2 MAC access lists for non-IP traffic. Note that the extended IP access lists that are available on the Catalyst 2950 do not have all the options available on a router. For example, you cannot use the access list to match a range of port numbers.

QOS Section 5
Queuing

Although classification and marking do a great job of categorizing traffic, these tools in isolation do not alter the behavior of traffic. Other QoS mechanisms, however, can reference those markings and make decisions based on them. Queuing mechanisms, for example, can make forwarding and bandwidth allocation decisions based on a packet's marking.

These flash cards review the characteristics of various queuing mechanisms. In addition, you are challenged to recall specific syntax to configure queuing, with the primary emphasis being on Modular Quality of Service Command-Line Interface (MQC) approaches to queuing (that is, Class-Based Weighted Fair Queuing [CB-WFQ] and Low Latency Queuing [LLQ]).

Question 1

Why is queuing necessary on Cisco network devices?

Question 2

Identify a queuing mechanism that does not perform a QoS function, such as packet reordering.

Question 3

How many queues are available with the Priority Queuing (PQ) mechanism?

Question 1 Answer

When a device, such as a switch or a router, is receiving traffic faster than it can be transmitted, the device attempts to buffer the extra traffic until bandwidth is available, as opposed to dropping packets. This buffering process is called *queuing*.

Question 2 Answer

First-in first-out (FIFO) queuing is not truly performing QoS operations. As its name suggests, the first packet to come into the queue is the first packet that is sent out of the queue.

Question 3 Answer

Priority Queuing places traffic into one of four queues (high, medium, normal, or low). Each queue has a different level of priority, and higher-priority queues must be emptied before packets are emptied from lower-priority queues. This behavior can "starve out" some types of traffic.

Question 4

Describe the operation of *round robin queuing*.

Question 5

Custom Queuing (CQ) has a "deficit" issue, where it might send more than the configured number of bytes for a queue during a round. What similar queuing approach is designed to overcome this problem?

Question 6

What type of queuing is used in a router's hardware queue?

Question 4 Answer

Round robin queuing places traffic into multiple queues, and packets are removed from these queues in a round-robin fashion, which avoids the protocol starvation issue that PQ suffered from.

Question 5 Answer

Deficit Round Robin (DRR) keeps track of the number of extra bytes sent during a round and subtracts that number from the number of bytes that can be sent during the next round.

Question 6 Answer

The hardware queue, which is sometimes referred to as the transmit queue (TxQ), always uses FIFO queuing, and only when the hardware queue is full does the software queue handle packets. Therefore, queuing configuration only takes effect after the hardware queue has overflowed.

Question 7

What type of queuing do Cisco routers use, by default, on interfaces that run at speeds greater than 2.048 Mbps?

Question 8

What formula is used to calculate the weight of a packet, using Weighted Fair Queuing (WFQ), in IOS versions prior to 12.0(5)T?

Question 9

What is the syntax that configures WFQ in interface-configuration mode?

Question 7 Answer

FIFO is the default queuing method on interfaces that run at speeds greater than 2.048 Mbps. Although FIFO is supported widely on all IOS platforms, it can starve out traffic by allowing bandwidth-hungry flows to take an unfair share of the bandwidth.

Question 8 Answer

Prior to IOS 12.0(5)T, the formula for weight was as follows:

Weight = 4096 /(IP Prec. + 1)

In more recent versions of the IOS, the formula for weight is as follows:

Weight = 32384 /(IP Prec. + 1)

Question 9 Answer

Although WFQ has default settings, you can manipulate those settings with the following interface-configuration-mode command:

```
Router(config-if)#fair-queue [cdt [dynamic-queues [reservable-queues]]]
```

cdt identifies the Congestion Discard Threshold (CDT), which is the number of packets allowed in all WFQ queues before the router begins to drop packets attempting to enter the queue that currently has the most packets. With WFQ, each flow is placed in its own queue, up to a maximum number of queues defined by the **dynamic-queues** parameter. The **reservable-queues** parameter defines the number of queues made available to interface features such as Resource Reservation Protocol (RSVP).

Question 10

List two negative characteristics of WFQ.

Question 11

Which CB-WFQ command specifies a minimum amount of bandwidth (in kbps) to make available to a class of traffic?

Question 12

Which CB-WFQ command specifies a minimum amount of bandwidth to allocate to a class of traffic, based on a percentage of the interface's bandwidth?

Question 10 Answer

Although WFQ is easy to configure (for example, it is enabled by default on interfaces that run at or below 2.048 Mbps), and although WFQ is supported on all IOS versions, it does have its limitations. Specifically, WFQ cannot guarantee a specific amount of bandwidth for an application. Also, if more than 256 flows exist, more than one flow can be forced to share the same queue.

Question 11 Answer

You can make a specific amount of bandwidth available for classified traffic. To allocate a bandwidth amount, use the following command, noting that the units of measure are in kbps:

```
Router(config-pmap-c)#bandwidth bandwidth
```

Question 12 Answer

Instead of specifying an exact amount of bandwidth, you can specify a percentage of the interface bandwidth. To allocate a percentage of the interface bandwidth, use the following command:

```
Router(config-pmap-c)#bandwidth percent percent
```

Question 13

Explain the purpose of the following syntax:

```
Router(config-pmap-c)#bandwidth remaining percent percent
```

Question 14

In an MQC configuration, for which class-map can you enable WFQ?

Question 15

Which command can specify the number of packets that can be stored in a queue that is used by a class-map?

Question 13 Answer

As an alternative to allocating a percentage of the total interface bandwidth, you also have the option of allocating a percentage of the remaining bandwidth (that is, after other bandwidth allocations have already been made). To allocate a percentage of the remaining interface bandwidth, use the following command:

```
Router(config-pmap-c)#bandwidth remaining percent percent
```

Question 14 Answer

In an MQC configuration, WFQ is supported only for the **class-default** class-map. This class-map is created by default and is used to match any traffic that is not matched by a configured class-map.

Question 15 Answer

By default, each queue that CB-WFQ uses has a capacity of 64 packets. However, this limit is configurable with the following command:

```
Router(config-pmap-c)#queue-limit number_of_packets
```

Question 16

In an LLQ configuration, explain why traffic that is placed in the priority queue is also policed.

Question 17

Which LLQ command specifies an amount of bandwidth (in kbps) to make available for priority traffic?

Question 18

Which LLQ command uses a percentage of the interface's bandwidth to specify an amount of bandwidth to make available for priority traffic?

Question 16 Answer

In an LLQ configuration, when you place packets in the priority queue, you are not only allocating a bandwidth amount for that traffic, but you also are policing (that is, limiting the available bandwidth for) that traffic. The policing option is necessary to prevent high-priority traffic from starving out lower-priority traffic.

Question 17 Answer

In policy-map-class configuration mode, you can specify an exact amount of bandwidth (in kbps) to make available for priority traffic with the following command:

```
Router(config-pmap-c)#priority bandwidth
```

Question 18 Answer

Instead of configuring an exact amount of bandwidth to make available for a priority class of traffic, you can allocate a percentage of an interface's bandwidth with the following command:

```
Router(config-pmap-c)#priority percent percent
```

Question 19

Explain the purpose of the queues in a Catalyst 2950 switch.

Question 20

Which Catalyst 2950 queue can you configure as an "expedite" queue?

Question 21

On a Catalyst 2950, frames are queued based on their CoS values. Which command alters the default queue assignments?

Question 19 Answer

A Catalyst 2950 switch has four queues, and you can configure WRR to place frames with specific CoS markings into certain queues (for example, CoS values 0 and 1 are placed in queue 1).

Question 20 Answer

On the Catalyst 2950, you can designate queue 4 as an "expedite" queue, which gives priority treatment to frames in that queue. Specifically, the expedite queue must be empty before additional queues are serviced. This behavior can lead to protocol starvation.

Question 21 Answer

The following Catalyst 2950 command alters the default queue assignments:

```
Switch(config)#wrr-queue cos-map queue_number cos_value_1 cos_value_2
… cos_value_n
```

For example, the following command would map CoS values of 0, 1, and 2 to queue 1 on a Catalyst 2950:

```
Switch(config)#wrr-queue cos-map 1 0 1 2
```

Question 22

Identify the Catalyst 2950 command that assigns weights to each of the switch's four queues.

Question 23

Which Catalyst 2950 command can you use to view how the switch is mapping CoS values to Differentiated Services Code Point (DSCP) values, and vice versa?

Question 22 Answer

The weight that is assigned to a queue specifies how many packets are emptied from a queue, during each round robin cycle, relative to other queues. You can configure queue weights with the following command:

```
Switch(config)#wrr-queue bandwidth weight_1 weight_2 weight_3 weight_4
```

Remember that queue 4 on a Catalyst 2950 can be configured as an expedite queue (that is, a priority queue). To configure queue 4 as an expedite queue, set its weight to 0.

Question 23 Answer

The **show mls qos maps** command displays CoS-to-DSCP mappings and DSCP-to-CoS mappings. However, you can add the **cos-dscp** or **dscp-cos** option to the command to view a single set of mappings.

QOS Section 6
Weighted Random Early Detection (WRED)

The previous section addressed queuing, which is a congestion-management QoS mechanism. However, this section focuses on congestion avoidance. Specifically, you do not want a queue to fill to capacity, because all arriving traffic flows would be dropped and enter Transport Control Protocol (TCP) slow start. Some negative consequences arise from having multiple flows simultaneously enter TCP slow start. To prevent such an occurrence, you can configure Weighted Random Early Detection (WRED).

These flash cards review the need for WRED. You also must be familiar with the inner workings of the industry-standard Random Early Detection (RED) approach, in addition to the configuration of WRED. Even though WRED can be configured from interface-configuration mode or as part of a Modular Quality of Service Command-Line Interface (MQC) configuration, these flash cards focus specifically on WRED's MQC implementation. Finally, you need to recall the characteristics and configuration of the Explicit Congestion Notification (ECN) mechanism.

Question 1

What is TCP slow start?

Question 2

Which QoS tool does Cisco use to prevent a queue from filling to capacity?

Question 3

Describe the following WRED parameters: minimum threshold, maximum threshold, and Mark Probability Denominator (MPD).

Question 1 Answer

TCP slow start occurs if a sender does not receive an acknowledgment from its receiver within a certain time. When this occurs, the TCP window size is reduced to 1. The TCP window size then increases exponentially up to one-half of the original congestion window size, after which the window size increases linearly.

Question 2 Answer

Cisco IOS can use WRED to prevent a queue from filling to capacity by discarding traffic more aggressively as the queue begins to fill. Dropping decisions are made based on the traffic's priority markings.

Question 3 Answer

- The minimum threshold specifies the number of packets that must be in a queue before the queue considers discarding packets that have a particular marking.
- The probability of discard increases until the queue depth reaches the maximum threshold. After a queue depth exceeds the maximum threshold, all other packets with a particular marking that attempt to enter the queue are discarded.
- However, the probability of packet discard when the queue depth equals the maximum threshold is 1/(MPD). For example, if the MPD were set to 10, when the queue depth reached the maximum threshold, the probability of discard, for the specified marking, would be 1/10 (that is, a 10 percent chance of discard).

Question 4

When configuring WRED, you configure an MPD of 4 for traffic that is marked with a Differentiated Services Code Point (DSCP) value of 46. When the queue depth is at the maximum threshold for DSCP 46 traffic, what is the probability (in percent) that a packet marked with a DSCP value of 46 will be discarded?

Question 5

Identify the QoS marking that WRED references if the following command is issued:

```
Router(config-if)#random-detect
```

Question 6

Define *global synchronization.*

Question 4 Answer

The probability of packet discard when the queue depth equals the maximum threshold is 1/(MPD). Therefore, if the MPD = 4, the probability of discard is 1/4, which equals 0.25 (that is, 25 percent).

Question 5 Answer

The **dscp-based** or **prec-based** option can be used with the **random-detect** command to specify the QoS markings that WRED should reference when making discard decisions. However, if neither of these parameters is used, WRED defaults to referencing IP Precedence values.

Question 6 Answer

Global synchronization occurs when multiple TCP flows simultaneously go into TCP slow start. This can occur if a queue is full, because all newly arriving packets are discarded. Note that global synchronization is sometimes referred to as *TCP synchronization*.

Question 7

Describe the three drop modes of RED: no drop, random drop, and full drop.

Question 8

Besides policy-map-class configuration mode, list two other configuration modes from which WRED can be configured.

Question 9

Identify what is typically the best location in an enterprise network to enable WRED.

Question 7 Answer

The three drop modes of RED are as follows:

- "No drop" occurs if the queue depth is at or below the minimum threshold. In this mode, there is no chance of discard.
- "Random drop" occurs if the queue depth is above the minimum threshold and equal to or below the maximum threshold. The likelihood of discard depends on the queue depth and the MPD. When the queue depth equals the maximum threshold, the probability of discard is 1/MPD. If the queue depth currently equaled the maximum threshold and the MPD = 4, the probability of discard would be 1/4 = 0.25 = 25 percent.
- "Full drop" occurs if the queue depth the maximum threshold. In this mode, there is a 100 percent chance of discard.

Question 8 Answer

In addition to Class-Based WRED (CB-WRED), in which WRED is configured in policy-map-class configuration mode, WRED can be configured from interface-configuration mode or from virtual-circuit-configuration mode.

Question 9 Answer

WRED typically is used on router interfaces that are likely to experience congestion, such as a WAN interface. However, WRED can be enabled within the core of an enterprise network, too. Because WRED is not processor intensive (for example, it does not compare packets to an access list or alter bits in a packet's ToS byte), WRED could be enabled throughout an enterprise. However, it typically serves the greatest benefit at the WAN edge.

Question 10

What policy-map-class configuration-mode command enables WRED and specifies that the WRED profiles should be based on DSCP values, as opposed to IP Precedence values?

Question 11

Which WRED command specifies a minimum threshold of 24, a maximum threshold of 45, and an MPD of 10 for an IP Precedence value of 2?

Question 12

Which command can you use to see the WRED parameters that are associated with a particular interface using the MQC process?

Question 10 Answer

The **random-detect dscp-based** command is used in policy-map-class configuration mode to enable WRED for the class of traffic and to instruct WRED to use drop profiles based on DSCP values. If the **random-detect** command had been issued without the **dscp-based** option, WRED would base its drop profiles instead on IP Precedence values.

Question 11 Answer

The syntax to configure WRED parameters for an IP Precedence value is as follows:

```
Router(config-pmap-c)#random-detect precedence precedence_value
minimum-threshold maximum-threshold mark-probability-denominator
```

Therefore, in this example, the command would be as follows:

```
Router(config-pmap-c)#random-detect precedence 2 24 45 10
```

Question 12 Answer

To view the parameters of a policy-map (including WRED parameters) that are associated with an interface, use the command:

```
show policy-map interface interface-identifier
```

Question 13

Define *Explicit Congestion Notification (ECN)*.

Question 14

What are the names of the ECN bits that are located in the 2 right-most bit positions of the ToS byte?

Question 15

What happens to packets that are sent between two ECN-capable routers when the queue depth for those packets is below the minimum threshold?

Question 13 Answer

ECN indicates the presence of congestion through signaling rather than dropping. By using the 2 right-most bits in the ToS byte, an ECN-capable device can indicate whether congestion is being experienced. (Reference RFC 3168 for more information.)

Question 14 Answer

The 7th bit in the ToS byte is the ECN-Capable Transport (ECT) bit. The 8th bit in the ToS byte is the Congestion Experienced (CE) bit. Note that the bit combinations of 10 or 01 are viewed identically (that is, as an ECN-capable device that is not currently experiencing congestion).

Question 15 Answer

If the queue depth is below the WRED minimum threshold, the packets are sent normally, just as with WRED.

Question 16

What is being indicated when a packet is received with both of its ECN bits set to 1?

Question 17

What happens to packets that are sent between two ECN-capable routers when the queue depth is above the packets' maximum threshold?

Question 18

What happens when an ECN-marked packet is received by a router that is not ECN capable?

Question 16 Answer

The ECT bit that is being set to 1 indicates that the device that is sending the packet is capable of using ECN, and the CE bit that is being set to 1 indicates that congestion is currently being experienced. When a packet is received with both of its ECN bits (that is, the ECT and CE bits) set to 1, the sender is ECN capable and is currently experiencing congestion.

Question 17 Answer

If the queue depth is above the configured maximum threshold, the packets are dropped, just as with WRED.

Question 18 Answer

If a packet is received by a router that is not ECN capable, the destination router does not examine the 7th or 8th bits (that is, the ECT and CE bits). Therefore, the destination router treats the packet with normal WRED behavior, assuming that the destination router is configured for WRED.

Question 19

Under what configuration mode (or modes) can you configure ECN?

Question 20

Which command enables ECN?

Question 19 Answer

Even though you can configure WRED under interface-configuration mode or in virtual-circuit-configuration mode, you can configure ECN only under policy-map-class configuration mode.

Question 20 Answer

The command to enable ECN is as follows:

```
Router(config-pmap-c)#random-detect ecn
```

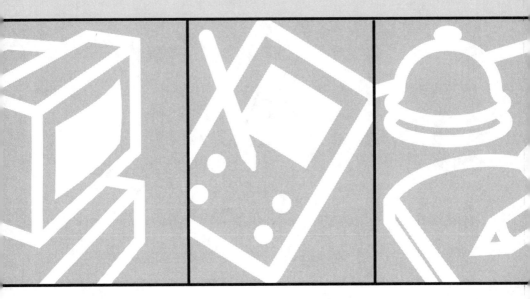

QOS Section 7
Traffic Conditioners

Not only do you want to allocate a *minimum* amount of bandwidth for specific traffic types, but you also might want to limit the amount of bandwidth that is available for specific applications. Traffic conditioners allow you to set a "speed limit" on specific types of traffic (that is, limit the amount of bandwidth that is available to those types of traffic). These flash cards review the details of the policing and shaping traffic-conditioning mechanisms.

These flash cards challenge you to recall the details surrounding the various flavors of Class-Based Policing (CB-Policing), including configuration syntax. You also must know the available options in a Class-Based Shaping (CB-Shaping) configuration and know how shaping is configured in a Frame Relay environment. For example, in a Frame Relay network, you might need your router to respond to Backward Explicit Congestion Notification (BECN) or Forward Explicit Congestion Notification (FECN) messages.

Question 1

Describe what a policing mechanism typically does to "exceeding" traffic.

Question 2

In what direction (or directions) can you apply policing mechanisms to an interface?

Question 3

Describe what a shaping mechanism does to traffic that exceeds the Committed Information Rate (CIR).

Question 1 Answer

A policing mechanism typically discards exceeding traffic. However, if bytes are available in the token bucket, you can configure policing mechanisms to transmit and remark traffic. The discarding of traffic can force Transport Control Protocol (TCP) retransmits, which might not maximize bandwidth usage. Therefore, policing mechanisms are recommended for use on higher-speed interfaces.

Question 2 Answer

You can apply policing mechanisms, unlike shaping mechanisms, in both the inbound and outbound directions on an interface.

Question 3 Answer

Unlike policing, shaping mechanisms buffer excess traffic and then send the traffic when bandwidth is again available. This buffering adds to overall delay, but it makes a more efficient use of the link's bandwidth. Therefore, shaping is recommended for use on slower-speed interfaces.

Question 4

Can you apply shaping mechanisms in the inbound direction of an interface, in the outbound direction, or both?

Question 5

Define the committed burst (Bc) traffic-conditioning parameter.

Question 6

What formula defines a CIR in terms of Bc and a timing interval (Tc)?

Question 4 Answer

Although you can apply policing mechanisms in both the inbound and outbound directions on an interface, you can apply shaping mechanisms only in the outbound direction.

Question 5 Answer

The Bc traffic-conditioning parameter defines the number of bits or bytes that are deposited into a token bucket during a timing interval. Shaping mechanisms measure Bc in bits, whereas policing mechanisms measure Bc in bytes.

Question 6 Answer

The CIR is given by the following formula:

$$CIR = Bc / Tc$$

For example, consider that you have a Bc of 8000 bits and a Tc of 0.125 seconds (that is, 1/8 of a second). In this example, you are sending 8000 bits (at line rate) 8 times a second (that is, 8000 * 8 = 64,000), for a grand total of 64,000 bps. The CIR can be calculated by the following formula:

$$CIR = 8000 / 0.125 = 64,000 \text{ bps}$$

Question 7

A policing mechanism is configured on an interface, and 500 bytes are currently in the token bucket. Two packets enter the router in the same timing interval. Both packets are 300 bytes in size. How does the policing mechanism handle the packets?

Question 8

Consider policing traffic to a single rate using a single token bucket. In this example, what defines *exceeding* traffic?

Question 9

Identify the two rates that are specified by a dual-rate policer.

Question 7 Answer

When the first packet arrives, 300 bytes are taken from the token bucket, leaving 200 bytes. When the second packet arrives, there are not sufficient tokens (that is, bytes) to send the packet, so the packet is discarded. Therefore, in this example, the first packet is transmitted and the second packet is dropped.

Question 8 Answer

With a single token bucket, the bucket has a capacity of Be bytes. Bytes are added to the bucket at a rate of Bc bytes per timing interval. However, if Bc does not equal Be, more than Bc bytes can be sent during a timing interval, provided that bytes already in the queue were left over (that is, unused) from a previous timing interval. An *exceed* action occurs when the number of bytes needed to transmit a packet requires more than Bc bytes to be removed from the bucket during a timing interval.

Question 9 Answer

With dual-rate policing, you have two token buckets. The first bucket is the Committed Information Rate (CIR) bucket, and the second bucket is the Peak Information Rate (PIR) bucket. These buckets are replenished with tokens at different rates, with the PIR bucket being filled at a higher rate.

Question 10

Define what is meant by a policing *multiaction*.

Question 11

What syntax is used to configure policing to a single rate?

Question 12

What syntax do you use to configure a dual-rate policer, where you specify traffic rates in bps?

Question 10 Answer

As the name suggests, a *multiaction* specifies more than one action to perform on conforming, exceeding, or violating traffic. An example of a multiaction would be specifying that exceeding traffic would not only be marked with a Differentiated Services Code Point (DSCP) value of AF11, but also that the traffic would have its Cell Loss Priority (CLP) bit set.

Question 11 Answer

You use the following syntax to police traffic to a single rate:

```
Router(config-pmap-c)#police cir [bc [be]] [conform-action action]
[exceed-action action] [violate-action action]
```

Note that if you specify the **violate** option, you use two token buckets. However, if you do not specify the **violate** option, you use a single token bucket.

Question 12 Answer

You use the following syntax to police traffic with a dual-rate policer, where the CIR and PIR traffic rates are in bps:

```
Router(config-pmap-c)#police cir cir [bc bc] [pir pir] [be be]
[conform-action action] [exceed-action action] [violate-action action]
```

Note that with a dual-rate policer, a packet can extract tokens only from the CIR bucket or the PIR bucket, but not both buckets.

Question 13

What syntax configures a dual-rate policer, where traffic rates are specified as percentages of the interface bandwidth?

Question 14

In a CB-Shaping configuration, what formula defines the peak rate?

Question 15

What syntax do you use in policy-map-class configuration mode to configure CB-Shaping?

Question 13 Answer

The following syntax polices traffic with a dual-rate policer, where the CIR and PIR traffic rates are specified as percentages of the interface bandwidth:

```
Router(config-pmap-c)#police cir percent percent [bc bc] [pir percent
percent] [be be] [conform-action action] [exceed-action action]
[violate-action action]
```

Note that on interfaces that can operate at more than one bandwidth (for example, serial interfaces), you should specify the bandwidth with the interface-configuration mode **bandwidth** command.

Question 14 Answer

CB-Shaping can shape traffic to an average rate, where Bc bits are added to the token bucket during each timing interval, or to a peak rate, where Bc + Be bits are added to the token bucket during each timing interval. Therefore, when shaping to a peak rate, the peak rate is defined as follows:

Peak Rate = CIR * [1 + (Be / Bc)]

Question 15 Answer

CB-Shaping is used in the outbound direction and is recommended for use on slower-speed interfaces. To configure CB-Shaping, use the following syntax in policy-map-class configuration mode:

```
Router(config-pmap-c)#shape {average | peak} percent percent [bc] [be]
```

Note that the **bc** and **be** parameters are in milliseconds when you use the **percent** option.

Question 16

Explain the purpose of the FECN bit.

Question 17

What policy-map-class configuration-mode command do you use to specify the minimum CIR (mincir) in a CB-Shaping configuration?

Question 16 Answer

The FECN bit is marked by a Frame Relay service provider on a frame that is traveling to a receiver. If the receiver is configured to respond to FECNs, upon receipt of a frame marked with an FECN bit, the receiver sends a Q.922 test frame back to the sender. This test frame then has its BECN bit marked by the service provider. When the sender receives this marked frame, if the sender is configured to respond to BECNs, it reduces its CIR by 25 percent.

Question 17 Answer

You use the **shape adaptive** *mincir* command to specify the lowest transmission rate that the router can reduce to in the presence of BECNs. Note that if the **shape adaptive** *mincir* command is configured in conjunction with Class-Based Weighted Fair Queuing (CB-WFQ), the minimum CIR value should not be less than the bandwidth that is allocated by CB-WFQ, with the **bandwidth** command.

QOS Section 8
QoS on Slow-Speed Links

Some QoS mechanisms are targeted toward making a more efficient use of slower-speed WAN links, where bandwidth is a scarce resource. The flash cards in this section review the roles of compression and Link Fragmentation and Interleaving (LFI) on Cisco's WAN links, not only to maximize throughput but also to reduce delay.

These flash cards challenge you to recall the theory and configuration that surround both Transport Control Protocol (TCP) and Real-Time Transport Protocol (RTP) Class-Based Header (CB-Header) compression. You should know when to apply specific LFI mechanisms and how to configure Multilink PPP (MLP) and FRF.12. Also, because delay is such a concern for the Cisco design, you should recall how to calculate serialization delay, given a link speed and frame size.

Question 1

List at least two approaches for performing payload compression.

Question 2

What is the goal of compression technologies?

Question 3

What is the approximate size of a compressed header using RTP header compression?

Question 1 Answer

Payload compression options include the following:

- **STAC**—Consumes more processor resources than Predictor
- **Predictor**—Consumes more memory resources than STAC
- **MPPC (Microsoft Point-to-Point Compression)**—Useful for Microsoft dialup clients

Question 2 Answer

Compression technologies attempt to increase throughput over a WAN link while reducing overall delay. However, on some lower-end routers, the processing time required to perform compression can increase the overall delay. Some routers, therefore, support hardware modules that offload compression tasks from the router's processor.

Question 3 Answer

RTP header compression reduces a voice packet's 40-byte header (containing IP, UDP, and RTP headers) to 2–4 bytes. Similarly, TCP header compression reduces a data packet's header to 3–5 bytes.

Question 4

List three LFI mechanisms that Cisco IOS supports.

Question 5

What policy-map-class configuration-mode command enables RTP header compression?

Question 6

Identify the type(s) of compression that are enabled by the following command:

```
Router(config-pmap-c)#compression header ip
```

Question 4 Answer

LFI mechanisms attempt to reduce the serialization delay that is experienced by small payloads on slow links by fragmenting larger payloads and then interleaving the small payloads among the fragments. Cisco IOS supports the following LFI mechanisms:

- **MLP**—Used on Point-to-Point Protocol (PPP) links
- **FRF.12**—Used on Voice over IP over Frame Relay (VoIPovFR) links
- **FRF.11 Annex C**—Used on Voice over Frame Relay (VoFR) links

Question 5 Answer

The following command enables RTP header compression for a class of traffic:

```
Router(config-pmap-c)#compression header ip rtp
```

Note that the other side of the link also must be enabled for RTP header compression in order for compression to occur.

Question 6 Answer

If you enter this command without the **tcp** or **rtp** arguments, you are enabling both TCP and RTP header compression.

Question 7

When you are configuring an LFI mechanism, what does Cisco recommend that the resulting serialization delay should be?

Question 8

How long does it take a 512-byte frame to exit a serial interface that is running at a speed of 128 kbps?

Question 9

When you are configuring LFI using MLP, what three ppp multilink commands are given in interface-configuration mode for the virtual multilink interface?

Question 7 Answer

When you are configuring an LFI mechanism, Cisco recommends a serialization delay of 10–15 ms. Also, Cisco recommends configuring LFI on link speeds of less than 768 kbps.

Question 8 Answer

To calculate the serialization delay for a frame, use the following formula:

Serialization Delay = (Frame_Size * 8) / Link_Speed

In this example, the serialization delay is as follows:

Serialization Delay = (512 * 8) / 128 = 32 ms

Question 9 Answer

To configure the LFI portion of MLP, issue the following **ppp multilink** commands in multilink-interface-configuration mode:

```
Router(config-if)#ppp multilink
```
(Configures fragmentation on the multilink interface)

```
Router(config-if)#ppp multilink interleave
```
(Shuffles the fragments together)

```
Router(config-if)#ppp fragment-delay [serialization_delay]
```
(Specifies how long it takes for a fragment to exit the interface, in milliseconds)

Question 10

When you configure FRF.12, your link speed is 64,000 bps. What fragment size should you configure to achieve a serialization delay of 10 ms?

Question 11

What map-class configuration-mode command do you use to specify the fragment size for an FRF.12 configuration?

Question 12

What command associates a Frame Relay map-class with an interface?

Question 10 Answer

You can perform some algebraic manipulations with the following formula to determine the desired frame size:

Serialization Delay = (Frame_Size * 8) / Link_Speed

In this example, the following equation results:

.010 = (Frame_Size * 8) / 64000

Rearranging terms yields the frame size, as follows:

(.010 * 64000) / 8 = Frame_Size = 80 bytes

Question 11 Answer

You configure FRF.12 using a Frame Relay map-class. After entering map-class configuration mode with the **map-class frame-relay** *name* command, you can specify a fragment size with the **frame-relay fragment** *fragment-size* command.

Question 12 Answer

The following command associates a map-class with either a Frame Relay interface or subinterface:

```
Router(config-if | config-subif)#frame-relay class name
```

Question 13

What command associates a Frame Relay map-class with a specific Data Link Connection Identifier (DLCI)?

Question 14

List at least one command that can display the fragment size that is being used in an FRF.12 configuration.

Question 13 Answer

A Frame Relay permanent virtual circuit (PVC) is known by a DLCI. To associate a Frame Relay map-class with a DLCI, use the following command:

```
Router(config-fr-dlci)#class name
```

Note that this syntax is different from the command that associates a Frame Relay map-class with an interface or subinterface.

Question 14 Answer

You can use the **show frame-relay fragment** command to view the fragment size. Also, you can use the **show frame-relay pvc** command to view the fragment size on a particular DLCI.

QOS Section 9
QoS Design Guidelines

Throughout the QoS Study Sheets, you were introduced to the constituents of the Cisco QoS framework. You learned how to configure each one and gained insight as to when it was appropriate to deploy a specific QoS mechanism. These flash cards primarily serve as reinforcement to this material. Finally, these flash cards address QoS considerations when selecting a service provider.

These flash cards do not focus on syntax. Rather, they test your recollection of the Cisco available QoS mechanisms and design best practices. In addition, service provider considerations, such as Service Level Agreements (SLAs), are reviewed.

Question 1

Which classification mechanism can look beyond Layer 3 or Layer 4 information, all the way up to Layer 7?

Question 2

The class of service (CoS) marking operates at what layer of the OSI model?

Question 3

Which two Layer 3 markings use the ToS byte in an IPv4 header?

Question 1 Answer

The Cisco Network-Based Application Recognition (NBAR) feature can classify multiple traffic types, even those that change ports (for example, stateful protocols). NBAR can even interrogate Layer 7 information, such as a URL string.

Question 2 Answer

You can mark traffic at Layer 2 using a CoS marking over trunk connections (that is, IEEE 802.1Q or ISL trunks). Eight possible values exist for CoS markings, in the range of 0 to 7. However, Cisco recommends that you never mark traffic with a CoS of 6 or 7, because those values are reserved.

Question 3 Answer

Both IP Precedence and Differentiated Services Code Point (DSCP) use bits from the type of service (ToS) byte to mark traffic at Layer 3. Specifically, IP Precedence uses the 3 leftmost bits in the ToS byte, and DSCP uses the 6 leftmost bits in the ToS byte.

Question 4

Low Latency Queuing (LLQ), Class-Based Weighted Fair Queuing (CB-WFQ), and Weighted Round Robin (WRR) fall under which category of QoS mechanisms?

Question 5

Name at least one congestion-avoidance mechanism that is available in the IOS.

Question 6

Class-Based Policing (CB-Policing) and Class-Based Shaping (CB-Shaping) fall under which category of QoS mechanisms?

Question 4 Answer

LLQ, CB-WFQ, and WRR are all considered congestion-management (that is, queuing) mechanisms. Congestion-management mechanisms determine how packets are emptied from a queue during periods of congestion. Both LLQ and WRR have the ability to give priority treatment to specified traffic types.

Question 5 Answer

The primary congestion-avoidance mechanism in the Cisco IOS is Weighted Random Early Detection (WRED). WRED prevents global synchronization by discarding packets, based on the packets' priority, before an output queue fills to capacity. Also, Explicit Congestion Notification (ECN) can be used to signal the presence of congestion.

Question 6 Answer

Traffic conditioners, such as policing and shaping mechanisms, can limit the amount of bandwidth that specific traffic uses. Policing can be applied both on the inbound and outbound direction on an interface, whereas shaping can be applied only in the outbound direction. Policing also can mark a packet based on the packet's bandwidth demand.

Question 7

FRF.12 falls under which category of QoS mechanisms?

Question 8

What is the Cisco design recommendation for the maximum packet loss for a voice call?

Question 9

List at least three criteria that are typically specified in an SLA.

Question 7 Answer

FRF.12 is a Link Fragmentation and Interleaving (LFI) mechanism—which is one type of link efficiency mechanism—that is used on Voice over IP over Frame Relay (VoIPovFR) links. Specifically, FRF.12 fragments large packets to a specific size and then interleaves smaller packets (for example, voice packets) among the fragments.

Question 8 Answer

Cisco recommends that you have no more than a 1 percent packet loss for a voice call. Also, the maximum one-way delay for a voice call should be no more than 150 ms.

Question 9 Answer

Parameters that are frequently specified in a service provider's SLA include the following:

- Latency
- Packet drops
- Variable delay
- Uptime
- Bandwidth availability

Question 10

Service providers that have Layer 3 awareness typically categorize customer traffic in how many classes?

Question 10 Answer

Some service providers have Layer 3 awareness. In such a situation, the SLA can specify how traffic is placed into the service provider's defined traffic classes, perhaps based on DSCP markings. Typically, service providers categorize traffic in up to three to five classes.

QOS Quick Reference Sheets

Why You Need Quality of Service (QoS)

The networks of yesteryear physically separated voice, video, and data traffic. Literally, these traffic types flowed over separate media (for example, leased lines or fiber-optic cable plants). Today, however, network designers are leveraging the power of the data network to transmit voice and video, thus achieving significant cost savings by reducing equipment, maintenance, and even staffing costs.

The challenge, however, with today's converged networks is that multiple applications are contending for bandwidth, and some applications such as, voice can be more intolerant of delay (that is, latency) than other applications such as, an FTP file transfer. A lack of bandwidth is the overshadowing issue for most quality problems.

When a lack of bandwidth exists, packets can suffer from one or more of the following symptoms:

- **Delay**—Delay is the time that is required for a packet to travel from its source to its destination. You might witness delay on the evening news, when the news anchor is talking through satellite to a foreign news correspondent. Because of the satellite delay, the conversation begins to feel unnatural.

- **Jitter**—Jitter is the uneven arrival of packets. For example, consider that in a Voice over IP (VoIP) conversation, packet 1 arrives. Then, 20 ms later, packet 2 arrives. After another 70 ms, packet 3 arrives, and then packet 4 arrives 20 ms behind packet 3. This variation in arrival times (that is, variable delay) is not dropping packets, but this jitter can be interpreted by the listener as dropped packets.

- **Drops**—Packet drops occur when a link is congested and a buffer overflows. Some types of traffic, such as User Datagram Protocol (UDP) traffic (for example, voice), are not retransmitted if packets are dropped.

Fortunately, quality of service (QoS) features that are available on Cisco routers and switches can recognize your "important" traffic and then treat that traffic in a special way. For example, you might want to allocate 128 kbps of bandwidth for your VoIP traffic and also give that traffic priority treatment.

Consider water that is flowing through a series of pipes with varying diameters. The water's flow rate through those pipes is limited to the water's flow rate through the pipe with the smallest diameter. Similarly, as a packet travels from its source to its destination, its effective bandwidth is the bandwidth of the slowest link along that path.

Effective Bandwidth

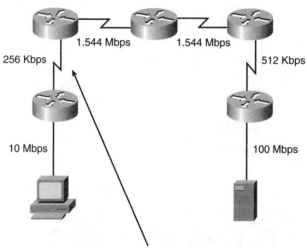

The weakest link between the two stations is
the effective bandwidth between those stations.

Because your primary challenge is a lack of bandwidth, the logical question is, "How do you increase available bandwidth?" A knee-jerk response to that question is often, "Add more bandwidth." Although adding more bandwidth is the best solution, it comes at a relatively high cost.

Compare your network to a highway system in a large city. During rush hour, the lanes of the highway are congested, but the lanes can be underutilized during other periods of the day. Instead of just building more lanes to accommodate peak traffic rates, the highway engineers add carpool lanes. Cars with two or more riders can use the reserved carpool lane. These cars have a higher priority on the highway. Similarly, you can use QoS features to give your mission-critical applications higher-priority treatment in times of network congestion.

Some of the QoS features that can address issues of delay, jitter, and packet loss include the following:

- **Queuing**—Queuing can send higher-priority traffic ahead of lower-priority traffic and make specific amounts of bandwidth available for those traffic types. Examples of queuing strategies that you consider later in these Quick Reference Sheets include the following:
  — Priority Queuing (PQ)
  — Custom Queuing (CQ)
  — Modified Deficit Round Robin (MDRR) queuing
  — Weighted Fair Queuing (WFQ)
  — Class-Based WFQ (CB-WFQ)
  — Low Latency Queuing (LLQ)
- **Compression**—By compressing a packet's header or payload, fewer bits are sent across the link. This effectively gives you more bandwidth.

QoS Basics

The mission statement of QoS could read something like "to categorize traffic and apply a policy to those traffic categories, in accordance with a QoS policy." Specifically, QoS configuration involves the following three basic steps:

Step 1 Determine network performance requirements for various traffic types. For example, consider the following design rules of thumb for voice, video, and data traffic:

Voice:

- No more than 150 ms of one-way delay

- No more than 30 ms of jitter

- No more than 1 percent packet loss

Video:

- No more than 150 ms of one-way delay for interactive voice applications (for example, video conferencing)

- No more than 30 ms of jitter

- No more than 1 percent packet loss

Data:

Applications have varying delay and loss characteristics. Therefore, data applications should be categorized into predefined "classes" of traffic, where each class is configured with specific delay and loss characteristics.

Step 2 Categorize traffic into specific categories. For example, you can have a category named "Low Delay," and you decide to place voice and video packets in that category. You can also have a "Low Priority" class, where you place traffic such as music downloads from the Internet. As a rule of thumb, Cisco recommends that you create no more that ten classes of traffic.

Step 3 Document your QoS policy, and make it available to your users. Then, for example, if a user complains that his network gaming applications are running slowly, you can point him to your corporate QoS policy, which describes how applications such as network gaming have "best-effort" treatment.

QoS Deployment

Cisco offers the following four basic approaches for QoS deployment in your network:

- **Command-Line Interface (CLI)**—The CLI is the standard IOS (or Cat OS) interface that configures routers or switches. CLI QoS features such as Priority Queuing (PQ) or Custom Queuing (CQ), which are configured through the CLI, have been available for many years.

- **Modular QoS CLI (MQC)**—Instead of using the CLI to configure QoS parameters for one interface at a time, the three-step MQC process allows you to (1) place packets into different classes, (2) assign a policy for those classes, and (3) apply the policy to an interface. Because the approach is modular, you can apply a single policy to multiple interfaces.

- **AutoQoS**—AutoQoS is a script that is executed on routers or switches that automates the process of QoS configuration. Specifically, this automatic configuration helps optimize QoS performance for VoIP traffic.

- **QoS Policy Manager (QPM)**—QPM, in conjunction with CiscoWorks, centralizes QoS configuration. Policies that are created with QPM can be pushed out to routers throughout an enterprise, thus reducing the potential for misconfiguration.

QoS Components

Cisco offers a wealth of QoS resources on its switch and router platforms. These resources are classified into one of three categories, which are discussed in this section. The category of QoS resources used most often in production, however, is the Differentiated Services category, which offers greater scalability and flexibility than the resources found in the Best-Effort or Integrated Services categories.

QoS Categories

All of the Cisco QoS features are categorized into one of the following three categories:

- **Best-Effort**—Best-Effort does not truly provide QoS, because there is no reordering of packets. Best-Effort uses the first-in first-out (FIFO) queuing strategy, where packets are emptied from a queue in the same order in which they entered it.
- **Integrated Services (IntServ)**—IntServ is often referred to as "Hard QoS," because it can make strict bandwidth reservations. IntServ uses signaling among network devices to provide bandwidth reservations. Resource Reservation Protocol (RSVP) is an example of an IntServ approach to QoS. Because IntServ must be configured on every router along a packet's path, the main drawback of IntServ is its lack of scalability.
- **Differentiated Services (DiffServ)**—DiffServ, as the name suggests, differentiates between multiple traffic flows. Specifically, packets are "marked," and routers and switches can then make decisions (for example, dropping or forwarding decisions) based on those markings. Because DiffServ does not make an explicit reservation, it is often called "Soft QoS." The focus of these Quick Reference Sheets is DiffServ, as opposed to IntServ or Best-Effort.

QoS Categories

- Best-Effort does not perform reordering of packets.
- DiffServ differentiates between flows and assigns policies to those flows.
- IntServ makes a strict bandwidth reservation for an application.

DiffServ

Now that you understand the importance that marking plays in a DiffServ QoS solution, you can learn how packets can be marked. Inside an IPv4 header is a byte called the *type of service (ToS) byte.* You can mark packets, using bits within the ToS byte, with either IP Precedence or Differentiated Service Code Point (DSCP) markings.

Type of Service (ToS) Byte

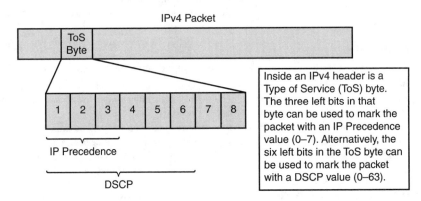

IP Precedence uses the 3 leftmost bits in the ToS byte. With 3 bits at its disposal, IP Precedence markings can range from 0 to 7. However, values 6 and 7 should not be used, because those values are reserved for network use.

For more granularity, you can choose DSCP, which uses the 6 leftmost bits in the ToS byte. Six bits yield 64 possible values (0 to 63). The challenge with so many values at your disposal is that the value you choose to represent a certain level of priority can be treated differently by a router or switch under someone else's administration.

To maintain relative levels of priority among devices, the Internet Engineering Task Force (IETF) selected a subset of those 64 values for use. These values are called *per-hop behaviors (PHBs)*, because they indicate how packets should be treated by each router hop along the path from the source to the destination.

The four categories of PHBs are as follows:

- **Default**—Traffic that only needs best-effort treatment can be marked with the Default PHB, which simply means that the 6 leftmost bits in the packet's ToS byte (that is, the DSCP bits) are all 0 (that is, a DSCP value of 0).
- **Expedited Forwarding (EF)**—The EF PHB has a DSCP value of 46. Latency-sensitive traffic, such as voice, typically has a PHB of EF.
- **Assured Forwarding (AF)**—The broadest category of PHBs is the AF PHB. Specifically, 12 AF PHBs exist, as shown in the following table.

PHB	Low Drop Preference	Medium Drop Preference	High Drop Preference
Class 1	AF11 (10) 001010	AF12 (12) 001100	AF13 (14) 001110
Class 2	AF21 (18) 010010	AF22 (20) 010100	AF23 (22) 010110
Class 3	AF31 (26) 011010	AF32 (28) 011100	AF33 (30) 011110
Class 4	AF41 (34) 100010	AF42 (36) 100100	AF43 (38) 100110

Notice that the Assured Forwarding PHBs are grouped into four classes. Examining these DSCP values in binary reveals that the 3 leftmost bits of all the Class 1 AF PHBs are 001 (that is, a decimal value of 1); the 3 leftmost bits of all the Class 2 AF PHBs are 010 (that is, a decimal value of 2); the 3 leftmost bits of all the Class 3 AF PHBs are 011 (that is, a decimal value of 3); and the 3 leftmost bits of all the Class 4 AF PHBs are 100 (that is, a decimal value of 4). Because IP Precedence examines these 3 leftmost bits, all Class 1 DSCP values would be interpreted by an IP Precedence–aware router as an IP Precedence value of 1. The same applies to the Class 2, 3, and 4 PHB values.

Within each AF PHB class are three distinct values, which indicate a packet's "drop preference." Higher values in an AF PHB class are more likely to be discarded during periods of congestion. For example, an AF13 packet is more likely to be discarded than an AF11 packet.

- **Class Selector (CS)**—To have backward compatibility with IP Precedence, you can use CS PHBs, because, just like IP Precedence, CS PHBs have 0s in the 4th, 5th, and 6th bits of the ToS byte. As an example, consider that your router uses DSCP markings, but you are sending packets to a router that only understands IP Precedence markings. That would be a great opportunity to use CS markings. You could send a packet marked with a DSCP value of 40, which is 101000 in binary. When that packet is received by the IP Precedence–aware router, its IP Precedence value is interpreted as 5, because only the 3 leftmost bits are considered, and because 101 in binary equals 5 in decimal.

QoS Tools

Now that you understand how markings can be performed with the DiffServ QoS model, realize that marking alone does not alter the behavior of packets. You must have a QoS tool that references those marking and alters the packets' treatment based on those markings. Following are some of the QoS tools that are addressed later in these Quick Reference Sheets:

- **Classification**—Classification is the process of placing traffic into different categories. Multiple characteristics can be used for classification. For example, POP3, IMAP, SMTP, and Exchange traffic could all be placed in an "EMAIL" class. Classification does not, however, alter bits in the frame or packet.
- **Marking**—Marking alters bits (for example, bits in the ToS byte) within a frame, cell, or packet to indicate how the network should treat that traffic. Marking alone does not change how the network treats a packet. Other tools (for example, queuing tools) can, however, reference those markings and make decisions based on them.
- **Congestion management**—When you hear the term *congestion management*, think *queuing*. These concepts are the same. When an interface's output software queue contains packets, the interface's queuing strategy determines how the packets are emptied from the queue. For example, some traffic types can be given priority treatment, and bandwidth amounts can be made available for specific classes of traffic.
- **Congestion avoidance**—If an interface's output queue fills to capacity, newly arriving packets are discarded (that is, "tail-dropped"), regardless of the priority that is assigned to the discarded packet. To prevent this behavior, Cisco uses a congestion avoidance technique called Weighted Random Early Detection (WRED). After the queue depth reaches a configurable level (that is, the minimum threshold) for a particular priority marking (for example, IP Precedence or DSCP), WRED introduces the possibility of discard for packets with those markings. As the queue depth continues to increase, the possibility of discard increases until a configurable maximum threshold is reached. After the queue depth has exceeded the maximum threshold for traffic with a specific priority, there is a 100 percent chance of discard for those traffic types.

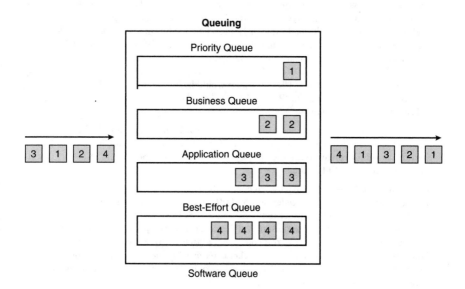

Queuing mechanisms determine in what order and in
what quantity specific packets are emptied from a queue.

- **Policing and shaping**—Sometimes, instead of making a minimum amount of bandwidth available for specific traffic types, you might want to limit the available bandwidth. Both policing and shaping tools can accomplish this objective. Collectively, these tools are called *traffic conditioners.*

Policing can be used in either the inbound or outbound direction, and it typically discards packets that exceed the configured rate limit, which you can think of as a "speed limit" for particular traffic types. Because policing drops packets, resulting in retransmissions, it is recommended for use on higher-speed interfaces. Policing mechanisms also allow you to rewrite packet markings (for example, IP Precedence markings).

Shaping can be applied only in the outbound direction. Instead of discarding traffic that exceeds the configured rate limit, shaping delays the exceeding traffic by buffering it until bandwidth becomes available. That is why shaping preserves bandwidth, as compared to policing, at the expense of increased delay. Therefore, shaping is recommended for use on slower-speed interfaces. Also, shaping does not have policing's ability to rewrite packet markings.

- **Link efficiency**—To make the most of the limited bandwidth that is available on slower-speed links, you can choose to implement compression or Link Fragmentation and Interleaving (LFI). Using header compression on smaller packets can dramatically increase a link's available bandwidth.

LFI addresses the issue of "serialization delay," which is the amount of time required for a packet to exit an interface. A large data packet, for example, on a slower-speed link could create excessive delay for a voice packet because of the time required for the data packet to exit the interface. LFI fragments the large packets and interleaves the smaller packets among the fragments, reducing the serialization delay that the smaller packets experience.

Link Efficiency Mechanisms

Header Compression

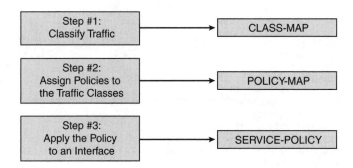

Link Fragmentation and Interleaving (LFI)

Basic QoS Configuration

Cisco continues to improve the ease and efficiency with which QoS mechanisms can be configured. This section addresses two of the Cisco more recent developments: MQC and AutoQoS.

Using MQC

One of the most powerful approaches to QoS configuration is the Modular Quality of Service Command-Line Interface (MQC). After you master the three basic steps of MQC, you can use them to configure a wide range of QoS tools, including queuing, policing, shaping, header compression, WRED, and marking.

Modular QoS CLI (MQC)

Step #1: Classify Traffic	→	CLASS-MAP
Step #2: Assign Policies to the Traffic Classes	→	POLICY-MAP
Step #3: Apply the Policy to an Interface	→	SERVICE-POLICY

The first step of MQC is to create class-maps, which categorize traffic types. The following command enters you into class-map configuration mode:

```
Router(config)#class-map [match-any | match-all] class-name
```

After you are in class-map configuration mode, you can specify multiple match statements to match traffic, and all traffic that meets the criteria that you specified with the **match** commands is categorized under the class-map. If multiple match statements are specified, by default, all match statements must be met before a packet is classified by the class-map. However, if you use the

match-any option, if any individual match condition is met, the packet is classified by the class-map. After the class-maps are defined, the first step of MQC is complete. The second step is to create a policy-map, which assigns characteristics (for example, marking) to the classified traffic.

To enter policy-map configuration mode, issue the following command:

```
Router(config)#policy-map policy-name
```

From policy-map configuration mode, enter policy-map-class configuration mode with the following command:

```
Router(config-pmap)#class class-name
```

From policy-map-class configuration mode, you can assign QoS policies to traffic that is classified by the class-map. You can also have a situation in which a packet matches more than one class-map. In that case, the first class-map that is identified in the policy-map is used. Up to 256 class-maps can be associated with a single policy-map.

Finally, in the third step of MQC, the policy-map is applied to an interface, Frame Relay map-class, or Asynchronous Transfer Mode (ATM) virtual circuit with the following command:

```
Router(config-if)#service-policy {input | output} policy-map-name
```

Following is an MQC example in which you are classifying various types of e-mail traffic (for example, SMTP, IMAP, and POP3) into one class-map. The KaZaa protocol, which is used frequently for music downloads, is placed in another class-map. Voice over IP (VoIP) traffic is placed in yet another class-map. Then, the policy-map assigns bandwidth allocations or limitations to these traffic types. The MQC example is as follows:

```
Router(config)#class-map match-any EMAIL
Router(config-cmap)#match protocol pop3
Router(config-cmap)#match protocol imap
Router(config-cmap)#match protocol smtp
Router(config-cmap)#exit
Router(config)#class-map MUSIC
Router(config-cmap)#match protocol kazaa2
Router(config-cmap)#exit
Router(config)#class-map VOICE
Router(config-cmap)#match protocol rtp
Router(config-cmap)#exit
Router(config)#policy-map QOS-STUDY
Router(config-pmap)#class EMAIL
Router(config-pmap-c)#bandwidth 128
Router(config-pmap-c)#exit
Router(config-pmap)#class MUSIC
Router(config-pmap-c)#police 32000
Router(config-pmap-c)#exit
Router(config-pmap)#class-map VOICE
Router(config-pmap-c)#priority 256
Router(config-pmap-c)#exit
Router(config-pmap)#exit
Router(config)#interface serial 0/1
Router(config-if)#service-policy output QOS-STUDY
```

Notice that the **QOS-STUDY** policy-map makes 128 kbps of bandwidth available to e-mail traffic. However, KaZaa version 2 traffic bandwidth is limited to 32 kbps. Voice packets not only have access to 256 kbps of bandwidth, but they also receive "priority" treatment, meaning that they are sent first (that is, ahead of other traffic) up to the 256-kbps limit.

The next logical question is, "What happens to all of the traffic that you did not classify?" Interestingly, the IOS created the **class-default** class-map, which categorizes any traffic that is not matched by one of the defined class-maps. Finally, in the previous example, the policy-map is applied in the outbound direction on the Serial 0/1 interface.

The following **show** commands can be used for verification and troubleshooting of an MQC configuration:

```
Router#show class-map [class-map-name]
```

(Used to view what a class-map is matching)

```
Router#show policy-map [policy-map-name]
```

(Used to view the policy that is applied to the classes within a policy-map)

```
Router#show policy-map interface interface-identifier [input | output]
```

(Used to view policy-map statistics for packets that are crossing a specific interface)

Using AutoQoS

Optimizing a QoS configuration for VoIP can be a daunting task. Fortunately, Cisco added a feature called *AutoQoS* to many of its router and switch platforms to automatically generate router-based or switch-based VoIP QoS configurations.

The following router platforms support AutoQoS:

- 1700 Series
- 2600 Series
- 3600 Series
- 3700 Series
- 7200 Series

Cisco also supports the AutoQoS feature on the following Catalyst switch series:

- 2950 (EI)
- 3550
- 4500
- 6500

On a router platform, the following command enables AutoQoS from either interface-configuration mode or from DLCI-configuration mode (for a Frame Relay circuit):

```
Router(config-if)#auto qos voip [trust] [fr-atm]
```

The **trust** option indicates that Auto QoS should classify voice traffic based on DSCP markings, instead of using NBAR. The **fr-atm** option enables the AutoQoS feature for Frame Relay–to–ATM links and is issued from DLCI-configuration mode.

Before enabling AutoQoS on a router interface, consider the following prerequisites:

- Cisco Express Forwarding (CEF) must be enabled, because AutoQoS uses NBAR, which requires the CEF feature.
- A QoS policy must not be attached to the interface.
- The correct bandwidth should be configured on the interface.
- An IP address must be configured on an interface if its speed is less than 768 kbps.
- The interface must not be administratively shut down.

Note that the interface's bandwidth determines which AutoQoS features are enabled. If an interface's bandwidth is less than 768 kbps, it is considered a low-speed interface. On a low-speed interface, AutoQoS configures Multilink PPP (MLP), which requires an IP address on the physical interface. AutoQoS takes that IP address from the physical interface and uses it for the virtual multilink interface that it creates.

To verify that AutoQoS is configured for a router interface, use the following command:

```
Router#show auto qos [interface interface-identifier]
```

Auto QoS

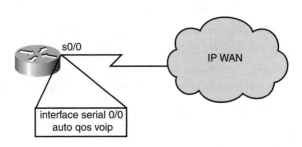

The Catalyst 6500 running in Hybrid mode (that is, using the Cat OS for switch functions) also supports AutoQoS. To enable AutoQoS on a Hybrid mode Catalyst 6500, you must first enable AutoQoS globally and then for a specific port. Following are the required commands:

```
Switch#set qos autoqos
```

(Globally enables AutoQoS)

```
Switch#set qos autoqos <mod/port> trust [cos | dscp]
```

(Enables AutoQoS for a specific port)

Note that the Catalyst 6500 can trust either CoS or DSCP values for its queuing decision. If the port is trusting DSCP markings, you can add the following command, which recognizes that the port is connected to a Cisco IP Phone or a Cisco SoftPhone (software that runs on a PC):

```
Switch#set port qos <mod/port> autoqos voip [ciscosoftphone | ciscoipphone]
```

The port must have Cisco Discovery Protocol (CDP) version 2 enabled to recognize an attached Cisco IP Phone. Although some switches do not recognize a Cisco SoftPhone, AutoQoS can be configured on Catalyst 2950 (EI) and 3550 switches, and the AutoQoS feature on these switches does recognize a Cisco IP Phone. To configure AutoQoS on these platforms, issue the following commands from interface-configuration mode:

```
Switch(config-if)#auto qos voip trust
```

(Configures the interface to trust CoS markings for classifying VoIP traffic)

```
Switch(config-if)#auto qos voip cisco-phone
```

(Detects the presence of a Cisco IP Phone, using CDP)

To troubleshoot and verify AutoQoS on a Catalyst switch, use the following commands:

```
Switch#show auto qos [interface interface-identifier]
```

(Displays the configuration that is applied by AutoQoS)

```
Switch#show mls qos interface [interface-identifier]
```

(Displays interface-level QoS statistics)

This section has broadly addressed the features that are enabled by AutoQoS. The specific features are shown in the following table.

QoS Mechanism	Router Feature	Switch Feature
Classification	NBAR and DSCP	Port trust states
Marking	CB-Marking	CoS-to-DSCP remarking
Congestion management	LLQ	WRR
Shaping	CB-Shaping or FRTS	—
Link efficiency	Header Compression and LFI	—

Traffic Classification and Marking

Classification and marking allow QoS-enabled networks to identify traffic types near the source and assign specific markings to those traffic types. This section addresses the need for and various approaches used to perform classification and marking.

Classification and Marking Basics

One of the first QoS mechanisms that you apply to your traffic is *classification*, which recognizes the types of traffic that are flowing across the network. For example, you might recognize Telnet, FTP, and HTTP traffic and categorize those applications together in a specific class of traffic.

Although classification is great, you probably do not want to configure classification on every router. Therefore, after the traffic is classified, you can "mark" it. At that point, other routers and switches in the network can reference those markings and make decisions (for example, forwarding or dropping decisions) based on those markings.

Some of these markings are Layer 2 (that is, the Data Link Layer) markings, whereas other markings are at Layer 3 (that is, the Network Layer). First, consider the Layer 2 markings.

On an Ethernet trunk, you can mark frames with a class of service (CoS) value. A CoS value can range from 0 through 7, although Cisco recommends that you never use 6 or 7. The bits that create the CoS marking depend on the type of trunk that is being used, as follows:

- **IEEE 802.1Q trunk**—Uses 3 bits in a Tag Control byte to mark a CoS value. (Note: This method is referred to as IEEE 802.1p.)
- **ISL trunk**—Uses 3 bits in the ISL header to mark a CoS value.

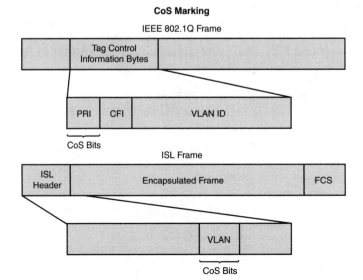

CoS Marking

Layer 2 markings also can extend to the WAN. Consider a Frame Relay network. Within a Frame Relay header is a bit called the *Discard Eligible (DE) bit,* which identifies frames that the service provider can drop during periods of congestion. You can leverage that DE bit to identify less important traffic that you send to the Frame Relay service provider. Similarly, you can mark the Cell Loss Priority (CLP) bit in an ATM cell to identify less important ATM traffic.

Service providers often use Multiprotocol Label Switching (MPLS) to forward traffic. Three bits in the MPLS label can be used to identify priority for traffic that is flowing through the service provider's cloud.

As mentioned earlier, Layer 3 markings are made possible by using bits within an IPv4 header's ToS byte. These markings are IP Precedence (which uses the 3 leftmost bits in the ToS byte) and DSCP (which uses the 6 leftmost bits in the ToS byte).

A major design issue to keep in mind is that a CoS marking from a trunk does not survive a route processor hop. So, if you are only using CoS markings to identify the priority of your traffic, those CoS markings should be "remarked" to a Layer 3 marking before the traffic passes through a route processor.

CoS Remarking

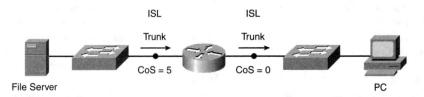

File Server

ISL   ISL

Trunk   Trunk

CoS = 5   CoS = 0

PC

Although Cisco recommends marking traffic as close to the source as possible, you typically do not want users setting their own priority markings. Therefore, you can use Catalyst switches to create a trust boundary, which is a point in the network that does not trust incoming markings. An exception to having a wiring closet switch acting as a trust boundary would be a Cisco IP Phone that is connected to the switch. Because the Cisco IP Phone performs priority marking, you can extend the trust boundary to the phone.

Modular Classification with MQC

Recall the previous discussion about the Cisco three-step MQC process for configuring QoS mechanisms. You can leverage this MQC approach to do classification and marking. First, consider classification using MQC. In class-map configuration mode, you can use the **match** command to categorize traffic based on any of the following criteria:

- Access control lists (ACLs)
- Existing markings (for example, CoS, IP Precedence, or DSCP)
- QoS group (a locally significant grouping of packets)
- Protocol (using NBAR)
- Traffic matching another class-map
- Incoming interface
- MAC address (source or destination)
- Range of UDP port numbers

In the following example, you are matching traffic based on a variety of the preceding criteria:

```
Router(config)#class-map match-any INT
Router(config-cmap)#match input-interface ethernet 0/0
Router(config-cmap)#match input-interface ethernet 0/1
```

```
Router(config-cmap)#exit
Router(config)#class-map ACL
Router(config-cmap)#match access-group 101
Router(config-cmap)#exit
Router(config)#class-map COS
Router(config-cmap)#match cos 0 1 2 3
Router(config-cmap)#exit
Router(config)#access-list 101 permit tcp any any eq 23
```

In this example, the **INT** class-map matches traffic that came into the router on any of the specified interfaces. The **ACL** class-map matches traffic that is matched by access-list 101. Finally, the **COS** class-map categorizes traffic with a CoS marking of 0, 1, 2, or 3.

Modular Marking with MQC

After you have classified your traffic using class-maps, you can use a policy-map to mark the traffic. Following is a listing of supported markings and the corresponding syntax:

- IP Precedence (**set ip precedence** *value*)
- DSCP (**set ip dscp** *value*)
- QoS group(**set ip precedence** *value*)
- MPLS experimental bits (**set mpls experimental** *value*)
- CoS value (**set cos** *value*)
- Frame Relay DE bit (**set fr-de**)
- ATM CLP bit (**set atm-clp**)

In the following example, you use MQC to remark CoS values that are entering a router to DSCP values:

CoS to DSCP Remarking

```
Router(config)#class-map HI-PRI
Router(config-cmap)#match cos 5 6 7
Router(config-cmap)#exit
Router(config)#class-map MED-PRI
Router(config-cmap)#match cos 2 3 4
Router(config-cmap)#exit
Router(config)#class-map LOW-PRI
Router(config-cmap)#match cos 0 1
Router(config-cmap)#exit
Router(config)#policy-map REMARK
Router(config-pmap)#class HI-PRI
Router(config-pmap-c)#set ip dscp af31
Router(config-pmap-c)#exit
Router(config-pmap)#class MED-PRI
Router(config-pmap-c)#set ip dscp af21
Router(config-pmap-c)#exit
Router(config-pmap)#class-map LOW-PRI
Router(config-pmap-c)#set ip dscp af11
Router(config-pmap-c)#exit
```

```
Router(config-pmap)#exit
Router(config)#interface fastethernet 0/1
Router(config-if)#service-policy input REMARK
```

In this example, traffic marked with CoS values of 5, 6, or 7 is classified in the **HI-PRI** class-map, whereas traffic with CoS values of 2, 3, or 4 goes into the **MED-PRI** class-map. Finally, CoS values of 0 and 1 are placed in the **LOW-PRI** class-map. The **REMARK** policy-map assigns a DSCP value of AF31 to the HI-PRI traffic, a DSCP value of AF21 to the MED-PRI traffic, and a DSCP value of AF11 to the LOW-PRI traffic. The third step of MQC applies a policy-map to an interface. In this case, you are applying the **REMARK** policy-map to the FastEthernet 0/1 interface in the inbound direction. It is critical that you apply the policy-map in the inbound direction. By doing so, you are remarking the CoS values before the route processor strips them.

As you learned earlier, to see what policies are applied to your class-maps, use the **show policy-map** command. Or, to see interface-specific statistics for a policy-map, the **show policy-map interface** *interface-identifier* command is appropriate.

Classifying with NBAR

The most powerful and flexible approach to classifying traffic is the Network Based Application Recognition (NBAR) feature. NBAR can look beyond Layer 3 and Layer 4 information, all the way up to Layer 7. Protocols that change port number (that is, stateful protocols) can be tracked, and even URL strings can be matched with NBAR.

Although the IOS comes with multiple NBAR application signatures, a continuing need exists for additional signature recognition. For example, even though your router might be able to recognize KaZaa traffic, it might not be able to recognize e-Donkey traffic. Fortunately, you can install Packet Description Language Modules (PDLMs) into the router's flash, and these PDLMs extend the IOS's ability to recognize traffic. PDLMs are available for download from http://www.cisco.com/cgi-bin/tablebuild.pl/pdlm.

Note that this site requires a Cisco.com login. Also, note that the context-sensitive help in the IOS might define the PDLM as Protocol Description Language Module instead of Packet Description Language Module.

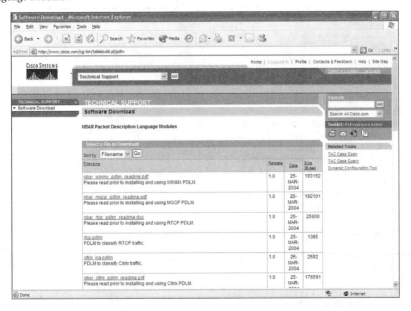

In addition to NBAR's usefulness in classifying, it can function as a protocol discovery tool. For example, NBAR protocol discovery could be enabled on an interface to determine the applications that are consuming the most bandwidth on that interface (that is, the "top talkers").

The following command configures NBAR protocol discovery:

```
Router(config-if)#ip nbar protocol-discovery
```

After NBAR has collected traffic statistics for an interface, use the following command to view the statistics:

```
Router#show ip nbar protocol-discovery
```

To use NBAR to classify traffic, as part of a class-map, use the keyword **protocol** in the **match** command, as follows:

```
Router(config-cmap)#match protocol protocol
```

You can reference the previously mentioned PDLM file with the following command:

```
Router(config)#ip nbar pdlm pdlm-file
```

In the following example, NBAR classifies KaZaa Version 2 traffic and HTTP traffic:

NBAR Example

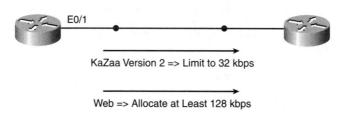

KaZaa Version 2 => Limit to 32 kbps

Web => Allocate at Least 128 kbps

NBAR can recognize stateful protocols (that is, protocols that change port numbers) and look beyond Layer 3 or Layer 4 information, including Layer 7 information.

```
Router(config)#class-map MUSIC
Router(config-cmap)#match protocol kazaa2
Router(config-cmap)#exit
Router(config)#class-map WEB
Router(config-cmap)#match protocol http
Router(config-cmap)#exit
Router(config)#policy-map NBARTEST
Router(config-pmap)#class MUSIC
Router(config-pmap-c)#police 32000
Router(config-pmap-c)#exit
Router(config-pmap)#class-map WEB
Router(config-pmap-c)#bandwidth 128
Router(config-pmap-c)#exit
Router(config-pmap)#exit
Router(config)#interface ethernet 0/1
Router(config-if)#service-policy output NBARTEST
```

In this example, KaZaa version 2 traffic is classified by the **MUSIC** class-map, whereas http traffic is classified by the **WEB** class-map. Then, the **NBARTEST** policy-map limits the MUSIC class to 32 kbps while allocating 128 kbps of bandwidth for the WEB class. Finally, the policy-map is applied outbound to the ethernet 0/1 interface.

Consider the priority that you should assign to web traffic. If you have an e-commerce site, as an example, web traffic might need varying levels of priority, depending on the content of the web traffic. The good news is that NBAR can recognize the content of web traffic using commands such as the following:

```
Router(config-cmap)#match protocol http url url-string
```

(Matches a string that is contained in the URL)

As an example, you could match traffic that contains the word *cisco* in the URL with the following command:

```
match protocol http url "*cisco*"
```

The asterisks are acting as wildcards, matching any characters before or after the word *cisco*.

QoS over Tunnel Connections

Virtual private networks (VPNs) are gaining tremendous popularity because of their ability to provide secure connectivity through a public network, such as an ISP. VPNs are made possible thanks to *tunneling*.

The challenge with QoS in a tunnel environment is that the tunnels encapsulate traffic, which hides the original information in a packet's header. After packets enter a tunnel, they have a tunnel header. Therefore, all packets have the same level of priority, because the classification of encapsulated packets is based on the tunnel header. The Cisco pre-classify feature overcomes this issue by applying QoS features to packets before they enter the tunnel. Pre-classification, however, is only necessary when you are classifying based on a criterion other than a packet's ToS byte. The IOS automatically copies bits from a packet's ToS byte into the ToS byte of the tunnel header.

Classification with Tunneling

After an IP packet is encapsulated in a tunnel, the original IP header
is concealed, and QoS classifications reference the tunnel header.

To enable the pre-classification feature, in tunnel-interface-configuration mode (or in crypto-map configuration mode for an IPSec tunnel), enter the following command:

```
qos pre-classify
```

QoS over BGP Networks

In a service provider environment, you might not want to use access-lists or other classification mechanisms through the service provider's network. An alternate option is to use QoS Policy Propagation Through BGP (QPPB).

QPPB lets you encode QoS information by assigning BGP attributes such as an autonomous system number, community string, or an IP prefix.

For example, instead of setting the IP Precedence marking to a 4 inside every packet, you could send the traffic with a certain community string. When the far-end autonomous system receives the traffic with that community string, it can mark those packets with an IP Precedence of 4.

In the following example for router R1, the community attribute determines how the IP Precedence value is set. Specifically, traffic with a community string of 20:1 has its IP Precedence set to a 2, and traffic with a community string of 20:2 has its IP Precedence set to a 3. The **bgp-policy source** command applies this policy to interface Serial 0/1.

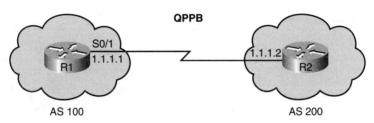

```
router bgp 100
table-map precedence-map
neighbor 1.1.1.2 remote-as 200
neighbor 1.1.1.2 send-community
!
route-map precedence-map permit 10
match community 1
set ip precedence 2
!
route-map precedence-map permit 20
match community 2
set ip precedence 3
!
ip community-list 1 permit 20:1
ip community-list 2 permit 20:2
!
interface serial 0/1
ip address 1.1.1.1 255.255.255.0
bgp-policy source ip-prec-map
```

Catalyst-Based Classification and Marking

You can perform classification and marking functions, not just on router platforms, but also on many Catalyst series switches. Even though QoS is considered primarily a WAN technology, proper QoS configuration in a enterprise network's infrastructure is also critical. For example, a switch might have interfaces that run at different speeds (for example, 10 Mbps and 1 Gbps). Such a scenario could lead to a switch queue overflowing. Also, traffic can enter a switch marked with a Layer 2 CoS value. These Layer 2 values do not pass through a route processor. Therefore, a Catalyst switch is an excellent place to perform CoS-to-DSCP remarking. So, when the traffic reaches the route processor, it has a Layer 3 marking, which can pass successfully through the route processor.

Applying QoS features at the edge of the network (for example, in a wiring closet) offers the following benefits:

- Provides immediate traffic classification
- Reduces congestion within the remainder of the network
- Eases the processor burden on the distribution and core routers

These Quick Reference Sheets primarily focus on the Catalyst 2950 Series of switches. You can configure the Catalyst 2950 ports to trust CoS or DSCP markings. However, by default, these ports are "untrusted," meaning that they disregard priority markings on incoming traffic. When a port is untrusted, traffic is assigned the configurable CoS value of the port.

The Catalyst 2950 can place frames in one of four queues. Later in these Quick Reference Sheets, you use these queues for Weighted Round Robin (WRR) queuing. For now, however, you should be familiar with how the switch places frames with various CoS markings into its four queues, as described in the following table.

Default Queue Assignment	
CoS Value	Queue
0 and 1	1
2 and 3	2
4 and 5	3
6 and 7	4

For internal QoS processing, all traffic (even non-IP traffic) is assigned an internal DSCP number. The default CoS-to-DSCP mappings are shown in the following table.

CoS-to-DSCP Mappings	
CoS Value	DSCP Value
0	0
1	8
2	16
3	24
4	32
5	40
6	48
7	56

Because the Catalyst 2950 uses CoS values to make queuing decisions, before the queuing process, the internal DSCP value is extrapolated to a CoS value. Although mappings are configurable, the default values are shown in the following table.

DSCP-to-CoS Mappings	
DSCP Values	CoS Value
0	0
8 and 10	1
16 and 18	2
24 and 26	3
32 and 34	4
40 and 46	5
48	6
56	7

With your understanding of the default switch behavior, you can explore how to manipulate the trust settings and the CoS-to-DSCP mappings. The following command tells a port what to trust:

```
Switch(config-if)#mls qos trust [cos [pass-through dscp] | device cisco-phone |
  dscp]
```

The **pass-through dscp** option does not modify the DSCP values (that is, remark them based on CoS values).

You can use the following command to assign a default CoS value for a port:

```
Switch(config-if)#mls qos cos {default-cos | override}
```

The **override** option applies the default CoS value to a frame, even though a frame might already have a CoS marking.

The following commands allow you to manipulate the default CoS-to-DSCP and DSCP-to-CoS mappings:

```
Switch(config)#mls qos map cos-dscp dscpvalue1 dscpvalue2 ... dscpvalue8
```

(Configures CoS-to-DSCP mapping)

For example:

```
Switch(config)#mls qos map cos-dscp 0 16 24 32 34 40 48 56
```

In this example, the eight DSCP values that are entered correspond to CoS values 0 through 7.

```
Switch(config)#mls qos map dscp-cos dscp-list to cos
```

(Configures DSCP-to-CoS mapping)

For example:

```
Switch(config)#mls qos map dscp-cos 16 28 24 26 to 1
```

DSCP to CoS Remarking

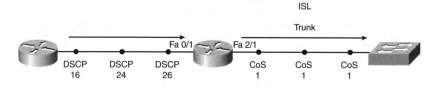

You can associate up to 13 DSCP values with a single CoS value.

The three-step MQC process can also be used on a Catalyst 2950 to perform classification and marking, without as many "match" options as are available on a router platform. Typically, you create a standard or extended IP access-list (or a Layer 2 MAC ACL for non-IP traffic). That access-list can then serve as the match criterion in a class-map. Note, however, that the extended IP access-lists that are available on the Catalyst 2950 do not have all the options that are available on a router. Specifically, you cannot use the access-list to match a range of port numbers.

In the following example, an extended IP access-list matches traffic that is destined for IP address 192.168.0.101. A policy-map then marks traffic that is destined for that host with a DSCP value of 34. Finally, the policy is applied to interface Gigabit Ethernet 0/3 in the inbound direction. The example is as follows:

```
Switch(config)#access-list 100 permit ip any host 192.168.0.101
Switch(config)#class-map CATCLASS
Switch(config-cmap)#match access-group 100
Switch(config-cmap)#exit
Switch(config)#policy-map CATPOLICY
Switch(config-pmap)#class CATCLASS
Switch(config-pmap-c)#set ip dscp 34
Switch(config-pmap-c)#interface gig 0/3
Switch(config-if)#service-policy input CATPOLICY
```

A switch's QoS interface configuration can be verified with the following command:

```
Switch#show mls qos interface interface-identifier
```

Use the following command to see how CoS and DSCP values are mapped to one another:

```
Switch#show mls qos maps [cos-dscp | dscp-cos]
```

Queuing

Sometimes referred to as congestion management, queuing mechanisms identify how traffic from multiple streams is sent out of an interface that is currently experiencing congestion. This section examines various approaches to queuing and emphasizes the queuing approaches configured via MQC.

Queuing Basics

When a device, such as a switch or a router, is receiving traffic faster than it can be transmitted, the device attempts to buffer the extra traffic until bandwidth is available. This buffering process is called *queuing*. You can use queuing mechanisms to influence in what order various traffic types are emptied from the queue.

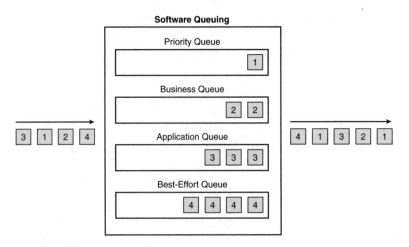

A software queuing mechanism is invoked
only after an interface's hardware queue overflows.

Congestion occurs not just in the WAN but also in the LAN. Mismatched interface speeds, for example, could result in congestion on a high-speed LAN. Points in the network in which you have aggregated multiple connections can result in congestion. For example, perhaps multiple workstations connect to a switch at Fast Ethernet speeds (that is, 100 Mbps), and the workstations are simultaneously transmitting to a server that is also connected through Fast Ethernet. Such a scenario can result in traffic backing up in a queue.

Although Cisco supports multiple queuing mechanisms, these Quick Reference Sheets primarily focus on CB-WFQ and LLQ. However, legacy queuing mechanisms are addressed first and include the following types:

- **FIFO queuing**—First-in first-out (FIFO) queuing is not truly performing QoS operations. As its name suggests, the first packet to come into the queue is the first packet sent out of the queue.

- **Priority Queuing (PQ)**—This type of queuing places traffic into one of four queues. Each queue has a different level of priority, and higher-priority queues must be emptied before packets are emptied from lower-priority queues. This behavior can "starve out" lower-priority traffic.
- **Round robin queuing**—This type of queuing places traffic into multiple queues, and packets are removed from these queues in a round-robin fashion, which avoids the protocol-starvation issue that PQ suffered from.
- **Weighted Round Robin (WRR) queuing**—This type of queuing can place a weight on the various queues, to service a different number of bytes or packets from the queues during a round-robin cycle. Custom Queuing (CQ) is an example of a WRR queuing approach.
- **Deficit Round Robin (DRR) queuing**—This type of queuing can suffer from a "deficit" issue. For example, if you configured CQ to removed 1500 bytes from a queue during each round-robin cycle, and you had a 1499-byte packet and a 1500-byte packet in the queue, both packets would be sent. This is because CQ cannot send a partial packet. Because the 1499-byte packet was transmitted and because another byte still had to be serviced, CQ would start servicing the 1500-byte packet. DRR keeps track of the number of extra bytes that are sent during a round and subtracts that number from the number of bytes that can be sent during the next round.

A router has two types of queues: a hardware queue and a software queue. The hardware queue, which is sometimes referred to as the transmit queue (TxQ), always uses FIFO queuing, and only when the hardware queue is full does the software queue handle packets. Therefore, your queuing configuration only takes effect during periods of interface congestion, when the hardware queue has overflowed. With this basic understanding of queuing, you begin to examine several queuing methods in more detail.

FIFO

Using FIFO in the software queue works just like FIFO in the hardware queue, where you are not truly performing packet manipulation. FIFO is the default queuing method on interfaces that run at speeds of greater than 2.048 Mbps.

Although FIFO is supported widely on all IOS platforms, it can starve out traffic by allowing bandwidth-hungry flows to take an unfair share of the bandwidth.

WFQ

Weighted Fair Queuing (WFQ) is enabled by default on slow-speed (that is, 2.048-Mbps and slower) interfaces. WFQ allocates a queue for each flow, for as many as 256 flows by default. WFQ uses IP Precedence values to provide a weighting to Fair Queuing (FQ). When emptying the queues, FQ does *byte-by-byte scheduling*. Specifically, FQ looks 1 byte deep into each queue to determine whether an entire packet can be sent. FQ then looks another byte deep into the queue to determine whether an entire packet can be sent. As a result, smaller traffic flows and smaller packet sizes have priority over bandwidth-hungry flows with large packets.

In the following example, three flows simultaneously arrive at a queue. Flow A has three packets, which are 128 bytes each. Flow B has a single 96-byte packet. Flow C has a single 70-byte packet. After 70 byte-by-byte rounds, FQ can transmit the packet from flow C. After an additional 26 rounds, FQ can transmit the packet from flow B. After an additional 32 rounds, FQ can transmit the first packet from flow A. Another 128 rounds are required to send the second packet from flow A. Finally, after a grand total of 384 rounds, the third packet from flow A is transmitted.

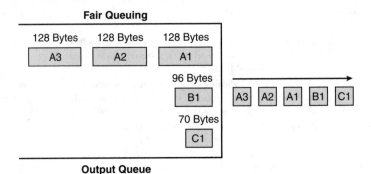

With WFQ, a packet's IP Precedence influences the order in which that packet is emptied from a queue. Consider the previous scenario with the addition of IP Precedence markings. In this scenario, flow A's packets are marked with an IP Precedence of 5, whereas flow B and flow C have default IP Precedence markings of 0. The order of packet servicing with WFQ is based on *sequence numbers,* where packets with the lowest sequence numbers are transmitted first.

The sequence number is the weight of the packet multiplied by the number of byte-by-byte rounds that must be completed to service the packet (just as in the FQ example). Cisco IOS calculates a packet's weight differently depending on the IOS version. Prior to IOS 12.0(5)T, the formula for weight was as follows:

$$\text{Weight} = 4096 / (\text{IP Prec.} + 1)$$

In more recent versions of the IOS, the formula for weight is as follows:

$$\text{Weight} = 32384 / (\text{IP Prec.} + 1)$$

Using the pre-IOS 12.0(5)T formula, the sequence numbers are as follows:

$$A1 = 4096 / (5 + 1) * 128 = 87381$$

$$A2 = 4096 / (5 + 1) * 128 + 87381 = 174762$$

$$A3 = 4096 / (5 + 1) * 128 + 174762 = 262144$$

$$B1 = 4096 / (0 + 1) * 96 = 393216$$

$$C1 = 4096 / (0 + 1) * 70 = 286720$$

Therefore, after the weighting is applied, WFQ empties packets from the queue in the following order: A1, A2, A3, C1, B1. With only FQ, packets were emptied from the queue in the order C1, B1, A1, A2, A3.

Although WFQ has default settings, you can manipulate those settings with the following interface-configuration-mode command:

```
Router(config-if)#fair-queue [cdt [dynamic-queues [reservable-queues]]]
```

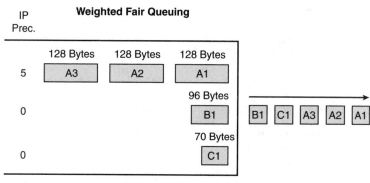

Output Queue

Sequence Number* = 4096/(IP Prec. + 1)

* In IOS 12.0(5)T and later, the Sequence Number = 32768/(IP Prec. + 1).

The *cdt* parameter identifies the Congestive Discard Threshold (CDT), which is the number of packets allowed in all WFQ queues before the router begins to drop packets that are attempting to enter the deepest queue (that is, the queue that currently has the most packets). The default CDT value is 64.

With WFQ, each flow is placed in its own queue, up to a maximum number of queues as defined by the *dynamic-queues* parameter. The default number of queues that is created dynamically (that is, dynamic-queues) is 256.

The *reservable-queues* parameter defines the number of queues that are made available to interface features such as RSVP. The default number of reservable queues is 0.

Although WFQ is easy to configure (for example, it is enabled by default on interfaces that run at or below 2.048 Mbps), and although WFQ is supported on all IOS versions, it has its limitations. Specifically, WFQ cannot guarantee a specific amount of bandwidth for an application. Also, if more than 256 flows exist, by default, more than one flow can be forced to share the same queue.

You can view statistics for WFQ with the **show interface** *interface-identifier* command. The output from this command not only verifies that WFQ is enabled on the specified interface, but it also shows such information as the current queue depth and the maximum number of queues allowed.

CB-WFQ

The WFQ mechanism made sure that no traffic was starved out. However, WFQ did not make a specific amount of bandwidth available for defined traffic types. You can, however, specify a minimum amount of bandwidth to make available for various traffic types using the CB-WFQ mechanism.

CB-WFQ is configured through the three-step MQC process. Using MQC, you can create up to 63 class-maps and assign a minimum amount of bandwidth for each one. Note that the reason you cannot create 64 class-maps is that the **class-default** class-map has already been created.

Traffic for each class-map goes into a separate queue. Therefore, one queue (for example, for CITRIX traffic) can be overflowing, while other queues are still accepting packets. Bandwidth allocations for various class-maps can be specified in one of three ways: bandwidth, percentage of bandwidth, and percentage of remaining bandwidth. The following paragraphs describe each of these allocations.

You can make a specific amount of bandwidth available for classified traffic. To allocate a bandwidth amount, use the following command, noting that the units of measure are in kbps:

```
Router(config-pmap-c)#bandwidth bandwidth
```

Instead of specifying an exact amount of bandwidth, you can specify a percentage of the interface bandwidth. For example, a policy-map could allocate 25 percent of an interface's bandwidth. Then, that policy-map could be applied to, for example, a Fast Ethernet interface and also to a slower-speed serial interface. To allocate a percentage of the interface bandwidth, use the following command:

```
Router(config-pmap-c)#bandwidth percent percent
```

As an alternative to allocating a percentage of the total interface bandwidth, you can also allocate a percentage of the remaining bandwidth (that is, after other bandwidth allocations have already been made). To allocate a percentage of the remaining interface bandwidth, use the following command:

```
Router(config-pmap-c)#bandwidth remaining percent percent
```

By default, each queue that is used by CB-WFQ has a capacity of 64 packets. However, this limit is configurable with the following command:

```
Router(config-pmap-c)#queue-limit number_of_packets
```

Although CB-WFQ queues typically use FIFO for traffic within a particular queue, the class-default queue can be enabled for WFQ with the following command:

```
Router(config-pmap-c)#fair-queue [dynamic-queues]
```

As noted earlier, CB-WFQ is configured through MQC. Therefore, the standard MQC verification and troubleshooting commands, such as **show policy-map interface** *interface-identifier*, are applicable for CB-WFQ.

By default, only 75 percent of an interface's bandwidth can be allocated. The remaining 25 percent is reserved for nonclassified or overhead traffic (for example, CDP, LMI, or routing protocols). This limitation can be overcome with the **max-reserved-bandwidth** *percentage* interface-configuration-mode command, where the *percentage* option is the percentage of an interface's bandwidth that can be allocated.

CB-WFQ is therefore an attractive queuing mechanism, thanks to its MQC configuration style and its ability to assign a minimum bandwidth allocation. The only major drawback to CB-WFQ is its inability to give priority treatment to any traffic class. Fortunately, an enhancement to CB-WFQ, called Low Latency Queuing (LLQ), does support traffic prioritization.

LLQ

Low Latency Queuing (LLQ) is almost identical to CB-WFQ. However, with LLQ, you can instruct one or more class-maps to direct traffic into a priority queue. Realize that when you place packets in a priority queue, you are not only allocating a bandwidth amount for that traffic, but you also are policing (that is, limiting the available bandwidth for) that traffic. The policing option is necessary to prevent higher-priority traffic from starving out lower-priority traffic.

Note that if you tell multiple class-maps to give priority treatment to their packets, all priority packets go into the same queue. Therefore, priority traffic could suffer from having too many priority classes. Packets that are queued in the priority queue cannot be fragmented, which is a consideration for slower-speed links (that is, link speeds of less than 768 kbps). LLQ, based on all the listed benefits, is the Cisco preferred queuing method for latency-sensitive traffic, such as voice and video.

You can use either of the following commands to direct packets to the priority queue:

```
Router(config-pmap-c)#priority bandwidth
```

(Note that the bandwidth units of measure are in kbps.)

```
Router(config-pmap-c)#priority percent percent
```

(Note that the *percent* option references a percentage of the interface bandwidth.)

Consider the following LLQ example.

LLQ Example

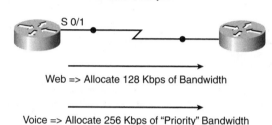

S 0/1

Web => Allocate 128 Kbps of Bandwidth

Voice => Allocate 256 Kbps of "Priority" Bandwidth

Whereas CB-WFQ allocates a specific bandwidth amount, LLQ can
allocate "priority" bandwidth amounts for specified traffic classes.

```
Router(config)#class-map SURFING
Router(config-cmap)#match protocol http
Router(config-cmap)#exit
Router(config)#class-map VOICE
Router(config-cmap)#match protocol rtp
Router(config-cmap)#exit
Router(config)#policy-map QOS_STUDY
Router(config-pmap)#class SURFING
Router(config-pmap-c)#bandwidth 128
Router(config-pmap-c)#exit
Router(config-pmap)#class-map VOICE
Router(config-pmap-c)#priority 256
Router(config-pmap-c)#exit
Router(config-pmap)#exit
Router(config)#interface serial 0/1
Router(config-if)#service-policy output QOS_STUDY
```

In this example, NBAR is being used to recognize http traffic, and that traffic is placed in the **SURFING** class. Note that NBAR is invoked with the following command:

```
Router(config-cmap)# match protocol
```

Voice packets are placed in the **VOICE** class. The **QOS_STUDY** policy-map gives 128 kbps of bandwidth to the http traffic while giving 256 kbps of priority bandwidth to voice traffic. Then the policy-map is applied outbound to interface serial 0/1.

Catalyst-Based Queuing

Some Cisco Catalyst switches also support their own queuing method, called Weighted Round Robin (WRR) queuing. For example, a Catalyst 2950 switch has four queues, and WRR can be configured to place frames with specific CoS markings into certain queues. (For example, CoS values 0 and 1 are placed in Queue 1.)

Weights can be assigned to the queues, influencing how much bandwidth the various markings receive. The queues are then serviced in a round-robin fashion. On the Catalyst 2950, queue number 4 can be designated as an "expedite" queue, which gives priority treatment to frames in that queue. Specifically, the expedite queue must be empty before any additional queues are serviced. This behavior can lead to protocol starvation.

On a Catalyst 2950, frames are queued based on their CoS values. The following command can be used to alter the default queue assignments:

```
Switch(config)#wrr-queue cos-map queue_number cos_value_1 cos_value_2 …
  cos_value_n
```

For example, the following command would map CoS values of 0, 1, and 2 to queue number 1 on a Catalyst 2950:

```
Switch(config)#wrr-queue cos-map 1 0 1 2
```

The weight that is assigned to a queue specifies how many packets are emptied from a queue during each round-robin cycle, relative to other queues. You can configure queue weights with the following command:

```
Switch(config)#wrr-queue bandwidth weight_1 weight_2 weight_3 weight_4
```

Remember that queue number 4 on a Catalyst 2950 can be configured as an expedite queue (that is, a priority queue). To configure queue number 4 as an expedite queue, set its weight to 0.

Following is an example of a WRR configuration.

Weighted Round Robin (WRR)

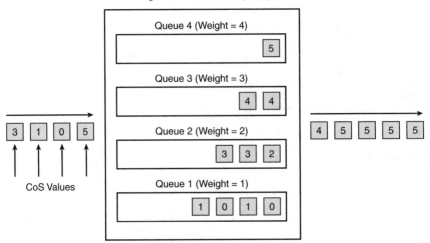

WRR "weights" queues to determine the relative amount of bandwidth available to each queue. In this example, Queue 4 has twice the available bandwidth of Queue 2.

```
Switch(config)#interface gig 0/5
Switch(config-if)#wrr-queue bandwidth 1 2 3 4
Switch(config-if)#wrr cos-map 4 5
```

In this example, the **wrr-queue** command is assigning the weights 1, 2, 3, and 4 to the switch's four queues. The first queue, with a weight of 1, for example, only gets one-third the bandwidth that is given to the third queue, which has a weight of 3. The **wrr cos-map 4 5** command is instructing frames that are marked with a CoS of 5 to enter the fourth queue.

To verify how a Catalyst 2950 is mapping CoS values to DSCP values (or vice versa), use the following command:

```
Switch#show mls qos maps [cos-dscp | dscp-cos]
```

You can use the following command to view the weight that is assigned to each queue:

```
Switch#show wrr-queue bandwidth
```

Another useful WRR command, which shows how CoS values are being mapped to switch queues shows is as follows:

```
Switch#show wrr-queue cos-map
```

Finally, you can see the QoS configuration for an interface (for example, trust state and the interface's default CoS value) with the following command:

```
Switch#show mls qos interface [interface-identifier]
```

Weighted Random Early Detection (WRED)

Whereas queuing provides congestion management, mechanisms such as WRED provide congestion avoidance. Specifically, WRED can prevent an output queue from ever filling to capacity, which would result in packet loss for all incoming packets. This section examines the need for and the configuration of WRED on Cisco routers.

How TCP Handles Drops

Recall from your early studies of networking technology how Transport Control Protocol (TCP) windowing functions. A sender sends a single segment, and if the sender receives a successful acknowledgment from the receiver, it then sends two segments (that is, a "windows size" of 2). If those two segments were acknowledged successfully, the sender sends four segments, and so on, increasing the window size exponentially.

However, if one of the segments is dropped, the TCP flow goes into TCP slow start, where the window size is reduced to 1. The TCP flow then exponentially increases its window size until the window size reaches half of the window size when congestion originally occurred. At that point, the TCP flow's window size increases linearly.

TCP slow start is relevant to QoS, because when an interface's output queue is full, all newly arriving packets are discarded (that is, "tail dropped"), and all of those TCP flows simultaneously go into TCP slow start.

Note that the process of multiple TCP flows simultaneously entering TCP slow start is called *global synchronization* or *TCP synchronization*. When TCP synchronization occurs, the link's bandwidth is underutilized, resulting in wasted bandwidth.

RED Basics

The purpose of Random Early Detection (RED) is to prevent TCP synchronization by randomly discarding packets as an interface's output queue begins to fill. How aggressively RED discards packets depends on the current queue depth.

The following three parameters influence when a newly arriving packet is discarded:

- Minimum threshold
- Maximum threshold
- Mark Probability Denominator (MPD)

The *minimum threshold* specifies the number of packets in a queue before the queue considers discarding packets. The probability of discard increases until the queue depth reaches the *maximum threshold*. After a queue depth exceeds the maximum threshold, all other packets that attempt to enter the queue are discarded.

However, the probability of packet discard when the queue depth equals the maximum threshold is 1/(MPD). For example, if the mark probability denominator were set to 10, when the queue depth reached the maximum threshold, the probability of discard would be 1/10 (that is, a 10 percent chance of discard).

Random Early Detection (RED)

As an output queue fills beyond the minimum threshold, RED begins to discard packets. Those packets are discarded more aggressively as the queue depth increases. When the queue depth exceeds the maximum threshold, all packets are discarded.

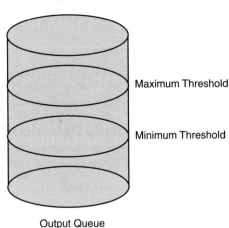

Maximum Threshold

Minimum Threshold

Output Queue

The minimum threshold, maximum threshold, and MPD comprise the RED profile. The following figure shows the three distinct ranges in a RED profile: no drop, random drop, and full drop.

RED Drop Ranges

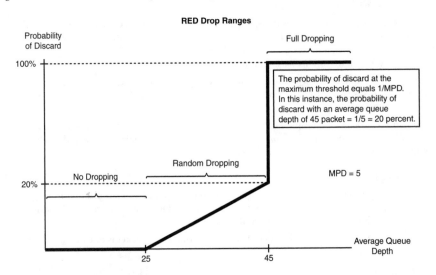

RED is most useful on router interfaces where congestion is likely. For example, a WAN interface might be a good candidate for RED.

CB-WRED

Cisco does not support RED, but fortunately it supports something better: Weighted Random Early Detection (WRED). Unlike RED, WRED has a profile for each priority marking. For example, a packet with an IP Precedence value of 0 might have a minimum threshold of 20 packets, whereas a packet with an IP Precedence of 1 might have a minimum threshold of 25 packets. In this example, packets with an IP Precedence of 0 would start to be discarded before packets with an IP Precedence of 1.

Although WRED can be configured from interface-configuration mode or from virtual-circuit-configuration mode, these Quick Reference Sheets focus on an MQC-based WRED configuration. To enable WRED and to specify the marking that WRED pays attention to (that is, IP Precedence or DSCP), issue the following policy-map-class configuration-mode command:

```
Router(config-pmap-c)#random-detect [dscp-based | prec-based]
```

If neither **dscp-based** nor **prec-based** is specified, WRED defaults to **prec-based**. After WRED is configured, the IOS assigns default minimum threshold, maximum threshold, and MPD values. However, you can alter those default parameters with the following commands:

```
Router(config-pmap-c)#random-detect precedence precedence_value minimum-
    threshold maximum-threshold mark-probability-denominator
```

(Used for prec-based WRED)

```
Router(config-pmap-c)#random-detect dscp dscp_value minimum-threshold maximum-
    threshold mark-probability-denominator
```

(Used for dscp-based WRED)

To reinforce this syntax, consider the following example, where the goal is to configure WRED for the **WREDTEST** class-map. After the class-map's queue depth reaches 25 packets, a DSCP value of AF13 might be discarded. Packets that are marked with a DSCP value of AF12 should not be discarded until the queue depth reaches 30 packets, and finally, packets that are marked with a DSCP value of AF11 should have no chance of discard until the queue depth reaches 35 packets. If the queue depth exceeds 100 packets, there should be a 100 percent chance of discard for these three DSCP values. However, when the queue depth is exactly 100 packets, the chance of discard for these various packet types should be 25 percent. Also, CB-WRED requires that CB-WFQ be configured for the interface. So, as an additional requirement, you make 25 percent of the interface's bandwidth available to the **WREDTEST** class of traffic.

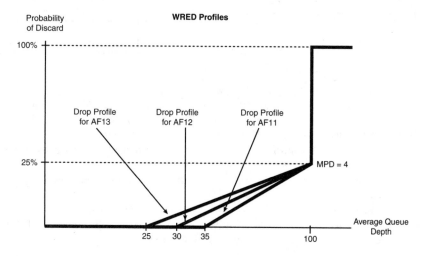

```
Router(config-pmap)#class WREDTEST
Router(config-pmap-c)#bandwidth percent 25
Router(config-pmap-c)#random-detect dscp-based
Router(config-pmap-c)#random-detect dscp af13 25 100 4
Router(config-pmap-c)#random-detect dscp af12 30 100 4
Router(config-pmap-c)#random-detect dscp af11 35 100 4
```

Examine the solution, and notice that the MPD is 4. This value was chosen to meet the requirement of a 25 percent chance of discard when the queue depth equals the maximum threshold (that is, $1/4 = .25$). Also, notice that a DSCP value of AF13 is dropped before a DSCP value of AF12, which is dropped before a DSCP value of AF11. This approach is consistent with the definition of the per-hop behaviors (PHBs), because the last digit in the Assured Forwarding (AF) DSCP name indicates its drop preference. For example, a value of AF13 would drop before a value of AF12.

To view the minimum threshold, maximum threshold, and MPD settings for the various IP Precedence or DSCP values, you can issue the **show policy-map interface** *interface-identifier* command.

ECN Configuration

WRED discards packets, and that is one way for the router to indicate congestion. However, routers can now indicate a congestion condition by signaling, using an approach called Explicit Congestion Notification (ECN).

ECN uses the 2 last bits in the ToS byte to indicate whether a device is ECN capable, and if so, whether congestion is being experienced.

Explicit Congestion Notification (ECN)

IPv4 Packet

Bit Combination	Meaning
00	Router is not ECN capable.
01	Router is ECN capable but is not experiencing congestion.
10	Router is ECN capable but is not experiencing congestion.
11	Router is ECN capable and is currently experiencing congestion.

ECT = ECN-Capable Transport
CE = Congestion Experienced

ECT Bit   CE Bit

Cisco routers can use ECN as an extension to WRED and mark packets that exceed a specified value, instead of dropping the packets. If the queue depth is at or below the WRED minimum threshold, the packets are sent normally, just as with WRED. Also, if the queue depth is above the WRED maximum threshold, all packets are dropped, just as with WRED.

But if the queue depth is currently in the range from the minimum threshold through the maximum threshold, one of the following things can happen:

- If both endpoints are ECN capable, the ECT and CE bits are set to a 1 and sent to the destination, indicating that the transmission rate should be reduced.
- If neither endpoints supports ECN, the normal WRED behavior occurs.
- A packet with its ECN and CE bits marked can reach a destination router that already has a full queue. In such an instance, the notification is dropped.

Use the following command to enable ECN:

```
Router(config-pmap-c)#random-detect ecn
```

Note that although WRED also can be configured in interface-configuration mode, ECN must be configured through MQC. Because ECN is configured by the three-step MQC process, the same verification and troubleshooting commands apply. Specifically, you can use the **show policy-map** and **show policy-map interface** *interface-identifier* commands to verify the ECN configuration.

Traffic Conditioners

QoS mechanisms can not only provide for the allocation of a minimum amount of bandwidth for specific traffic but also limit the amount of bandwidth made available to that traffic. This section discusses how policing and shaping mechanisms limit traffic rates.

Policing Versus Shaping

Instead of allocating bandwidth for applications, in some instances, you might want to restrict the amount of bandwidth that is available for specific traffic. For example, you might want to set a "speed limit" for users on the network who are downloading music files from the Internet.

QoS mechanisms that limit bandwidth are called *traffic conditioners*. The two categories of traffic conditioners are policing and shaping. Although both of these approaches limit bandwidth, they have different characteristics, as follows:

- **Policing**—Policing typically limits bandwidth by discarding traffic that exceeds a specified rate. However, policing also can remark traffic that exceeds the specified rate and attempt to send the traffic anyway. Because policing's drop behavior causes TCP retransmits, it is recommended for use on higher-speed interfaces. Also, note that policing can be applied inbound or outbound on an interface.

- **Shaping**—Shaping limits excess traffic, not by dropping it but by buffering it. This buffering of excess traffic can lead to delay. Because of this delay, shaping is recommended for slower-speed interfaces. Unlike policing, shaping cannot remark traffic. As a final contrast, shaping can be applied only in the outbound direction on an interface.

The question becomes this: How do you send traffic out of an interface at a rate that is less than the physical clock rate of the interface? It is impossible for an interface to send at a rate that is slower than the line rate. However, you can send at an "average" rate that is less than the clock rate by using policing or shaping tools that do not transmit all the time. Specifically, these tools send a certain number of bits or bytes at line rate, and then they stop sending until a specific timing interval (for example, 1/8 of a second) is reached. When the timing interval is reached, the interface again sends a specific amount of traffic at line rate, it stops, and then it waits for the next timing interval to occur. This process continually repeats, allowing an interface to send an average bandwidth that can be below the physical speed of the interface. This average bandwidth is called the Committed Information Rate (CIR). The number of bits (the unit of measure that is used with shaping tools) or bytes (the unit of measure that is used with policing tools) that is sent during a timing interval is called the Committed Burst (Bc). The timing interval is written as Tc.

For example, consider that you have a physical line rate of 128 kbps, but the CIR is only 64 kbps. Also consider that there are eight timing intervals in a second (that is, Tc = 1/8 of a second = 125 ms), and during each of those timing intervals, 8000 bits (that is, the committed burst parameter) are sent at line rate. Therefore, over the period of a second, 8000 bits were sent (at line rate) eight times, for a grand total of 64,000 bits per second, which is the CIR.

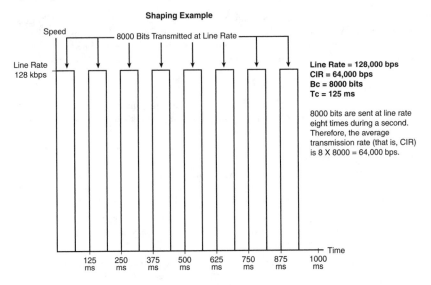

Shaping Example

Speed

8000 Bits Transmitted at Line Rate

Line Rate
128 kbps

Line Rate = 128,000 bps
CIR = 64,000 bps
Bc = 8000 bits
Tc = 125 ms

8000 bits are sent at line rate
eight times during a second.
Therefore, the average
transmission rate (that is, CIR)
is 8 X 8000 = 64,000 bps.

Time

125 ms   250 ms   375 ms   500 ms   625 ms   750 ms   875 ms   1000 ms

However, if all the Bc bits (or bytes) were not sent during a timing interval, you have an option to "bank" those bits and use them during a future timing interval. The parameter that allows this storing of unused potential bandwidth is called the Excess Burst (Be) parameter. The Be parameter in a shaping configuration specifies the maximum number of bits or bytes that can be sent in excess of the Bc during a timing interval, if those bits are indeed available. For those bits or bytes to be available, they must have gone unused during previous timing intervals. Policing tools, however, use the Be parameter to specify the maximum number of bytes that can be sent during a timing interval. Therefore, in a policing configuration, if the Bc equals the Be, no excess bursting occurs. If excess bursting does occur, policing tools consider this excess traffic as *exceeding traffic*. Traffic that conforms to (that is, does not exceed) the specified CIR is considered by a policing tool to be *conforming traffic*. As part of your policing configuration, you can specify what action to take when traffic conforms to the CIR and what other action to take when the traffic exceeds the CIR.

The relationship between the Tc, Bc, and CIR is given with the following formula:

CIR = Bc / Tc

Alternatively, the formula can be written as follows:

Tc = Bc / CIR

Therefore, if you want a smaller timing interval, you could configure a smaller Bc.

To illustrate the operation of traffic conditioners, Cisco allows the metaphor of a "token bucket," where you place Bc tokens in the bucket during each timing interval. Also, the bucket can hold a total of Be tokens. In a policing configuration, traffic that requires no more than the Bc number of bits or bytes to be transmitted is called *conforming traffic*. Traffic that requires more than the Bc number of bits or bytes is said to be *exceeding traffic*.

Consider a policing example, where 500 bytes are currently in the token bucket. A packet comes through requiring 300 bytes. The bytes are removed from the bucket, and the packet is sent. Then, before the bucket has been replenished with more tokens, another 300-byte packet comes along. Because only 200 bytes remain in the bucket, the packet cannot be sent and is discarded.

Token Bucket

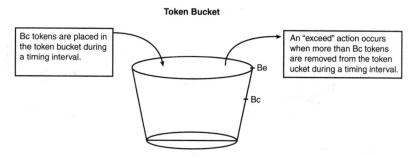

Bc tokens are placed in the token bucket during a timing interval.

An "exceed" action occurs when more than Bc tokens are removed from the token ucket during a timing interval.

This illustration describes how policing functions with a *single token bucket;* however Cisco supports a *dual token bucket.*

With a dual token bucket, two buckets exist. The first bucket has a depth of Bc, and the second bucket has a depth of Be. If a packet can be forwarded using bytes in the Bc bucket, it is said to be *conforming.* If the packet cannot be forwarded using the bytes in the Bc bucket, but it can be forwarded using the bytes in the Be bucket, it is said to be *exceeding.* If the packet cannot be forwarded using either of the buckets individually, it is said to be *violating.* Realize, however, that a violating packet can still be transmitted if it can be forwarded using the combined bytes in both the Bc and Be buckets.

Dual Token Bucket

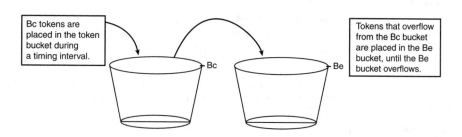

Bc tokens are placed in the token bucket during a timing interval.

Tokens that overflow from the Bc bucket are placed in the Be bucket, until the Be bucket overflows.

Instead of policing traffic to a single rate, Cisco also supports dual-rate policing. With dual-rate policing, you still have two token buckets. The first bucket is the Committed Information Rate (CIR) bucket, and the second bucket is the Peak Information Rate (PIR) bucket. These buckets are replenished with tokens at different rates, with the PIR bucket being filled at a faster rate.

When a packet arrives, the dual-rate policer checks to see whether the PIR bucket has enough tokens (that is, bytes) to send the packet. If there are not sufficient tokens, the packet is said to be *violating,* and it is discarded. Otherwise, the policer checks to see whether the CIR bucket has enough tokens to forward the packet. If the packet can be sent using the CIR bucket's tokens, the packet is *conforming.* If the CIR bucket's tokens are not sufficient, but the PIR bucket's tokens are sufficient, the packet is said to be *exceeding*, and the exceed action (for example, transmit with a DSCP value of AF11) is applied.

Dual-Rate Token Bucket

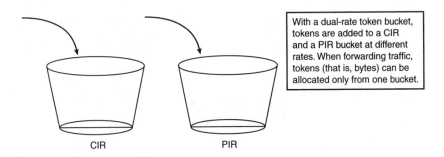

With a dual-rate token bucket, tokens are added to a CIR and a PIR bucket at different rates. When forwarding traffic, tokens (that is, bytes) can be allocated only from one bucket.

With a policing mechanism, you can specify various actions to perform based on whether a packet is conforming, exceeding, or violating. Examples of these actions are as follows:

- **Transmit**—Send the packet on to the scheduler.
- **Drop**—Discard the packet.
- **Mark**—Set priority bits for the packet.
- **Multiaction**—Perform more than one action, such as mark the packet with a DSCP value of AF12 and set the CLP bit to a 1.

CB-Policing Configuration

First, consider the configuration of Class-Based Policing (CB-Policing) for a single rate. You can configure CB-Policing with the following command:

```
Router(config-pmap-c)#police cir [bc [be]] [conform-action action] [exceed-
action action] [violate-action action]
```

Note that you do not have to specify the Bc or Be values. If you specify only the CIR, the IOS calculates Bc as CIR/32 or 1500 (whichever is higher). Also, the default Be value equals Bc, meaning that the token bucket never holds more than Bc bytes.

In the following example, you want to limit web traffic to 100 kbps and Telnet traffic to 50 kbps on interface Ethernet 0/0.

CB-Policing

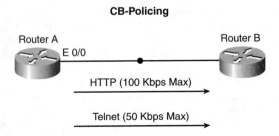

```
RouterA(config)#class-map WEB
RouterA(config-cmap)#match protocol http
```

```
RouterA(config-cmap)#exit
RouterA(config)#class-map TELNET
RouterA(config-cmap)#match protocol telnet
RouterA(config-cmap)#exit
RouterA(config)#policy-map POLICING_EXAMPLE
RouterA(config-pmap)#class WEB
RouterA(config-pmap-c)#police 100000
RouterA(config-pmap-c)#exit
RouterA(config-pmap)#class-map TELNET
RouterA(config-pmap-c)#police 50000
RouterA(config-pmap-c)#exit
RouterA(config-pmap-c)#exit
RouterA(config-pmap)#exit
RouterA(config)#interface Ethernet 0/0
RouterA(config-if)#service-policy output POLICING_EXAMPLE
```

As mentioned earlier, you can configure dual-rate CB-Policing, where you police to two distinct rates: the CIR and PIR. The following command configures dual-rate CB-Policing:

```
Router(config-pmap-c)#police cir cir [bc bc] [pir pir] [be be] [conform-action
    action] [exceed-action action] [violate-action action]
```

Similar to CB-WFQ and LLQ, dual-rate CB-Policing allows you to limit the bandwidth of specific traffic by a percentage of an interface's bandwidth. This can be accomplished with the following command:

```
Router(config-pmap-c)#police cir percent percent [bc bc] [pir percent percent]
    [be be] [conform-action action] [exceed-action action] [violate-action action]
```

CB-Shaping Configuration

One of two approaches can be used when configuring Class-Based Shaping (CB-Shaping): shaping to average and shaping to peak. When you configure CB-Shaping to shape to average, you only want to send traffic at the CIR. However, if you configure shaping to peak, you are attempting to send above the CIR, if bandwidth is available. Specifically, when you shape to peak, instead of just adding Bc bits to the token bucket during each timing interval, you are adding Bc + Be bits to the token bucket. The peak rate is given by the following formula:

$$\text{Peak Rate} = \text{CIR} * [1 + (\text{Be/Bc})]$$

Although shaping to peak can squeeze out some extra bandwidth from a WAN connection, it also can lead to multiple packet drops. Therefore, you should judiciously choose between the average and peak options.

Following is the command to configure CB-Shaping:

```
Router(config-pmap-c)#shape {average | peak} cir [bc] [be]
```

Like CB-Policing, CB-Shaping can specify its CIR as a percentage of interface bandwidth, with the following command:

```
Router(config-pmap-c)#shape {average | peak} percent percent [bc] [be]
```

Consider the following CB-Shaping example, where you are shaping one class-map to average and another class-map to peak:

```
Router(config)#class-map AVERAGECLASS
Router(config-cmap)#match protocol telnet
Router(config-cmap)#exit
Router(config)#class-map PEAKCLASS
Router(config-cmap)#match protocol http
Router(config-cmap)#exit
Router(config)#policy-map AVERAGEPOLICY
```

```
Router(config-pmap)#class AVERAGECLASS
Router(config-pmap-c)#shape average 64000
Router(config-pmap-c)#exit
Router(config-pmap)#exit
Router(config)#policy-map PEAKPOLICY
Router(config-pmap)#class PEAKCLASS
Router(config-pmap-c)#shape peak 64000
```

In this example, the **AVERAGEPOLICY** policy-map is shaping Telnet traffic to average, meaning that Telnet traffic is shaped to the CIR of 64 kbps. However, that is not the case for the **PEAK-POLICY** policy-map.

The **PEAKPOLICY** policy-map is shaping traffic to a peak rate of CIR * [1 + (Be/Bc)]. Because you let the IOS calculate the Bc and Be values, they are equal, which means that you are shaping to a rate of 64000 * (1 + 1) = 128 kbps.

Enabling CB-Shaping for Frame Relay Networks

On Frame Relay networks, you might need not only to shape your traffic, but you might also need your router to respond to congestion occurring in the service provider's cloud, by reducing the CIR to a lower value.

When a service provider becomes congested and needs to discard frames, it first discards frames with their Discard Eligible (DE) bit set to a 1. The service provider also can request that the sending router slow its transmission rate, by marking the Backward Explicit Congestion Notification (BECN) bit to a 1, in a frame going back to the sender. When this occurs, if the router is configured to respond to BECNs, the router reduces its CIR by 25 percent. If the router receives another BECN in the next time interval, it decreases its transmission rate by 25 percent of the current rate. This behavior can continue until the rate drops to the router's configured minimum CIR.

Backward Explicit Congestion Notification (BECN)

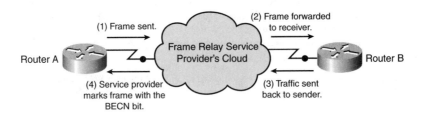

When Router A receives a frame marked with
a BECN bit, it reduces its CIR by 25 percent.

You can, however, encounter a situation in which the vast majority of the traffic is from one router to another router (that is, with little, if any, return traffic). In such a situation, the service provider cannot mark the BECN bit in a frame going back to the sender, because no (or very few) frames are going back to the sender. To remedy this situation, the service provider can mark the Forward Explicit Congestion Notification (FECN) bit in a frame that is destined for the receiver. If the receiver is configured to respond to FECNs, it generates a Q.922 test frame and sends it back to the sender. This test frame gives the service provider the opportunity to mark a frame's BECN bit, in an attempt to make the sender slow its transmission rate.

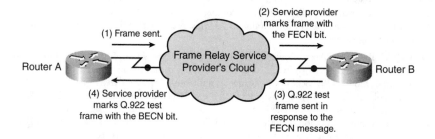

Forward Explicit Congestion Notification (FECN)

Router A

(1) Frame sent.

Frame Relay Service Provider's Cloud

(2) Service provider marks frame with the FECN bit.

Router B

(4) Service provider marks Q.922 test frame with the BECN bit.

(3) Q.922 test frame sent in response to the FECN message.

Instead of waiting for Router B to send traffic back to Router A, the service provider marks a frame going to Router B with a FECN bit. This bit causes Router B to send a Q.922 test frame back to Router A. The service provider marks the BECN bit in this frame to ask Router A to reduce its CIR.

After a sender has slowed its transmission rate because of BECNs, 16 timing intervals must elapse before the sender begins to increase its transmission rate. When the sender does begin to increase its transmission rate, it does so at a much more cautious rate than when it reduced its rate. Specifically, the sender only increases its transmission rate by (Be + Bc) / 16 bits per timing interval.

Consider the following example, where CB-Shaping is being combined with CB-WFQ to allocate at least one amount of bandwidth, while shaping (that is, limiting the traffic rate) to a higher bandwidth.

```
Router(config)#policy-map FRAMESHAPE
Router(config-pmap)#class FRAMECLASS
Router(config-pmap-c)#shape average 128000
Router(config-pmap-c)#shape adaptive 96000
Router(config-pmap-c)#bandwidth 96
```

In this example, traffic classified by the **FRAMECLASS** class-map is shaped to an average rate of 128 kbps. Also, the **shape adaptive** *mincir* command is used to specify the minimum value to which the CIR can drop in the presence of BECNs. In this example, the router can reduce its transmission rate to a CIR of 96 kbps. (Note that the units of measure for the *mincir* parameter are bits per second.) Also, CB-WFQ specifies that at least 96 kbps of bandwidth is available for this class of traffic. Note that, as shown in the previous example, minimum CIR (as specified by the **shape adaptive** command) should not be less than the bandwidth that is allocated by CB-WFQ.

QoS on Slow-Speed Links

In this section, you make the most of your limited bandwidth on lower-speed WAN interfaces. Specifically, you are introduced to compression technologies, which send fewer bits across the link, and link fragmentation and interleaving technologies, which fragment large payloads to reduce the serialization delay that is experienced by smaller payloads.

Tools for Using Bandwidth Efficiently

The two broad categories of compression are as follows:

- **Payload compression**—Reduces the payload size, using approaches such as STAC, Predictor, or MPPC.
- **Header compression**—Reduces the size of the TCP and RTP headers.

The goal of compression technologies is to increase the throughput over a WAN link while reducing the delay. However, particularly with payload-compression approaches, the time that is required by lower-end routers to run the compression algorithm can increase the overall delay. Fortunately, these routers can have hardware acceleration modules that you can add to dramatically improve the router's ability to perform compression in a timely manner. For example, a Compression Advanced Integration Module (CAIM) is available to offload compression tasks from 2600 Series routers.

These Quick Reference Sheets, however, focus on header compression. With header compression, a header typically is reduced from approximately 40 bytes in size to approximately 3 to 5 bytes [for Transport Control Protocol (TCP) header compression] or 2 to 4 bytes [for Real-Time Transport Protocol (RTP) header compression]. However, the routers technically are not doing compression. Rather, these routers cache information that does not change during a conversation, such as source and destination IP addresses and TCP/UDP port numbers. The compressed header then carries such information as UDP checksums and a session context ID (CID), which identifies which flow the packet is a part of.

RTP Header Compression

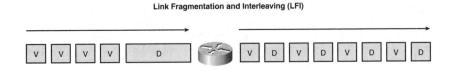

Another QoS mechanism that is useful for slower link speeds is Link Fragmentation and Interleaving (LFI). Consider a 1500-byte data frame that is being sent out of a 64-kbps serial interface. The interface, in this case, needs 187 ms just to place that data frame on the wire. If a smaller packet were sitting behind that data frame (for example, a voice frame), that frame might have already experienced excessive "serialization" delay before it was ever placed on the wire. LFI mechanisms fragment larger payloads to specified fragment sizes and then interleave the smaller payloads in among the fragments, greatly reducing the serialization delay that is experienced by the smaller payloads.

Link Fragmentation and Interleaving (LFI)

The three primary LFI mechanisms supported by Cisco are as follows:

- **Multilink PPP (MLP)**—Used on PPP links
- **FRF.12**—Used on Voice over IP over Frame Relay (VoIPovFR) links
- **FRF.11 Annex C**—Used on Voice over Frame Relay (VoFR) links

TCP and RTP Header Compression

Although header compression has been supported in the IOS for some time, IOS 12.2(13)T introduced Class-Based Header (CB-Header) Compression, which allows you to configure compression using the three-step MQC approach. CB-Header Compression is the focus of these Quick Reference Sheets.

Before configuring header compression, realize that header compression is most effective for slow links that are carrying packets with relatively small payloads, such as voice or Telnet traffic.

CB-Header Compression can be configured from policy-map-class configuration mode with the following command:

```
Router(config-pmap-c)#compression header ip [tcp | rtp]
```

Note that if you do not specify **tcp** or **rtp,** this command performs both TCP and RTP header compression. Unlike previous versions of header compression, you do not need to specify the maximum number of simultaneous compressed sessions supported. With CB-Header Compression, the number of connections is determined automatically by the IOS.

Consider the following CB-Header Compression example:

```
Router(config)#class-map VOICE
Router(config-cmap)#match protocol rtp
Router(config-cmap)#exit
Router(config)#policy-map COMPRESS
Router(config-pmap)#class VOICE
Router(config-pmap-c)#compression header ip rtp
Router(config-pmap-c)#exit
Router(config-pmap)#exit
Router(config)#interface serial 0/1
Router(config-if)#service-policy output COMPRESS
```

In this example, you are matching voice traffic (that is, RTP packets) using NBAR. Then, you are applying CB-Header Compression to those RTP packets with the **COMPRESS** policy-map. The policy-map is then applied outbound to interface serial 0/1. Because you configured header compression using the MQC approach, the same verification commands that you learned earlier (that is, **show policy-map** and **show policy-map interface** *interface-identifier*) are still applicable.

Using MLP and FRF.12 for LFI

The serialization delay goal that you have when configuring an LFI mechanism is in the range of 10 to 15 ms. To determine the serialization delay for a specific frame size on a specific link speed, use the following formula:

$$\text{Serialization Delay} = (\text{Frame\_Size} * 8) / \text{Link\_Speed}$$

The reason that you multiply the frame size by 8 is to convert bytes into bits. Consider a frame size of 512 bytes on a link speed of 128 kbps, as follows:

$$\text{Serialization Delay} = (512 * 8) / 128 = 32 \text{ ms}$$

Although Cisco supports FRF.11 Annex C as an LFI mechanism for VoFR networks, these Quick Reference Sheets focus on the configuration of Multilink PPP (MLP) and FRF.12. First, consider the configuration of MLP.

Multilink PPP, by default, fragments traffic. You can leverage that fact and run MLP, even over a single link. You perform the MLP configuration under a virtual multilink interface, and then you can assign one or more physical interfaces to the multilink group. The physical interface does not have an IP address assigned, but the virtual multilink interface does. Typically, you use a single interface as a member of the multilink group. Following is the syntax to configure MLP:

```
Router(config)#interface multilink multilink_interface_number
```

(Creates a virtual multilink interface.)

```
Router(config-if)#ip address ip_address subnet_mask
```

(Assigns an IP address to the virtual multilink interface.)

```
Router(config-if)#ppp multilink
```

(Configures fragmentation on the multilink interface.)

```
Router(config-if)#ppp multilink interleave
```

(Shuffles the fragments together.)

```
Router(config-if)#ppp fragment-delay serialization_delay
```

(Specifies how long it will take for a fragment to exit the interface, in milliseconds. Note that the IOS automatically calculates the appropriate packet size to meet the specified serialization delay.)

```
Router(config-if)#encapsulation ppp
```

(Enables ppp encapsulation on the physical interface.)

```
Router(config-if)#no ip address
```

(Removes the IP address from the physical interface.)

```
Router(config-if)#multilink-group multilink_group_number
```

(Associates the physical interface with the multilink group.)

In the following example, the goal is to configure MLP on routers R1 and R2 so that you are achieving a serialization delay of 10 ms on their serial 0/0 interfaces.

Multilink PPP

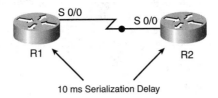

10 ms Serialization Delay

```
R1(config)#interface multilink 1
R1(config-if)#ip address 10.1.1.1 255.255.255.0
R1(config-if)#ppp multilink
R1(config-if)#ppp multilink interleave
R1(config-if)#ppp fragment-delay 10
R1(config-if)#exit
R1(config)#interface serial 0/0
R1(config-if)#encapsulation ppp
R1(config-if)#no ip address
R1(config-if)#multilink-group 1

R2(config)#interface multilink 1
R2(config-if)#ip address 10.1.1.2 255.255.255.0
R2(config-if)#ppp multilink
R2(config-if)#ppp multilink interleave
R2(config-if)#ppp fragment-delay 10
R2(config-if)#exit
R2(config)#interface serial 0/0
R2(config-if)#encapsulation ppp
R2(config-if)#no ip address
R2(config-if)#multilink-group 1
```

To verify the MLP configuration, you can use the **show interfaces multilink** *interface-identifier* command. The output from this command shows how many interleaves have been performed. Therefore, this is an excellent command to verify that MLP is indeed functioning.

FRF.12 is configured as part of a Frame Relay map-class. Unlike MLP, where you can specify a desired serialization delay, with FRF.12, you must specify the size that you want to fragment frames to. As a rule of thumb, divide the line speed by 800 to get a fragment size that results in a 10-ms serialization delay. For example, on a 64,000-bps link, divide 64,000 by 800 to get 80. This means that if you specify a fragment size of 80, your fragments will have a serialization delay of 10 ms.

Following is the syntax to configure FRF.12:

```
Router(config)#map-class frame-relay name
```

(Creates the map-class and enters map-class configuration mode.)

```
Router(config-map-class)#frame-relay fragment fragment-size
```

(Specifies the size to which FRF.12 will fragment frames. Note that the IOS does not automatically calculate the fragment size based on a specified delay, as the MLP mechanism did.)

```
Router(config-if)#frame-relay traffic-shaping
```

(Enables Frame Relay traffic shaping on the physical interface.)

```
Router(config-if | config-subif)#frame-relay class name
```

(Associates the map-class with an interface or a subinterface.)

```
Router(config-fr-dlci)#class name
```

(Associates the map-class with a Frame Relay DLCI.)

In the following example, you configure FRF.12 to create a serialization delay of 10 ms on a link that is clocked at a rate of 64 kbps. The map-class then is applied to DLCI 101. Because FRF.12 is configured as a part of Frame Relay traffic shaping, you also specify a CIR of 64 kbps and a Bc of 640.

FRF.12

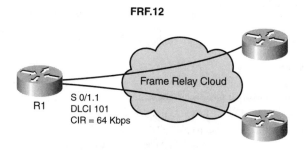

```
R1(config)#map-class frame-relay FRF12-EXAMPLE
R1(config-map-class)#frame-relay cir 64000
R1(config-map-class)#frame-relay bc 640
R1(config-map-class)#frame-relay fragment 80
R1(config-map-class)#exit
R1(config)#interface serial 0/1
R1(config-if)#frame-relay traffic-shaping
R1(config-if)#interface serial 0/1.1 point-to-point
R1(config-subif)#frame-relay interface-dlci 101
R1(config-fr-dlci)#class FRF12-EXAMPLE
```

You can use the **show frame-relay fragment** command to view the fragment size that is being used. Also, use the **show frame-relay pvc** command to view the fragment size that is used on a particular DLCI.

QoS Design Guidelines

This section reviews, in a design context, many of the concepts presented earlier in these Quick Reference Sheets. For example, voice, data, and video applications each have unique design guidelines. These guidelines are examined in this section.

Classification Review

As a review, recall how you performed classification and marking early on in these Quick Reference Sheets. Using the three-step MQC approach, you saw how to classify traffic by such characteristics as an incoming interface, an access-list match, or an NBAR. The Network Based Application Recognition (NBAR) classification mechanism offered the most granular classification, because NBAR can look beyond Layer 3 or Layer 4 information, all the way up to Layer 7.

Marking could then be done at Layer 2 or Layer 3 using markings such as CoS (at Layer 2), IP Precedence (at Layer 3), or DSCP (at Layer 3).

Type of Service (ToS) Byte

IPv4 Packet

ToS Byte

1	2	3	4	5	6	7	8

IP Precedence

DSCP

Inside an IPv4 header is a Type of Service (ToS) byte. The three left bits in that byte can be used to mark the packet with an IP Precedence value (0–7). Alternatively, the 6 left bits in the ToS byte can be used to mark the packet with a DSCP value (0–63).

Queuing Review

Marking traffic alone does not change the behavior of the traffic. To influence the traffic's behavior, you can use the following other QoS mechanisms:

- **Queuing** (for example, LLQ, CB-WFQ, and WRR)
- **Congestion avoidance** (for example, WRED and ECN)
- **Compression** (for example, TCP and RTP CB-Header Compression)
- **Traffic conditioning** (for example, CB-Policing and CB-Shaping)
- **Link efficiency** (for example, Link Fragmentation and Interleaving mechanisms such as MLP and compression mechanisms, such as RTP)

With the coverage of each of these QoS mechanisms, you can now select the appropriate tool or tools for a specific application. For example, if you wanted to give specific traffic priority treatment, you could use LLQ on a router or WRR on certain Catalyst switch platforms.

On a lower-speed WAN link, where bandwidth is scarce, you might choose to use TCP or RTP CB-Header Compression. In addition, you enable the appropriate LFI mechanism for the media that you are working with to reduce serialization delay that smaller payloads experience.

Cisco recommends that you perform classification and marking as close to the source as possible. However, you typically do not want to trust a user device's markings. Therefore, you establish a "trust boundary," where you determine the component (for example, a switch or an IP phone) that you trust to assign appropriate markings to traffic. The scheduling of packets (for example, queuing) can be formed on any device (for example, switch or router) that supports packet scheduling. However, link efficiency mechanisms are typically deployed on WAN links, where bandwidth conservation might be more of an issue.

Application-Specific QoS

Some of your applications have specific QoS guidelines that you should adhere to in the design process. For example, voice and interactive video traffic are latency sensitive and might require priority treatment. Following are a few design rules of thumb for voice and interactive video traffic:

- One-way delay of no more than 150 ms
- Packet loss of no more than 1 percent
- Jitter of no more than 30 ms
- Should be given priority treatment

Data applications vary widely in their needs. Therefore, each application on the network should be placed into a specific traffic category, where that application is sharing a policy with other applications that have similar QoS requirements.

QoS in a Service Provider Environment

As a final consideration in these QoS Quick Reference Sheets, consider some of the questions to ask when selecting a service provider. When negotiating with a service provider, you will probably put your agreement in writing in a document called a Service Level Agreement (SLA). An SLA stipulates specific service parameters that the service provider must adhere to a certain percentage of the time. For example, the SLA might state that 90 percent of the time, your traffic will experience no more than 150 ms of one-way delay. Parameters that are frequently specified in an SLA include the following:

- Latency
- Packet drops
- Variable delay
- Uptime
- Bandwidth availability

If your service provider only provides Layer 2 service over, for example, a Frame Relay cloud, the service provider will not be inspecting your Layer 3 markings. Therefore, it would be up to you as the customer to apply QoS features (for example, LLQ, CB-Header Compression, and LFI) to your frames before they enter the service provider's cloud.

However, some service providers do have Layer 3 awareness. In such a situation, the SLA can specify how your traffic is placed in the service provider's defined traffic classes, perhaps based on your DSCP markings. Typically, service providers can categorize your traffic in up to three to five classes.

PART II   CVOICE

CVOICE Section I
Overview of Legacy and IP Telephony Networks

Mastery of IP telephony technologies requires a foundational understanding of legacy telephony technologies. For example, our voice-enabled routers need to interface with existing PBX and PSTN equipment. Therefore, you need to understand the inner workings of these technologies.

The flash cards in this section review the basic call setup procedures in a legacy telephony environment. Also, a variety of ports are available on the Cisco voice-enabled routers for connecting with existing telephony equipment. In these flash cards, you are challenged to distinguish between various interface types (for example, FXS, FXO, T1, and E1). In addition, your knowledge of basic telephony terminology is confirmed.

Question 1

Define a *local loop* as it applies to legacy telephony environments.

Question 2

What types of connections are used to interconnect phone switches (for example, one CO switch to another CO switch or a CO switch to a Private Branch Exchange [PBX])?

Question 3

What type of phone switch is most appropriate for a company that has 30 to 40 users?

Question 1 Answer

Local loops connect customer locations to a local central office (CO) over a pair of wires called *tip and ring*. The local loop carries both signaling information and voice traffic.

Question 2 Answer

Phone switches are interconnected through trunks. These trunks come in various forms, including analog (for example, Foreign Exchange Office [FXO]) and digital (for example, T1).

Question 3 Answer

Although PBXs typically support from 20 to 20,000 users, a more cost-effective solution for 30 to 40 users is a key system.

Question 4

List the three basic steps to establish an end-to-end call in the legacy telephony environment.

Question 5

Describe common channel signaling (CCS) as it relates to call signaling.

Question 6

Describe channel-associated signaling (CAS) as it relates to call signaling.

Question 4 Answer

The three basic steps to establish an end-to-end voice call are as follows:

Step 1   A phone goes off-hook and sends digits to the local phone switch.

Step 2   The local phone switch examines the dialed digits, makes a forwarding decision, and sends signaling information to the destination phone switch.

Step 3   The destination phone switch signals the destination phone by sending ringing voltage to the phone.

Question 5 Answer

CCS has a channel that is dedicated to signaling. For example, in an Integrated Services Digital Network (ISDN) circuit, the D channel is dedicated to signaling.

Question 6 Answer

CAS can use framing bits from a few of the channels to serve as signaling bits. Sometimes this is called *robbed-bit signaling*.

Question 7

How does a phone switch know that a loop-start phone has gone off-hook?

Question 8

Describe the operation of ground-start signaling.

Question 9

How does E&M wink start signal that a device is ready to receive digits?

Question 7 Answer

When a phone goes off-hook in a loop-start environment, it closes a circuit inside the phone, which causes "loop current" to flow through the tip-and-ring leads. When the phone switch sees that the loop current is flowing, the switch knows that the phone has gone off-hook.

Question 8 Answer

Ground-start signaling causes a phone switch to seize a line after the phone temporarily grounds the "ring" side of the circuit. Ground-start signaling often is used with PBXs and pay phones.

Question 9 Answer

E&M wink start indicates that a device (for example, a PBX) is ready to receive digits when the polarity on an E&M circuit is reversed and then quickly flipped back to the original polarity. E&M wink start often is used with PBX-to-PBX connections.

Question 10

What type of multiplexing transmits multiple conversations by sending the conversations at different frequencies?

Question 11

What is the purpose of a gateway in a packet telephony network?

Question 12

What type of device can attach to a Foreign Exchange Station (FXS) port on voice-enabled routers?

Question 10 Answer

Frequency-division multiplexing (FDM) allows multiple conversations to be sent at the same time using different frequencies. For example, dense-wavelength-division multiplexing (DWDM) uses FDM by simultaneously sending multiple light frequencies over a fiber-optic cable.

Question 11 Answer

Gateways can forward calls among different types of networks. For example, a call from an IP phone could be forwarded through a gateway to the Public Switched Telephone Network (PSTN).

Question 12 Answer

An FXS port allows you to connect plain old telephone service (POTS) devices to a router. For example, you could attach a traditional analog phone, speakerphone, or fax machine to an FXS port on a Cisco router, and that FXS port can act like a PBX or a CO switch. For example, an FXS port can provide dial tone when the phone goes off-hook, interpret dialed digits, and send ringing voltage to the attached phone.

Question 13

What type of analog port in a Cisco voice-enabled router can receive dial tone, dial digits, place calls, and answer incoming calls?

Question 14

How many channels in an E1 circuit are typically usable for voice paths?

Question 15

In a centralized IP telephony deployment, where all Cisco CallManagers (CCMs) are located at the headquarters office, what IOS router feature maintains basic connectivity for Cisco IP Phones at the remote sites in the event of a WAN failure?

Question 13 Answer

An FXO port in a Cisco voice-enabled router can place calls, answer calls, receive dial tone, and dial digits, similar to an analog phone.

Question 14 Answer

E1 interfaces have 32 channels. However, regardless of the CAS or CCS approach, only 30 of the channels are typically available for voice paths.

Question 15 Answer

Survivable Remote Site Telephony (SRST) allows a Cisco IOS router to perform basic CCM functions. Therefore, even if an IP phone at a remote site lost connectivity with the CCM at a headquarters location, the IP phone would still have basic functionality.

CVOICE Section 2
The Mechanics of Analog and Digital Voice Circuits

Now that you have been introduced to basic signaling approaches in the previous section, the flash cards in this section address analog and digital signaling approaches with greater specificity. Also, the process of encoding analog waveforms is addressed, in addition to special situations when you must send fax or modem signals.

Sending voice packets across the LAN does not create a significant bandwidth impact. However, on the WAN, where bandwidth is a much more precious resource, you need to compress your encoded voice to preserve bandwidth. The flash cards in this section review various voice-encoding and -compression schemes and quality measurements. Also, signaling methodologies among various locations in the network (for example, between Private Branch Exchanges [PBXs], between central office [CO] switches, and between customer equipment and the CO) are addressed.

Question 1

List three categories of signaling that are used to complete an end-to-end analog voice call.

Question 2

Describe how pulse dialing can indicate a dialed digit to a phone switch.

Question 3

Describe how DTMF dialing can indicate a dialed digit to a phone switch.

Question 1 Answer

Three types of signaling that are used to complete an end-to-end analog voice call are as follows:

- **Supervisor signaling** (for example, on-hook or off-hook conditions)
- **Address signaling** (for example, dialing digits with pulse or dual-tone multifrequency [DTMF] dialing)
- **Information signaling** (for example, tones that indicate the status of a call, such as a busy signal)

Question 2 Answer

Pulse dialing rapidly opens and closes the tip-and-ring circuit. This series of open and closed circuit conditions within specific timing parameters indicates a dialed digit.

Question 3 Answer

With DTMF, two simultaneous frequencies are generated, and the phone interprets this combination of frequencies as a dialed digit. For example, the combination of a 697-Hz tone and a 1209-Hz tone indicates a dialed digit of 1.

Question 4

What is the most common type of E&M signaling?

Question 5

Identify the primary cause of echo in an analog voice network.

Question 6

According to the Nyquist Theorem, how many samples per second should be taken to accurately sample a waveform whose highest frequency is 4 kHz?

Question 4 Answer

Although Cisco supports three types of E&M signaling (that is, wink start, immediate start, and delay start), the most common type of E&M signaling is wink start.

Question 5 Answer

Echo is usually a result of an impedance mismatch in a 2-wire–to–4-wire circuit. These circuits are found commonly in analog phones and phone switches.

Question 6 Answer

The Nyquist Theorem states that you should sample a waveform at twice the waveform's highest frequency. In this example, the highest frequency is 4000 Hz. Therefore, you should sample the waveform at a rate of 2 * 4000 = 8000 samples per second.

Question 7

What is the name of the process of taking Pulse Amplitude Modulation (PAM) samples and converting them into digits, which can then be transmitted across a digital network?

Question 8

Which codec that you typically use in a LAN environment encodes using PCM?

Question 9

How much bandwidth is required to transmit voice using the G.729 codec, not including overhead?

Question 7 Answer

The process of assigning digits to PAM samples is known as *quantization*. An alternate correct answer, which describes the entire sampling and conversion process, is Pulse Code Modulation (PCM).

Question 8 Answer

The G.711 codec uses 64 kbps of bandwidth to transport voice, not including overhead. No compression is being performed with G.711. Rather, G.711 uses PCM.

Question 9 Answer

The G.729 codec requires 8 kbps of bandwidth to transmit voice over a Cisco network. Note that this 8-kbps value does not include overhead. Therefore, G.729 provides a significant bandwidth savings over G.711, which requires 64 kbps of bandwidth for voice, not including overhead.

Question 10

How does G.729a differ from G.729?

Question 11

How does G.729b differ from G.729?

Question 12

Which time slot does an E1 circuit typically use for signaling?

Question 10 Answer

Although both G.729 and G.729a require 8 kbps of bandwidth, not including overhead, to transmit voice packets, G.729a is less processor intensive. However, as a trade-off, the reduced load on the router's processor produces a slight degradation in voice quality for G.729a, as opposed to G.729.

Question 11 Answer

G.729b adds voice activity detection (VAD) support to G.729. Specifically, if the router detects that neither party in a conversation has spoken within a certain period of time (that is, 250 ms by default), the router preserves bandwidth by suppressing the transmission of silence.

Question 12 Answer

Regardless of whether you are using a CCS approach or a CAS approach, on an E1 circuit, the 17th time slot typically is used for signaling. Sometimes, you might see this written as "TS16," which means "time slot 16." The time slot is 16 for the 17th channel because time slot numbering begins at 0.

Question 13

What is the purpose of a mean opinion score (MOS)?

Question 14

In a T.37 fax store-and-forward topology, what roles do Cisco routers play?

Question 15

Distinguish between the Digital Private Network Signaling System (DPNSS) and Signaling Transport (SIGTRAN).

Question 13 Answer

To measure quality, you can use an MOS, which uses a "trained ear" to judge the quality of voice after passing through the codec that is being tested. MOS values range from 1, for unsatisfactory quality, to 5, for no noticeable quality degradation. For toll-quality voice, however, an MOS value in the range of 4 is appropriate.

Question 14 Answer

With the T.37 approach, a Cisco router (called an *on ramp*) can convert fax data into a TIFF attachment in an e-mail message and transmit that attachment to a store-and-forward e-mail server. This server then can deliver the fax e-mail message to an *off-ramp* Cisco router, which initiates a session with the destination fax machine.

Question 15 Answer

You can use the DPNSS protocol to interconnect PBXs. European PBX vendors developed DPNSS in the early 1980s, which was before Integrated Services Digital Network (ISDN) standards had been established. Numerous Cisco IOS gateways can function in a DPNSS network, because DPNSS can run over a standard ISDN interface.

CO switches typically use Signaling System 7 (SS7) as the signaling protocol between CO switches. For the Cisco Voice over IP (VoIP) networks, you can use SIGTRAN to send SS7 messages over an IP network. Specifically, SIGTRAN transports these SS7 messages using a Layer 4 protocol called Stream Control Transport Protocol (SCTP).

CVOICE Section 3
Configuring Router Voice Ports

As a follow-up to the theory that surrounds voice ports in previous sections, the flash cards in this section address how to configure voice ports, in both analog and digital environments. The configurations also demonstrate how to improve the quality of the voice calls by reducing echo and by making the volume in the Voice over IP (VoIP) network consistent with the volume that users experience in a Private Branch Exchange (PBX) environment.

The flash cards in this section primarily focus on syntax. Therefore, you should be comfortable with configuring Foreign Exchange Station (FXS), Foreign Exchange Office (FXO), E&M, and T1 interfaces. In addition, you are challenged with verification and troubleshooting commands.

Question 1

A call that originates and terminates on the same router is categorized as what type of call?

Question 2

Describe a Private Line Automatic Ringdown (PLAR) call.

Question 3

From what configuration mode would you issue the impedance 600r command?

Question 1 Answer

A local call originates on a phone that is connected to the same router as the destination phone. This is as opposed to an *on-net* call, in which the source and destination phones are attached to different routers in a network.

Question 2 Answer

A PLAR call occurs when a user lifts the handset on a phone and the phone automatically connects to a predetermined number. For example, a security phone in a parking lot might allow a user to lift the handset and be connected directly to the security office. Such a phone call would be considered a PLAR call.

Question 3 Answer

You issue the **impedance 600r** command from within voice-port configuration mode for an analog voice port. The purpose of the command is to have the impedance of the voice port match the impedance of the equipment that is connected to the voice port. Echo is reduced by matching the impedance. The *r* in the command indicates that the 600 ohms of impedance is purely resistive. (That is, it does not have a capacitive component.)

Question 4

Which command would you issue in voice-port configuration mode for an FXS interface to change the ringing pattern that is sent to the phone?

Question 5

Explain the purpose of the echo-cancel coverage 32 command.

Question 6

What is the purpose of the nonlinear feature?

Question 4 Answer

The ringing pattern that is sent from an FXS port to a phone defaults to 2 seconds on and 4 seconds off. However, you can create a distinctive ringing pattern by using the **ring cadence** *pattern* command, which is issued in voice-port configuration mode.

Question 5 Answer

By default, a voice port can store 8 ms of the analog waveform that it sent to the attached equipment. If that same waveform is seen again, within the 8-ms window, coming back from the attached equipment, the waveform is interpreted as echo. This time period is called the *cancel coverage*. The **echo-cancel coverage 32** command extends the echo cancel coverage to the maximum value of 32 milliseconds.

Question 6 Answer

The nonlinear feature suppresses all incoming waveforms from the phone until the volume is loud enough to be interpreted as speech. Note that this feature can lead to "clipping" when the other party begins to speak.

Question 7

Which voice-port configuration-mode command configures an FXO port for pulse dialing?

Question 8

Which E&M voice-port configuration command specifies that the voice path uses four wires?

Question 9

What is specified with the voice-port configuration command timeouts initial 20?

Question 7 Answer

To configure an FXO port for pulse dialing, use the **dial-type pulse** command from voice-port configuration mode.

Question 8 Answer

On an E&M port, voice is not carried over the E&M leads themselves. Rather, voice is transmitted over tip-and-ring leads. Some implementations give the tip-and-ring leads their own return path. Specifically, four wires are used to transmit voice. The E&M voice-port configuration-mode command **operation 4-wire** specifies that four wires are used to transmit voice.

Question 9 Answer

The FXS voice-port configuration command **timeouts initial 20** gives the caller 20 seconds to dial his first digit before the dial tone is removed. The **timeouts interdigit** command, however, specifies the maximum number of seconds allowed between dialed digits.

Question 10

The ring number 3 command is specified in voice-port configuration mode for which type of voice port?

Question 11

What voice-port configuration command configures an E&M port for wink start signaling?

Question 12

In what configuration mode would you enter the framing esf command?

Question 10 Answer

The **ring number** 3 command specifies that an FXO port should answer an incoming call (that is, go off-hook) after it receives three rings. The default setting causes an FXO port to answer after a single ring.

Question 11 Answer

Cisco IOS supports three E&M signaling types: wink start, immediate start, and delay start. The voice-port configuration-mode command **signal wink-start** specifies wink start signaling for an E&M voice port.

Question 12 Answer

T1 parameters, such as framing and linecoding, are configured under controller-configuration mode as opposed to interface- or voice-port configuration mode. From controller-configuration mode, you can configure T1 parameters such as framing, line coding, and clocking. However, you can issue voice-port configuration-mode commands for the individual channels of the T1.

Question 13

What transparent common-channel signaling (T-CCS) command instructs a router to use the G.Clear codec when transmitting a specified signaling channel?

Question 14

Which command would you enter to configure a T1 to use B8ZS line coding?

Question 15

Which command could you issue to view the settings for the voice ports on a router (for example, the codec that is currently being used by a voice port)?

Question 13 Answer

The dial-peer configuration-mode command **codec clear-channel** allows proprietary signaling information to pass transparently through a router, with no codec manipulation, by using the G.Clear codec. This command, part of a T-CCS configuration, is designed to allow proprietary signaling information from a PBX to be transmitted across an IP WAN.

Question 14 Answer

T1s are configured from controller-configuration mode. From that mode, you can issue the **linecode b8zs** command to specify B8ZS line coding for a T1.

Question 15 Answer

The **show voice port** command displays voice-port settings on a router. For a more concise view of installed voice ports (for example, a listing of voice ports and their current on-hook/off-hook conditions), you can use the **show voice port summary** command.

Question 16

What is the csim start command used for?

Question 16 Answer

The **csim start** *number* command can instruct a gateway to dial a number. For example, you could enter the command **csim start 5551212** to cause the router to place a call to a destination phone number of 555-1212. This command is "hidden," meaning that it does not appear in the IOS's context-sensitive help. Cisco also warns that this command occasionally causes a router to crash. Therefore, use this command with caution.

CVOICE Section 4
Configuring Router Dial Peers

Voice-enabled routers need to be trained how to forward phone calls to their appropriate destinations. One approach is to configure dial peers that associate a phone number or a range of phone numbers with an address. This address might be an IP address, or it might be a physical port (for example, a Foreign Exchange Station [FXS] port) that is attached to equipment, such as a phone or a Private Branch Exchange (PBX).

The flash cards in this section test your knowledge of dial peer configuration, for both plain old telephone service (POTS) and Voice over IP (VoIP) dial peers. In addition, you should be familiar with wildcard usage to match a range of phone numbers. Digit manipulation (for example, prepending digits to a dialed number) is also addressed. These flash cards verify your understanding of Private Line Automatic Ringdown (PLAR) and PLAR Off-Premise Extension (PLAR-OPX) configuration. Finally, dial plans are reviewed.

Question 1

Two phones connect to different routers, and the routers are separated by an IP WAN. How many dial peers must you create to support calls between the phones, allowing either phone to initiate a call?

Question 2

When you are configuring a POTS dial peer, what two parameters typically are specified in dial-peer configuration mode?

Question 3

The dial-peer voice 1111 pots command enters you into dial-peer configuration mode for a POTS dial peer. Identify what the "1111" indicates.

Question 1 Answer

To support phone calls between phones that are attached to two routers, you need a total of four dial peers, two from the perspective of each router. Specifically, each router needs a POTS dial peer to point to the locally attached phone, and each router needs a VoIP dial peer to point to the remote router.

Question 2 Answer

When you are configuring a POTS dial peer, you typically identify the phone number with the **destination-pattern** command. In addition, you point to the physical port to which the POTS device is attached with the **port** command.

Question 3 Answer

When you are creating a POTS dial peer with the **dial-peer voice 1111 pots** command, the "1111" is a locally significant tag. Although you might want to have this tag match the phone number to which the dial peer is pointing, this is not necessary.

Question 4

In dial-peer configuration mode for a POTS dial peer, you want to identify FXS port 1/1/1. Which command should you use?

Question 5

You are configuring a VoIP dial peer, and you want to match a destination pattern (that is, a phone number) of 2222. Which command should you issue in VoIP dial-peer Which mode?

Question 6

Which H.323 VoIP dial-peer configuration-mode command should you enter to point to an IP address of 1.1.1.2?

Question 4 Answer

To point to the physical port to which a POTS device is attached, issue the **port** *port_address* command in dial-peer configuration mode. In this example, with FXS port 1/1/1, you should issue the **port 1/1/1** command in POTS dial-peer configuration mode.

Question 5 Answer

The **destination-pattern** *number* command identifies a phone number for a dial peer. Interestingly, this command applies to both POTS and VoIP dial peers. In this example, with a destination pattern of 2222, you would issue the **destination-pattern 2222** command in the VoIP dial-peer configuration mode. Note that a hyphen is required between "destination" and "pattern."

Question 6 Answer

A VoIP dial peer uses the **session target ipv4:***ip_address* command to identify the remote IP address to which voice packets should be sent. Note that unlike the **destination-pattern** *number* command, you do not place a hyphen between "session" and "target." Also, notice that you must prepend the IP address with the "ipv4:" syntax. Therefore, in this example, you should enter **session target ipv4:1.1.1.2** in dial-peer configuration mode.

Question 7

The "T" wildcard in a destination pattern represents a dial string of any length. When you are using a "T" in the destination pattern, how do you indicate that your dial string is complete?

Question 8

You want to create a destination pattern that matches numbers in the range 5000 to 5999. Using the period wildcard (that is, "."), what would your destination pattern be?

Question 9

The destination pattern "1[2-3]45" represents what dialed digits?

Question 7 Answer

When you are using the "T" wildcard, the voice-enabled router forwards the call if you have not dialed a digit for 10 seconds, by default, or if you press the "#" key to indicate the end of the dial string. The "T" wildcard often is used when matching the variety of dial-string lengths necessary to support various Public Switched Telephone Network (PSTN) calls (for example, with and without an area code).

Question 8 Answer

The period wildcard in a destination pattern represents any dialed digit. To represent the range of numbers 5000 to 5999, you need any four-digit number that begins with a 5. Using the period wildcard, you can use the 5... destination pattern.

Question 9 Answer

When you are configuring a destination pattern, you can use brackets to represent a range of numbers. In this example, "1[2-3]45" represents a four-digit number whose second digit is either a 2 or a 3. Specifically, this destination pattern represents the following dialed digits: 1245 and 1345.

Question 10

List at least three commands that you can use to match inbound dial peers.

Question 11

Which inbound dial peer command uses caller ID to identify the calling number?

Question 12

You have two dial peers, a VoIP and POTS dial peer, that have matching destination patterns. However, the VoIP dial peer has a preference of 0, whereas the POTS dial peer has a preference of 1. Assuming that both paths are available, which one will be used?

Question 10 Answer

In addition to the **destination-pattern** and **port** commands, you can use the **incoming called-number** and **answer-address** commands to match inbound dial peers.

Question 11 Answer

The **answer-address** command, which matches inbound dial peers, leverages caller ID information to identify the calling number. This can be an appropriate solution when you want to direct calls to different customer service agents, based on the source of the phone call. For example, you might want to route calls that originate in Mexico to customer service agents who speak Spanish.

Question 12 Answer

When more than one dial peer matches a single destination pattern, you can influence which dial peer will be chosen with the **preference** *number* command. Lower preference numbers are preferred over higher preference numbers. In this example, the VoIP dial peer is used, because it has a lower preference number than the POTS dial peer. Valid numbers for the preference command are 0 to 10.

Question 13

What is accomplished with the forward-digits 9 command?

Question 14

The num-exp 311 2222 command is issued in global-configuration mode. What does the router do when a caller dials 311?

Question 15

In which configuration mode would you enter the connection plar 2222 command?

Question 13 Answer

By default, voice-enabled routers only forward digits that are not explicitly matched in a destination pattern (that is, digits that match wildcards). You can override this default behavior with the **forward-digits** *number* dial-peer configuration-mode command. In this example, the **forward-digits 9** command instructs the router to forward the 9 rightmost digits, regardless of the digits that explicitly are matched by the destination pattern.

Question 14 Answer

The number expansion feature allows a caller to dial a number, but the router translates the dialed number into another predefined number, which is the number that the router is actually dialed. To accomplish this, you can use the **num-exp** *dialed_number translated_number* command. In this example, with the **num-exp 311 2222** command, when a caller dials 311, the router actually dials 2222, which has been defined previously with a dial peer.

Question 15 Answer

PLAR allows a user to pick up the handset of a phone and have the attached voice-enabled router automatically place a call to a predefined number. In this example, with the **connection plar 2222** command, when a particular voice port notices that the attached device is off-hook, a call is completed automatically to 2222. Because a voice port initiates the PLAR phone call, the **connection plar 2222** command is issued from voice-port configuration mode.

Question 16

A North American dial plan number has ten digits. What are the first three digits used for?

Question 17

The number 859-555-1212 uses the North American dial plan. What do the numbers "555" indicate?

Question 18

List at least three questions that you should ask when designing a customer's dial plan.

Question 16 Answer

The first three digits in the ten-digit North American dial plan are used for an area code, which typically is associated with a geographic location within North America.

Question 17 Answer

In the number 859-555-1212, "555" is the central office code, which is also known as the *NXX code*. This code identifies a central office location within the area that is specified by the area code.

Question 18 Answer

Consider the following questions when designing a dial plan for a customer:

- Where is the dial-plan logic located?
- Can the numbers in the dial plan be reached by multiple paths?
- Should you use digit translations to make dial plans have a consistent feel you?
- Does an attached voice-mail system require a different number of digits than an extension?
- When do area codes need to be dialed?
- How can the dial plan support different countries?

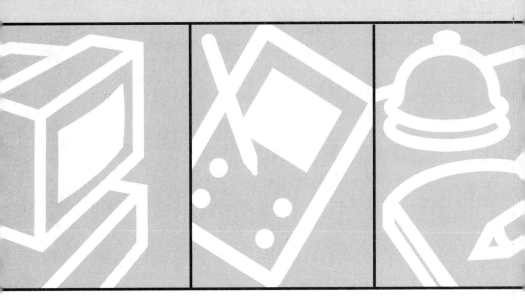

CVOICE Section 5
Voice over IP Design Considerations

The flash cards in this section review several design issues that surround Voice over IP (VoIP). For example, you should be familiar with the characteristics of IP networks and how to handle voice packets over such networks. Also, numerous protocols are required to support an end-to-end voice call. For example, whereas voice packets are carried through Real-Time Transport Protocol (RTP), gateways might need their own gateway control protocol (for example, H.323).

You also are challenged to recall details regarding other voice-over-data technologies, such as Voice over Frame Relay (VoFR) and Voice over ATM (VoATM). In addition to codec selection, several other factors impact a voice call's bandwidth requirement. These flash cards test your understanding of these other factors. Finally, your understanding of security considerations in a VoIP design is verified.

Question 1

The Internet Protocol (IP) is considered connectionless. What is meant by the term *connectionless?*

Question 2

IP networks support multiple paths between a source and destination. What benefits does this characteristic offer to VoIP networks?

Question 3

The Real-Time Transport Protocol maps to which layer of the OSI model?

Question 1 Answer

A *connectionless* protocol, such as IP, does not provide reliable delivery of packets. However, connection-oriented protocols, such as Transport Control Protocol (TCP), can add reliability. Voice packets are carried through User Datagram Protocol (UDP), which is considered to be unreliable. As a result, if a voice packet is dropped, a mechanism does not exist to retransmit the dropped packet.

Question 2 Answer

Because IP networks can have multiple paths between the source and destination devices, VoIP packets can be load balanced across the links. Also, having multiple links adds fault tolerance to the design.

Question 3 Answer

RTP carries voice packets and maps to Layer 4 (that is, the transport layer) of the OSI model.

Question 4

RTP packets are encapsulated inside what protocol?

Question 5

Voice packets might arrive at the destination router out of order, because IP networks support multiple paths between source and destination devices. Which protocol provides sequence information to the destination router so that the voice packets can be played out in the correct order?

Question 6

Identify the three main quality challenges in a VoIP network.

Question 4 Answer

RTP packets are encapsulated inside User Datagram Protocol (UDP). Interestingly, RTP and UDP both map to Layer 4 of the OSI model. Also, note that because RTP relies on UDP for transport, the RTP packets are "unreliable," meaning that dropped packets are not retransmitted.

Question 5 Answer

An RTP header contains sequence information. This sequence information can be referenced by the destination router to reorder the packets.

Question 6 Answer

The three main challenges faced when implementing a VoIP network are as follows:

- **Delay**—Too much delay can make a conversation feel unnatural.
- **Jitter**—Jitter is variable delay, where interpacket arrival times vary. This variation in delay can lead to gaps in the conversation.
- **Drops**—When packets are dropped in a VoIP conversation, they are not retransmitted. However, the Cisco router can attempt to mask the packet drops by interpolating how the voice packet would have sounded. Still, too many dropped packets can distort the conversation.

Question 7

When configuring a VoFR dial peer, what does the "session target" identify?

Question 8

Identify the main advantage that VoFR and VoATM have over VoIP.

Question 9

Which formula is used to calculate the bandwidth that is required for a VoFR call?

Question 7 Answer

In a VoFR network, the "session target" command identifies a local Data Link Connection Identifier (DLCI), which is the identifier of a permanent virtual circuit (PVC).

Question 8 Answer

VoFR and VoATM operate at Layer 2 of the OSI model. As a result, these technologies do not have the IP, UDP, and RTP headers that are present in VoIP. The combined size of these headers is approximately 40 bytes. Therefore, this reduction in header overhead is the primary advantage of VoFR and VoATM over VoIP. Also, VoFR can identify voice and prevent inadvertent voice fragmentation; voice fragmentation can occur in a VoIP network.

Question 9 Answer

The per-call bandwidth requirement for a VoFR call can be calculated with the following formula:

Per_Call_Bandwidth = Codec_Bandwidth * (Payload + Overhead) / Payload

The units of measure for "Codec_Bandwidth" are bps, whereas the "Payload" and "Overhead" parameters are measured in bytes.

Question 10

What is the default payload size for a voice frame that uses the G.729 codec on a VoFR network?

Question 11

What is the size of an Asynchronous Transfer Mode (ATM) cell?

Question 12

Which formula is used to calculate the bandwidth that is required for a VoATM call?

Question 10 Answer

On a VoFR network, a voice frame that uses the G.729 codec (which requires 8 kbps of bandwidth for voice) is 30 bytes in size, by default.

Question 11 Answer

An ATM cell is 53 bytes in size. The cell is composed of 48 bytes of payload and 5 bytes of header. If a voice payload does not fill the 48 bytes of payload space in a cell, the remainder of the 48 bytes is filled with padding, which can lead to an inefficient use of bandwidth.

Question 12 Answer

The per-call bandwidth requirement for a VoATM call can be calculated with the following formula:

$$Per\_Call\_Bandwidth = Codec\_Bandwidth * (Number\_of\_Cells * 53) / Payload$$

The units of measure for "Codec_Bandwidth" are bps, whereas "Payload" is measured in bytes.

Question 13

How many cells are required to transmit a voice sample using the G.711 codec in a VoATM network (assuming a default sample size)?

Question 14

List at least two considerations when selecting a gateway for a VoIP network.

Question 15

List three Layer 5 VoIP protocols that VoIP gateway use.

Question 13 Answer

The G.711 codec requires six ATM cells to send a single voice sample. However, the G.729 codec requires only a single cell to send a voice sample.

Question 14 Answer

Selecting a gateway for a VoIP network involves several considerations, such as the following:

- Do you need an analog or a digital gateway?
- What specific ports are required on the gateway?
- What signaling protocol does the gateway need to support?
- Does the gateway need to support Survivable Remote Site Telephony (SRST)?

Question 15 Answer

Layer 5 of the OSI model, the session layer, is responsible for the setup and teardown of sessions. In the VoIP context, gateway control protocols set up and tear down sessions. Typical gateway control protocols include the following:

- H.323
- Media Gateway Control Protocol (MGCP)
- Session Initiation Protocol (SIP)

Question 16

In a Cisco VoIP network, what range of UDP ports is used for the Real-Time Transport Protocol (RTP) and the Real-Time Transport Control Protocol (RTCP)?

Question 17

What is the default payload size of a G.729 voice packet on a VoIP network (in bytes)?

Question 18

What is the default length of a voice sample that is included in a VoIP packet (in milliseconds)?

Question 16 Answer

In a Cisco VoIP network, RTP and RTCP protocols use UDP ports in the range 16,384 to 32,767. Note that RTP uses the even-numbered ports in that range, whereas RTCP uses the odd-numbered ports.

Question 17 Answer

On a VoIP network, the default payload size of a G.729 voice packet is 20 bytes.

Question 18 Answer

By default, a VoIP packet includes 20 ms of voice.

Question 19

A VoIP packet has an IP, UDP, and RTP header. What is the typical combined size of these headers?

Question 20

How much bandwidth is required for a voice payload (not including overhead) using the G.711 codec?

Question 21

On what link speeds should you use RTP header compression?

Question 19 Answer

A VoIP packet typically includes a 20-byte IP header, an 8-byte UDP header, and a 12-byte RTP header, for a combined header size of 40 bytes. However, you can use RTP header compression (cRTP) to reduce the header size to 2 or 4 bytes.

Question 20 Answer

The G.711 codec requires 64 kbps of bandwidth for the voice payload. However, you typically should use the G.729 codec over WAN links, because the G.729 codec requires only 8 kbps of bandwidth for the voice payload.

Question 21 Answer

RTP header compression (cRTP) is recommended for use on link speeds of less than 2 Mbps. By performing header compression, you can reduce the 40-byte header size on a VoIP packet to 2 or 4 bytes.

Question 22

How large is an Ethernet header?

Question 23

Which type of firewall can watch an H.323 negotiation and determine which UDP port to allow through the firewall to transmit the voice packets?

Question 24

How much additional overhead is placed on a VoIP packet when the packet is transmitted through a Virtual Private Network (VPN)?

Question 22 Answer

An Ethernet header is 18 bytes in size. However, for WAN links, you typically use Multilink PPP (MLP) or Frame Relay (FR). Both MLP and FR headers are 6 bytes in size.

Question 23 Answer

A stateful firewall can monitor protocols, such as H.323, which can shift port numbers after the session begins. In the example of a VoIP call, H.323 uses TCP protocols (that is, H.225 and H.245) to perform call setup. The voice then is streamed using a UDP port in the port range 16,384 to 32,767. A stateful firewall that monitors the call setup can learn dynamically which UDP port to allow through the firewall.

Question 24 Answer

VPNs can tunnel VoIP packets securely. However, a variety of VPN technologies exist, meaning that the additional overhead varies, depending on the VPN that is implemented. However, as a rule, you typically add 30 to 60 bytes of overhead per VoIP packet when you transmit the packet over a VPN.

Question 25

Define "SAFE" in the context of security.

Question 25 Answer

The Secure Architecture For Enterprise (SAFE) is the Cisco model for security design. The main goal of the Cisco SAFE blueprint is to provide best-practice information for designing and implementing secure networks. Specifically, the SAFE blueprint seeks to detect and defend against intrusions into the network, to control which traffic can enter and leave the network, and to protect data as it travels through the network. For more information on the Cisco SAFE blueprint, visit http://www.cisco.com/go/safe.

CVOICE Section 6
Gateway Protocols

Gateway control protocols determine how a Cisco IOS gateway sets up a call to a destination that is located across an IP WAN. The flash cards in this section address three gateway control protocols that IOS gateways use. Specifically, your knowledge of H.323, the Session Initiation Protocol (SIP), and the Media Gateway Control Protocol (MGCP) is verified.

Beyond the theory of gateway control protocols, you must understand the configuration and verification of these protocols. Some protocols can be better suited for some topologies than others. For example, MGCP is well suited for a service provider environment, because Cisco CallManagers (CCMs) can be located at the service provider's centralized location.

Question 1

Define the ultimate goal of call control protocols (also known as gateway control protocols), such as H.323, MGCP, and SIP.

Question 2

Describe the centralized call control deployment.

Question 3

Describe the distributed call control deployment.

Question 1 Answer

The ultimate goal of call control protocols is to allow Real-Time Transport Protocol (RTP) streams to flow directly between endpoints. To reach that goal, the call control protocols perform signaling between voice gateways. After the gateways agree on a set of parameters, voice streams (that is, RTP streams) flow directly between the endpoints (that is, gateways).

Question 2 Answer

In a centralized call control environment, CCMs are located only in a central location. Gateways at remote sites communicate with the centralized CCMs over an IP WAN. Survivable Remote Site Telephony (SRST) often is used at the remote locations to preserve functionality of the IP phones that are located at the remote locations.

Question 3 Answer

In a distributed call control environment, CCMs are located at each remote site and at the central site. This deployment model offers greater scalability and fault tolerance than the centralized deployment model.

Question 4

List at least two pros and two cons of the centralized call control deployment.

Question 5

List at least two pros and two cons of the distributed call control deployment.

Question 6

Which H.323 protocol is responsible for performing a "capabilities exchange"?

Question 4 Answer

Centralized call control environments have the following characteristics:

Pros:

- Less expensive
- Easier to maintain

Cons:

- Single point of failure
- Less scalable
- Use WAN bandwidth for call setup

Question 5 Answer

Distributed call control environments have the following characteristics:

Pros:

- More fault tolerant.
- Do not consume WAN bandwidth for call setup.
- More scalable.

Cons:

- Require additional equipment.
- More work is required to perform updates.

Question 6 Answer

The two major protocols used by H.323 to establish a call are H.225 and H.245. H.225 performs call setup and Registration, Admission, and Status (RAS) functions. H.245 performs call control, including a capabilities exchange, in which endpoints agree on call parameters.

Question 7

List at least three physical components that can make up an H.323 network.

Question 8

In the context of H.323, what does the acronym RAS stand for?

Question 9

H.323 gatekeepers use the RAS channel to communicate with which H.323 components?

Question 7 Answer

H.323 networks can consist of the following physical components:

- Terminals
- Gateways
- IP-to-IP gateways
- Gatekeepers
- Multipoint Control Units (MCUs)

Question 8 Answer

H.323 gatekeepers (GKs) can communicate with H.323 gateways (GWs) or other H.323 GKs using the Registration, Administration, and Status (RAS) channel.

Question 9 Answer

H.323 gatekeepers use the RAS channel to communicate with other H.323 GKs or H.323 GWs.

Question 10

Which command do you enter in global-configuration mode to enable an IOS router as an H.323 gateway?

Question 11

Which session target command on an H.323 gateway is used to point to an H.323 gatekeeper?

Question 12

Describe the purpose of the show call active voice command.

Question 10 Answer

To enable an IOS router as an H.323 gateway, you can enter the **gateway** command in global-configuration mode.

Question 11 Answer

H.323 gateways use the RAS channel to communicate with an H.323 gatekeeper. To point a dial peer to an H.323 gatekeeper, you can use the **session target ras** dial-peer configuration-mode command.

Question 12 Answer

The **show call active voice** command displays details for current voice calls.

Question 13

List at least three types of SIP servers.

Question 14

Identify two types of SIP UAs.

Question 15

A SIP request message goes from which SIP user agent to which other SIP user agent?

Question 13 AnswerAnswer 13

SIP networks can use one or more of the following SIP servers:

- **Proxy server**—Performs forwarding for a User Agent Client (UAC)
- **Registrar server**—Registers the location of current clients
- **Redirect server**—Informs the User Agent (UA) of the next server to contact
- **Location server**—Performs address resolution for SIP proxy and redirect servers

Question 14 AnswerAnswer 14

SIP is a peer-to-peer protocol. These peers are called User Agents (UAs). Two types of UAs are as follows:

- **User Agent Clients (UACs)**—Initiate the connection by sending INVITE messages
- **User Agent Servers (UASs)**—Reply to INVITE messages

Question 15 AnswerAnswer 15

A SIP request is a message from a SIP User Agent Client (UAC) to a SIP User Agent Server (UAS). Conversely, a SIP response is a message from a UAS to a UAC. Note that these SIP messages are sent in clear text.

Question 16

A basic SIP call setup begins with a client sending what type of message to a server?

Question 17

When you are configuring a Voice over IP (VoIP) dial peer for a SIP user agent, you can use the session target sip-server command. Where is the "sip-server" specified?

Question 18

Which command tells a dial peer to use version 2 of the SIP protocol?

Question 16 Answer

Basic SIP call setup begins when the SIP client sends an INVITE message to a SIP server. Note that a SIP IP phone can act as either a client or a server, depending on whether the IP phone is originating or terminating a call.

Question 17 Answer

The dial-peer configuration-mode command **session target sip-server** tells the dial peer to use a SIP server that is defined under sip-ua configuration mode. For example, in sip-ua configuration mode, the **sip-server dns:SERVER1** command specifies a server with a DNS name of "SERVER1."

Question 18 Answer

In dial-peer configuration mode, you can use the **session protocol sipv2** command to instruct the VoIP dial peer to use version 2 of the SIP protocol.

Question 19

List at least two categories of MGCP components.

Question 20

What are the two parts of an MGCP endpoint name?

Question 21

List at least two categories of MGCP concepts.

Question 19 Answer

Three categories of MGCP components are as follows:

- **Endpoints**—An endpoint is where you interface between the VoIP network and the traditional telephony network.
- **Gateways**—Gateways are in charge of converting audio between a VoIP network and a circuit-switched network.
- **Call agents**—A call agent is the intelligence of an MGCP network and controls the gateways and their endpoints.

Question 20 Answer

An endpoint name looks much like an e-mail address (for example, circuitID@mgcpgw.ciscopress.com) and is composed of two parts: a locally significant name of the endpoint (before the "@" sign) and the DNS name of the MGCP gateway (after the "@" sign).

Question 21 Answer

The logical pieces that make up an MGCP network are called *concepts*. Three categories of MGCP concepts are as follows:

- **Call**—A call is formed when two or more endpoints are interconnected.
- **Events**—An event is what an endpoint has been instructed (by the call agent) to watch for. As an example, an FXS port might notice the event of an attached POTS device going off-hook.
- **Signal**—A call agent instructs an endpoint to send a specific signal when a certain event occurs. For example, after the event of a POTS phone going off-hook, the FXS port might send the signal of "dial tone" to the phone.

Question 22

What is an MGCP package?

Question 23

What is the purpose of an MGCP digit map?

Question 24

Describe how MGCP switchover and switchback offers increased availability to an MGCP gateway?

Question 22 Answer

An *MGCP package* is a grouping of relevant events and signals. For example, a line package contains events and signals that are used on subscriber lines, such as an off-hook event and a dial-tone signal.

Question 23 Answer

An *MGCP digit map* is a copy of an MGCP call agent's dial plan that is downloaded to an MGCP gateway. The MGCP gateway can collect digits and find a matching pattern, without having to forward each dialed digit to the call agent.

Question 24 Answer

MGCP switchover and switchback uses two or more call agents (for example, CCMs). When a GW does not see MGCP messages from a call agent for a period of time, it sends keepalive packets, and if it does not get a response, the GW attempts to establish a connection with a backup CCM. If the primary CCM comes back up, the GW can be configured to switch back to the primary CCM.

Question 25

Which command would you use to point an MGCP gateway to a call agent that is located at IP address 10.1.1.1?

Question 26

Instead of a destination-pattern command, which command do you use when configuring an MGCP dial peer to indicate that the port is controlled by an MGCP call agent?

Question 27

Which command can you use to view information about current connections on an MGCP gateway?

Question 25 Answer

The command to point an MGCP gateway to a call agent is **mgcp call-agent** *ip_address*. Therefore, you would enter the **mgcp call-agent 10.1.1.1** command to point to a call agent that is located at IP address 10.1.1.1.

Question 26 Answer

When configuring an MGCP dial peer, you use the **application MGCPAPP** command instead of a **destination-pattern** command to indicate that a dial peer is controlled by an MGCP call agent.

Question 27 Answer

You can use the **show mgcp connection** command to view information about current connections on an MGCP gateway.

Question 28

Which call control protocol uses ASN.1 for call control messages?

Question 29

What is an IP-to-IP gateway?

Question 28 Answer

H.323 uses Abstract Syntax Notation 1 (ASN.1) for call control messages, whereas both MGCP and SIP send call control messages in clear text.

Question 29 Answer

An IP-to-IP gateway allows different VoIP networks to interconnect. For example, if two companies had their own internal VoIP network with their own service provider, an IP-to-IP gateway could allow the two companies to join their VoIP networks. This solution requires no extension number overlapping between the two companies.

CVOICE Section 7
Ensuring Voice Quality

One of the most critical aspects in designing a Voice over IP (VoIP) network is ensuring that the quality of the voice is at least similar to the quality that users are accustomed to in a Private Branch Exchange (PBX) environment. Therefore, the flash cards in this section review how you measure and maintain voice quality in VoIP networks.

These flash cards specifically address overcoming jitter and delay in Cisco VoIP networks. Quality of service (QoS) strategies for both the LAN and the WAN are reviewed. Your knowledge of Call Admission Control (CAC) approaches is verified, and you are challenged to recall the steps that are involved in bandwidth provisioning.

Question 1

Define a jitter buffer.

Question 2

Which commands can you use to specify the maximum size of the jitter buffer, while allowing the jitter buffer to dynamically adjust its size based on network conditions?

Question 3

Which commands can you use to statically specify the size of the jitter buffer?

Question 1 Answer

A *jitter buffer* stores packets as they come into a router and then plays the packets out in a smooth fashion. When packets are in the jitter buffer, you can record them based on Real-Time Transport Protocol (RTP) sequence numbers.

Question 2 Answer

The dial-peer configuration-mode command **playout-delay mode adaptive**, along with the **playout-delay maximum *size*** command, can specify, in milliseconds, the maximum size of the jitter buffer, while allowing the jitter buffer to adjust its size dynamically based on network conditions.

Question 3 Answer

You can use the **playout-delay mode fixed** and the **playout-delay nominal** *size* dial-peer configuration-mode commands to statically specify the size of a jitter buffer.

Question 4

Which command should you use to view jitter conditions that a voice call is experiencing currently?

Question 5

Of the following delay components, which are fixed delay components and which are variable delay components?

- Coder delay
- Queuing delay
- Serialization delay
- Propagation delay

Question 6

What is the maximum time that is typically required for a G.729 codec to perform coding on a voice packet?

Question 4 Answer

You can view current jitter conditions that a voice call is experiencing by using the **show call active voice** command.

Question 5 Answer

Fixed delay components do not vary during a call. However, variable delay components can vary during a call. For example, congestion in a service provider's cloud can vary, or the number of packets that are queued in the local router can vary. Following are a few examples of delay components:

- Coder delay—Fixed
- Queuing delay—Variable
- Serialization delay—Fixed
- Propagation delay—Fixed

Question 6 Answer

A digital signal processor (DSP) typically supports up to four calls. If a DSP is supporting only one call, it can perform G.729 coding in 2.5 ms; however, if a DSP is supporting four calls simultaneously, it can take 10 ms to perform G.729 coding. For design purposes, you should use the worst-case time of 10 ms.

Question 7

How much serialization delay does a 1500-byte frame experience while exiting a 64-kbps serial interface?

Question 8

On a Voice over IP over Point-to-Point Protocol (PPP) network, which Link Fragmentation and Interleaving (LFI) mechanism is appropriate?

Question 9

On a Voice over IP over Frame Relay (VoIPovFR) network, which LFI mechanism is appropriate?

Question 7 Answer

To calculate serialization delay, you convert the bytes into bits by multiplying by 8; then you divide by the line rate. In this example, the calculation is as follows:

Serialization Delay = (1500 * 8) / 64000 = 0.1875 = 187.5 ms

Question 8 Answer

Multilink PPP (MLP) is the appropriate LFI mechanism on a Voice over IP over PPP network. Note that MLP does not require multiple links. You can use MLP even over a single link, because MLP can fragment payloads and interleave smaller payloads among the fragments.

Question 9 Answer

FRF.12 is the appropriate LFI mechanism on a VoIPovFR network. Note that FRF.12 is configured in a map-class as part of a Frame Relay Traffic Shaping (FRTS) configuration.

Question 10

Describe how Weighted Round Robin (WRR) forwards packets out of switch queues.

Question 11

Cisco recommends a 2Q1T approach for Catalyst switch queues. What is indicated by 2Q1T?

Question 12

Describe the differences between the QoS IntServ and DiffServ approaches.

Question 10 Answer

WRR assigns weights to a switch's queues, and these weights determine the relative amounts of bandwidth available to each of the queues. As an example, consider that queue 1 has a weight of 1 and queue 4 has a weight of 4. In this example, queue 4 receives four times as much bandwidth as queue 1 because of the queue weightings.

Question 11 Answer

A 2Q1T approach indicates that a switch can place frames into one of two queues and that each of those queues has a single threshold. Having a single threshold means that a queue does not discard frames until the queue is filled to capacity.

Question 12 Answer

IntServ uses signaling to request network resources for the duration of an application. However, DiffServ typically differentiates between traffic flows, marks packets, and makes dropping or forwarding decisions based on those markings.

Question 13

Which bits in the type of service (ToS) byte are used for Differentiated Services Code Point (DSCP) markings?

Question 14

List at least four QoS areas that define different types of QoS mechanisms.

Question 15

If you mark voice packets with a DSCP value of 46, how does the behavior of the voice packets change, by default?

Question 13 Answer

DSCP uses the 6 left-most bits in an IPv4 header's ToS byte. These bits give DSCP 64 possible values, in the range 0 to 63.

Question 14 Answer

Most QoS mechanisms can be placed into one of the following areas:

- Classification and marking
- Congestion avoidance
- Congestion management
- Traffic conditioning
- Signaling
- Link efficiency mechanisms

Question 15 Answer

By default, just marking a packet does not change its behavior. However, other QoS mechanisms, such as Low Latency Queuing (LLQ) and Weighted Random Early Detection (WRED), can reference the marking and make forwarding or dropping decisions based on it.

Question 16

LLQ and Class-Based Weighted Fair Queuing (CB-WFQ) are categorized under which area of QoS mechanisms?

Question 17

What is the Cisco preferred queuing approach for voice traffic?

Question 18

What is the main difference between LLQ and CB-WFQ?

Question 16 Answer

LLQ and CB-WFQ are both queuing mechanisms. All queuing mechanisms are considered congestion-management QoS mechanisms.

Question 17 Answer

Cisco recommends LLQ for latency-sensitive applications such as voice. LLQ is configured through the three-step Modular QoS CLI (MQC) process and can give priority treatment to voice packets, while not starving out lower-priority packets.

Question 18 Answer

LLQ and CB-WFQ are both queuing mechanisms that are configured through the three-step MQC process. The primary difference between these two approaches is that CB-WFQ does not have a priority queuing mechanism, but LLQ does.

Question 19

List the three steps in an MQC configuration.

Question 20

What is the purpose of traffic shaping?

Question 21

Describe how the Resource Reservation Protocol (RSVP) can reserve bandwidth for a voice call.

Question 19 Answer

The MQC approach to configuring QoS mechanisms involves the following three steps:

Step 1   Categorize traffic under different class-maps.

Step 2   Assign policies to the traffic classes through a policy-map.

Step 3   Associate a policy-map with an interface using the **service-policy** command.

Question 20 Answer

Traffic shaping is a traffic-conditioning mechanism that limits traffic to a specific rate and buffers (that is, delays) excess traffic. Traffic shaping often is used when different ends of a permanent virtual circuit (PVC) are running at different rates. By shaping both ends of the PVC to the same rate, you avoid oversubscription.

Question 21 Answer

The RSVP is an IntServ approach to QoS, where routers use signaling between routers to set up bandwidth reservations, one reservation in each direction, for the duration of a voice call.

Question 22

Describe the purpose of LFI.

Question 23

On what link speeds should LFI be used?

Question 24

Describe the purpose of RTP Header Compression (cRTP).

Question 22 Answer

LFI takes large payloads, fragments them, and interleaves smaller packets among the fragments to reduce serialization delay for latency-sensitive traffic.

Question 23 Answer

LFI is best suited for link speeds of less than 768 kbps, where a 1500-byte data frame could cause excessive serialization delay.

Question 24 Answer

cRTP takes a 40-byte VoIP header and compresses it to 2 or 4 bytes. cRTP is recommended for use on link speeds of less than 2 Mbps.

Question 25

List the three categories of CAC mechanisms.

Question 26

Describe the operation of measurement-based CAC mechanisms.

Question 27

What is indicated by the grade of service (GoS)?

Question 25 Answer

CAC mechanisms prevent too many phone calls from oversubscribing network resources, which would result in poor voice quality for all calls. The three categories of CAC mechanisms are as follows:

- Local CAC mechanisms
- Measurement-based CAC mechanisms
- Resource-based CAC mechanisms

Question 26 Answer

Measurement-based CAC mechanisms send Service Assurance Agent (SAA) probes into the network to determine network conditions. A request to place a phone call across the IP WAN then is permitted or denied based on the probes' results.

Question 27 Answer

GoS is the probability that a call will be blocked because of bandwidth oversubscription. Typically, you use a GoS of P(.01), which indicates a 1 percent probability of a blocked call during your busiest hour.

Question 28

Define an Erlang.

Question 29

What is the Cisco recommended congestion-avoidance mechanism?

Question 30

Under what configuration modes can you enter the auto qos voip command on a Cisco router?

Question 28 Answer

An *Erlang* is defined as one hour of conversation. For example, two phone calls that last 30 minutes each would equal one Erlang.

Question 29 Answer

The Cisco congestion-avoidance tool of choice is WRED, which begins to discard packets periodically as the queue depth increases. These discard decisions are made based on IP Precedence or DSCP markings. Therefore, lower-priority packets are discarded more aggressively than higher-priority packets.

Question 30 Answer

The **auto qos voip** command automatically executes a series of QoS configuration commands, which depend on the configured interface bandwidth. For example, on a PPP interface that is running at less than 768 kbps, the AutoQoS feature automatically configures LLQ, cRTP, MLP, and even a Simple Network Management Protocol (SNMP) configuration, where quality issues can be reported to an SNMP network management server. You can issue this command from either the interface configuration mode or from Data Link Connection Identifier (DLCI) configuration mode (for a Frame Relay PVC).

Question 31

How does MGCP CAC make call admission control decisions?

Question 32

What is Perceptual Evaluation of Speech Quality (PESQ), as it relates to voice quality?

Question 31 Answer

MGCP CAC can make call admission control decisions based on available router resources, SAA probe results, and available network bandwidth.

Question 32 Answer

Like Perceptual Speech Quality Measurement (PSQM), PESQ uses test equipment to measure voice quality, as opposed to a "trained ear." However, PESQ attempts to match mean opinion scores (MOSs). For example, if a codec had an MOS of 3.92, it should have a PESQ score of 3.92. However, the maximum value on the PESQ scale is 4.5, whereas the MOS scale reaches 5.0.

CVOICE
Quick Reference Sheets

Overview of Legacy and IP Telephony Networks

Introduction

Understanding emerging Voice over IP (VoIP) technologies requires a solid understanding of legacy telephony networks. Therefore, the Quick Reference Sheets in this section review many of the terms and concepts that surround legacy and packet telephony networks, and those technologies are then contrasted with IP Telephony technologies.

Legacy Telephony Networks

The Public Switched Telephone Network (PSTN) is at the heart of the legacy telephony network. PSTN components include the following items:

- Edge devices (for example, phones) are used by customers to interface with the PSTN.
- Local loops connect customer locations to a local central office (CO) over a pair of wires called *tip and ring*.
- Phone switches allow one phone to connect to another phone by dialing a phone number. The switch interprets the dialed digits and interconnects the dialing phone's local loop with the destination phone's local loop. The "phone company" has switches that are located in COs. However, companies can have their own phone switches [for example, Private Branch Exchanges (PBXs) or key systems] located locally.
- Trunks interconnect phone switches.

Companies that have their own phone switches can select between PBXs or key systems. PBXs are typically more scalable than key systems, supporting 20 to 20,000 phones. PBX users in the United States typically dial a 9 to access an outside line. However, key systems traditionally have buttons on a key phone that the user presses to access a specific outside line. For example, you might have been in a store and heard an intercom announcement such as, "Kevin, pick up line 2." In that example, Kevin would go to a "key phone" and press the line 2 button to access the call. Because of their scalability limitations, key systems typically support a maximum of 30 to 40 users.

Call signaling makes it possible to place an end-to-end voice call. Consider the following steps that are used to establish an end-to-end voice call:

Step 1   A phone goes off-hook and sends digits to the local phone switch.

Step 2   The local phone switch examines the dialed digits, makes a forwarding decision, and sends signaling information to the destination phone switch.

Step 3   The destination phone switch signals the destination phone by sending ringing voltage to the phone.

When a user dials digits on an analog phone, those digits can be communicated to the local phone switch using either dual-tone multifrequency (DTMF) or pulse dialing. DTMF sends tones that are composed of two frequencies, whereas pulse dialing rapidly opens and closes the local loop to indicate dialed digits.

With digital circuits, such as T1s or E1s, multiple conversations can be carried in different channels on the same circuit. Each of these digital channels needs bits for signaling information. Common approaches include the following:

- **Common channel signaling (CCS)**—Has a channel that is dedicated to signaling. For example, in an Integrated Services Digital Network (ISDN) circuit, the D channel is dedicated to signaling.
- **Channel associated signaling (CAS)**—Can use framing bits from a few of the channels to serve as signaling bits. Sometimes this is called *robbed-bit signaling*.

Analog circuits have their own signaling mechanisms, such as the following:

- **Loop-start**—Causes a phone switch to seize a line when loop current is flowing
- **Ground-start**—Causes a phone switch to seize a line after the phone temporarily grounds the "ring" side of the circuit
- **E&M wink start**—Seizes a line when the polarity on an E&M circuit is reversed and then quickly flipped back to the original polarity

Digital circuits can use multiplexing techniques to place multiple conversations on a single link. For example, time-division multiplexing can give a "time slice" to a specific channel, and by "taking turns," you can send 24 conversations across a single link.

Frequency-division multiplexing (FDM) allows multiple conversations to be sent at the same time using different frequencies. For example, dense-wavelength-division multiplexing (DWDM) simultaneously sends multiple light frequencies over a fiber-optic cable.

Packet Telephony Networks

Many companies that have PBXs at more than one site and interconnect those PBXs through the PSTN are migrating to a packet telephony network. A *packet telephony network* allows companies to preserve their existing investment in PBX technologies, while eliminating the recurring expense for the trunks that interconnect their PBXs. Specifically, companies can connect their PBXs to routers that are already interconnected through a wide-area network (WAN). The PBXs can then send their signaling information and voice calls over the WAN.

Call-forwarding intelligence can reside in the routers. For increased scalability, however, you can configure routers to point to external call agents. Such a topology lays the foundation for other packet telephony technologies, including the following:

- IP phones have an Ethernet connection that sends and receives voice calls.
- Call agents replace much of the functionality that was provided previously by the PBX. For example, a call agent can be configured with route plans that dictate how voice calls are forwarded. The Cisco CallManager (CCM) is an example of a call agent.

- Gateways can forward calls between different types of networks. For example, a call from an IP phone could be forwarded through a gateway to the PSTN.
- Gatekeepers keep track of WAN resources and, based on available resources, either permit or deny a request to place a call across the WAN. In addition, the gatekeeper can provide E.164 number resolution.
- Multipoint Control Units (MCUs) contain digital signal processor (DSP) resources and can support the mixing of audio streams in a conference call.

Simply placing a voice call across a WAN does not guarantee the quality of the voice call. Data applications, for example, tend to be more forgiving of dropped or delayed packets than applications such as voice or video. Therefore, the *quality of service (QoS)* technology is an integral part of Cisco VoIP designs, and an entire section in these Quick Reference Sheets focuses on QoS technologies.

IP Telephony Networks

Although *packet telephony* is more of a generic term, covering Voice over IP (VoIP), Voice over Frame Relay (VoFR), and Voice over ATM (VoATM), the primary focus of these Quick Reference Sheets is creating IP-based telephony networks using VoIP technologies. Therefore, with the foundational understanding of legacy and packet telephony networks, you delve into some of the components of IP Telephony. First, you consider the analog interfaces that are available on voice-enabled routers.

A Foreign Exchange Station (FXS) port allows you to connect plain old telephone service (POTS) devices to a router. For example, you could attach a traditional analog phone, speakerphone, or fax machine to an FXS port on a Cisco router, and that FXS port can act like a PBX or CO switch. For example, an FXS port can provide a dial tone when the phone goes off-hook, interpret dialed digits, and send ringing voltage to the attached phone.

A Foreign Exchange Office (FXO) port connects to a phone switch (for example, a PBX or the PSTN). The FXO port can connect into the traditional tip-and-ring connection that comes from a CO or a PBX. Because it is acting as a phone, an FXO port can go off-hook, dial digits, and answer incoming calls.

E&M is the third type of analog port, and this port interconnects PBXs. The "E" and "M" originally referred to "earth" and "magneto," although you can think of "ear" and "mouth" to better visualize the receive and transmit functions of E&M.

Analog Port Types

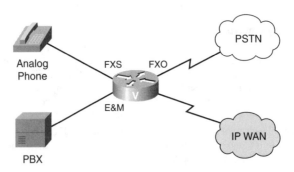

Two primary digital ports (that is, interfaces) are the T1 and E1 interfaces. A T1 interface can send 24 voice channels using channel associated signaling (CAS). Alternatively, with a common channel signaling (CCS) approach, where one channel is dedicated to signaling information, a T1 interface can carry 23 voice channels.

E1 interfaces have 32 channels. However, regardless of the CAS or CCS approach, only 30 of the channels are typically available for voice paths.

Integrated Services Digital Network (ISDN) interfaces are great examples of digital CCS, where one channel is dedicated to signaling. The two flavors of ISDN are Basic Rate Interface (BRI) and Primary Rate Interface (PRI). A BRI has two 64-kbps "B" channels (that is, bearer channels) that carry the voice, video, or data. For signaling, a BRI has a single "D" channel. PRIs, however, are based on T1 or E1 interfaces, where either 23 or 30 voice channels are available.

These digital and analog interfaces just described provide connectivity from Cisco routers to legacy telephony networks. However, we now consider how IP phones connect into this topology.

Some of the Cisco IP Phones are actually three-port switches. One port connects to the IP phone itself and a second port connects to a Catalyst switch in the wiring closet; the third port can connect to a PC. By having a port that connects to a PC, the IP phone allows the PC to daisy-chain through the phone, back to the switch, thus eliminating the need for extra wiring for the IP phone. As the IP phone forwards its voice packets and the PC's data packets back to the wiring closet switch, the IP phone can place the different packets in different virtual LANs (VLANs) and give the packets different priority markings. As discussed in the section "Ensuring Voice Quality," later in these Quick Reference Sheets, those priority markings that are assigned by the IP phone can be referenced by switches or routers, which can make forwarding or dropping decisions based on those markings. Cisco IP Phones register with a Cisco CallManager (CCM), which acts as a call agent.

When you have multiple sites (for example, a main headquarters site and remote office sites) that contain IP phones, those CCMs can be located centrally at the headquarters location. In such an example, IP phones at the remote sites register with CCMs over the WAN link. If the WAN were to go down, these phones would lose connectivity with the headquarters site. To preserve basic service for those IP phones at remote sites, you can configure Survivable Remote Site Telephony (SRST), which allows a Cisco router to stand in for a CCM and perform basic functions in the event of a WAN outage.

Centralized Deployment Model

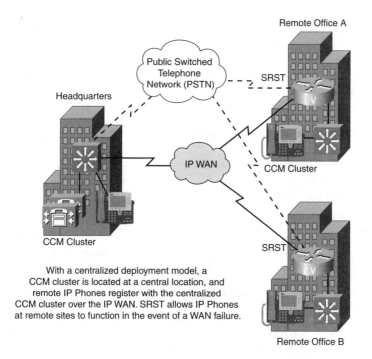

With a centralized deployment model, a CCM cluster is located at a central location, and remote IP Phones register with the centralized CCM cluster over the IP WAN. SRST allows IP Phones at remote sites to function in the event of a WAN failure.

Although a centralized deployment can minimize the number of CCMs that must be purchased, the IP WAN is a potential point of failure. Therefore, you can choose a distributed deployment model, in which you have CCMs at all remote offices. In this example, if a WAN link were to fail, the remote offices' IP phones maintain connectivity to local CCMs, and they still can route calls out to the PSTN by leveraging, for example, FXO ports on a Cisco router acting as a gateway.

Distributed Deployment Model

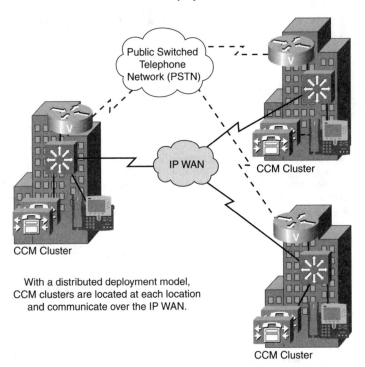

With a distributed deployment model,
CCM clusters are located at each location
and communicate over the IP WAN.

The Mechanics of Analog and Digital V oice Circuits

Introduction

In the previous section, you were introduced to analog and digital voice connections. Now, the material gets more specific and examines the electrical characteristics of these connections.

Analog Voice

First, consider the following types of signaling that are present in the analog telephony world:

- **Supervisory signaling**—Indicates the on-hook or off-hook condition of a phone, based on whether loop current is flowing. In addition, "ringing" is considered to be supervisory signaling. Ringing voltage is sent from the phone switch to alert the destination phone that it is receiving an incoming call. In the United States, the pattern of ringing (that is, *ring cadence*) is 2 seconds on and 4 seconds off.

- **Address signaling**—Allows a phone to dial (that is, specify the address of) a destination phone. The older method of dialing digits was with a rotary phone, which used "pulse" dialing. Pulse dialing rapidly opens and closes the tip-and-ring circuit. This series of open and closed circuit conditions within specific timing parameters indicates a dialed digit.

A more efficient approach to address signaling is dual-tone multifrequency (DTMF) dialing. With DTMF, two simultaneous frequencies are generated, and this combination of frequencies is interpreted by the phone switch as a dialed digit. For example, the combination of a 697-Hz tone and a 1209-Hz tone indicates a dialed digit of 1.

- **Information signaling**—Like DTMF, information signaling uses combinations of frequencies to, in this case, indicate the status of a call (that is, to provide information to the caller). For example, a busy signal is a combination of a 480-Hz tone and a 620-Hz tone, with on/off times of 0.5/0.5 seconds.

In the previous section, you were introduced to the concept of a *trunk*, which interconnected phone switches. Also, you saw how loop-start signaling seized a line when loop current began to flow, and how ground-start signaling seized a line by giving its tip lead a ground potential. However, consider E&M signaling more closely. Five types of E&M signaling exist (that is, Type I through Type V), and these types define such things as the number of wires used for an E&M circuit and the polarity of those wires. Note that the voice path does not use the E&M leads. The E&M leads are intended only for signaling.

With E&M, three types of signaling can occur over the E&M leads: wink start, immediate start, and delay start. However, the most common type of E&M signaling is wink start. With wink-start signaling, the calling equipment (for example, the router) seizes a line by applying voltage to its M lead. The called equipment (for example, the PBX) "winks" by toggling its M lead on and off. When the calling equipment sees this wink, it sends its dialed digits across the voice path.

Voice ports on voice-enabled Cisco routers also can help you with the problem of echo. An impedance mismatch in a 2-wire–to–4-wire hybrid circuit (such as those found in analog phones) is the typical cause of echo. Fortunately, Cisco routers can listen to the analog voice waves that are being sent out of, for example, an FXS port. If that same waveform comes back into the router (within 8 ms by default on pre-IOS 12.3 platforms), the router interprets the waveform as echo and cancels the echo by internally playing an inverse waveform (that is, a waveform that is 180 degrees out of phase with the echo waveform).

Echo Cancellation

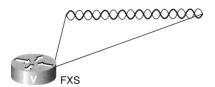

Analog
Phone

The Cisco router can, by default, store 8 ms of transmitted waveforms. If a received waveform matches the stored waveform, the router can internally play an inverse waveform (that is, 180 degrees out of phase) to cancel this echo waveform.

Digitizing the Spoken Voice

To transmit the spoken voice across a digital network or an IP network, you need to digitize the analog speech patterns. In this section, you see how this conversion happens. Also, you might want to conserve WAN bandwidth by compressing those now-digitized voice packets.

To digitize an analog waveform, you periodically take samples of the analog waveform's amplitude. However, the question is this: How many samples should you take? The Nyquist Theorem, developed by Harry Nyquist in 1933, says that you need to sample at a rate that is at least twice as high as the highest frequency that is being sampled. For voice, in theory, the highest sampled frequency is 4 kHz. Therefore, the Nyquist Theorem indicates that you need to take 8000 samples per second, which means that you need to take a sample every 125 microseconds.

Sampling

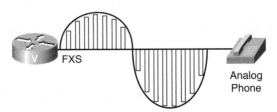

According to the Nyquist Theorem, you should sample a waveform at least twice as many times as the highest frequency. For example, if the highest frequency you wanted to sample were 4000 Hz, sample at twice that rate. Specifically, you should sample 4000 * 2 = 8000 samples per second.

These samples, consisting of a single frequency, have amplitudes equaling the amplitudes of the sampled signaling at the instant of the sampling. This is called Pulse Amplitude Modulation (PAM). The next step is to take these PAM amplitudes and assign them a number, which can be sent in binary form. The process of assigning a number to an amplitude is called *quantization*.

Linear Quantization

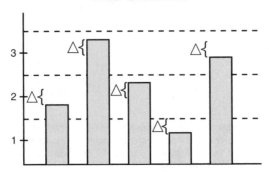

After Pulse Amplitude Modulation (PAM) samples, you need to quantize these samples (that is, assign numbers to represent their amplitudes). However, if you use a linear scale (as shown), the quantization error (as indicated by the deltas) causes distortion in the voice. This distortion is especially noticeable at lower volumes. Therefore, instead of a linear scale, use a logarithmic scale, which has more measurement intervals at lower volumes.

To assign a number to these samples, you establish logarithmic thresholds, and you assign numbers to samples whose amplitudes fall between specific thresholds. Because this process is really "rounding off" to a threshold value, you are introducing *quantization error,* which adds noise (that is, hissing) to the signal. This hissing is reduced, because a logarithmic scale is being used, and small signals are more likely to occur than large signals. Also, large signals tend to mask the noise.

After the analog waveforms have been digitized, you might want to save WAN bandwidth by compressing those digitized waveforms. The processes of encoding and decoding these waveforms are defined by *codecs.* The various forms of waveform compression are as follows:

- **Pulse Code Modulation (PCM)**—Does not actually compress the analog waveform. Rather, PCM samples and performs quantization (as previously described) with no compression. The G.711 codec uses PCM.

- **Adaptive Differentiated PCM (ADPCM)**—Uses a "difference signal." Instead of encoding an entire sample, ADPCM can send the difference in the current sample versus the previous sample. G.726 is an example of an ADPCM codec.

- **Conjugate Structure Algebraic Code Excited Linear Predication (CS-ACELP)**—Dynamically builds a codebook based on the speech patterns. It then uses a "look-ahead buffer" to see whether the next sample matches a pattern that is already in the codebook. If it does, the codebook location can be sent, instead of the actual sample. G.729 is an example of a CS-ACELP codec.

- **Low-Delay Conjugate Excited Linear Predication (LDCELP)**—Is similar to CS-ACELP. However, LDCELP uses a smaller codebook, resulting in less delay but requiring more bandwidth. G.728 is an example of an LDCELP codec.

Working with Cisco products, you normally use G.711 (which requires 64 kbps of bandwidth for voice payload) in the LAN environment and G.729 (which requires 8 kbps of bandwidth for voice payload) over the WAN. G.729 has a couple of variants. Although all forms of G.729 require 8 kbps of bandwidth, G.729a uses a less-complex algorithm, which saves processor resources with slight quality degradation. G.729b enables voice activity detection (VAD), which suppresses the sending of silence if a party in the conversation does not speak for, by default, 250 ms.

Codecs vary in their bandwidth requirements, and in their quality. To measure quality, you can use a mean opinion score (MOS), which uses a "trained ear" to judge the quality of voice after passing through the codec that is being tested. MOS values range from 1, for unsatisfactory quality, to 5, for no noticeable quality degradation. For toll-quality voice, however, an MOS value in the range of 4 is appropriate. The G.711 codec has an MOS value of 4.1. Accompanied by a significant bandwidth savings, G.729 has an MOS of 3.92, while the less-processor-intensive G.729a has an MOS of 3.9.

The challenge with MOS is that at its essence, it is based on opinion. Another approach to quality measurement is Perceptual Speech Quality Measurement (PSQM), which digitally measures the difference in the original signal and the signal after it passes through a codec.

Digital Signaling

Previously, you reviewed how analog signaling (for example, loop-start) functions. Next, consider digital signaling. On a T1 circuit, each frame (including the framing bit) is 193 bits. Typically, you use a framing approach called extended super frame (ESF), which groups 24 of those standard 193-bit frames together. Because the frames are grouped, you do not need all 24 framing bits. Therefore, you can use robbed-bit signaling (that is, channel associated signaling [CAS]) to send signaling information in the framing bit of every sixth frame. Specifically, you can use the framing bit from frames 6, 12, 18, and 24 in an ESF for signaling purposes.

Alternately, T1s can use common channel signaling (CCS), which supports 23 voice channels and one channel, the 24th channel, that is dedicated to carrying only signaling information.

An E1 circuit has 32 channels, and you can use up to 30 of them for voice. The first channel (that is, time slot 0) is used for framing information; the 17th channel (that is, time slot 16 or TS 16) carries signaling information.

In a CAS implementation, one frame might use channel 17 to carry signaling information for channels 2 and 18, while the next frame uses channel 17 to carry signaling information for channels 3 and 19.

With a CCS E1 implementation, the 17th channel (that is, TS 16) is dedicated to carrying signaling information for all other channels that use a protocol called Q.931. ISDN is an example of a CCS technology, which reserves its D channel to carry signaling information.

Whereas the Q.931 signaling protocol is often used from a customer site to a CO, the Q-Signaling (QSIG) protocol is a standards-based approach to signaling between different PBX vendors.

You can also encounter the Digital Private Network Signaling System (DPNSS) protocol, which also can interconnect PBXs. DPNSS was developed by European PBX vendors in the early 1980s, which was before ISDN standards were established. Numerous Cisco IOS gateways can function in a DPNSS network, because DPNSS can run over a standard ISDN interface.

COs typically use Signaling System 7 (SS7) as the signaling protocol between CO switches. For VoIP networks, you can use Signaling Transport (SIGTRAN) to send SS7 messages over an IP network. Specifically, SIGTRAN transports these SS7 messages using a Layer 4 protocol called Stream Control Transport Protocol (SCTP).

The Challenge of Compressing Nonvoice Streams

Although codecs such as G.729 do a great job of compressing voice, they are not designed to compress nonvoice signals such as fax or modem tones. Fax and modem information can be transmitted using G.711 without a problem, but the G.729 codec corrupts these signals to a point where they cannot be interpreted.

Fax Transmission with G.729

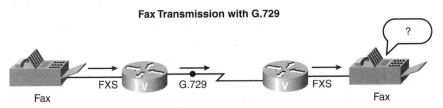

Because the G.729 CODEC is designed to compress human speech, fax or modem signals cannot be successfully sent across a network that compresses the fax or modem tones using the G.729 Codec.

Cisco has a proprietary solution for this situation, called Cisco Fax Relay. With Cisco Fax Relay, the router's DSPs hear the fax tones and do not compress those tones using G.729. A similar industry-standard approach is T.38 Fax Relay. As an additional benefit, Cisco routers can send faxes to PCs and servers that are configured with T.38 fax software.

Another approach to sending faxes across the WAN is T.37 Fax Store and Forward. With the T.37 approach, a Cisco router (called an *on-ramp*) can convert fax data into a TIFF attachment in an e-mail message and transmit that attachment to a store-and-forward e-mail server. This server can then deliver the fax e-mail messages to an off-ramp Cisco router, which initiates a session with the destination fax machine.

To transmit modem tones across a WAN when you have specified the G.729 codec for voice traffic, you can use *modem relay,* which sends modem information through the Simple Packet Relay Transport (SPRT). The last-hop router then remodulates the data and sends it to the destination router.

Confi guring Router V oice Por ts

Introduction

Now that you understand, in theory, the operation of various voice interfaces, in this section, you review the configuration of these interfaces on Cisco voice-enabled routers. First, consider the following categories of voice calls:

- **Local calls**—Occur when both the calling and called phones are attached to the same router.
- **On-net calls**—Span more than one router. Specifically, the calling phone is attached to one router, and the called phone attaches to a different router. In this case, routers are part of the same network.
- **Off-net calls**—Originate on a router but terminate on the PSTN.
- **Private Line Automatic Ringdown (PLAR) calls**—Occur when a caller picks up a phone and the phone automatically dials a preconfigured number.
- **PBX-to-PBX calls**—Are on-net calls, where the source and destination are PBXs.
- **CallManager-to-CallManager calls**—Occur when IP phones register with Cisco CallManagers (CCMs) and one CCM forwards a call to another CCM.
- **On-net to off-net calls**—Originally intend to be on-net calls. However, because of conditions such as WAN oversubscription or a WAN outage, the call is diverted off-net (for example, to the PSTN).

Analog Voice Ports

A phone connects to an FXS port, just as a phone would connect to a PBX or the PSTN. Therefore, you can configure parameters such as signal type (that is, loop-start or ground-start), ring pattern, impedance (to match the impedance of the connecting device), and call progress tones (for example, what a busy signal sounds like). Consider the following FXS configuration example.

FXS Port Configuration

An FXS port acts like a phone switch. Specifically, it can provide such features as dial tone and ringing voltage, and it has the ability to recognize dialed digits.

```
Router(config)#voice-port 1/1/1
Router(config-voiceport)#signal loopstart
Router(config-voiceport)#impedance 600r
Router(config-voiceport)#ring cadence pattern02
Router(config-voiceport)#output attenuation -2
Router(config-voiceport)#input gain 3
Router(config-voiceport)#echo-cancel coverage 32
```

In this example, voice port 1/1/1 is an FXS port, and you are specifying that it should use loop-start signaling, as opposed to ground-start. Also, the impedance is set to 600 ohms resistive (that is, no capacitive component). The ringing pattern is set to the predefined **pattern02**, which specifies a cadence of 1 second on and 4 seconds off. Because you want the volume of VoIP calls to be approximately the same as the volume of the calls in a PBX environment (to make the VoIP network as transparent to the users as possible), you can make gain and attenuation adjustments. In this example, you are attenuating the volume of calls that are being sent out of the port to the attached phone by 2 decibels (dB), with the **output attenuation** command. The **input gain** command, in this example, is increasing the volume of the waveforms that are coming from the phone into the router by 3 dB.

To combat echo, instead of the default 8-ms period of time during which a router can recognize an incoming waveform as echo, you are increasing the coverage to 32 ms, with the **echo-cancel coverage** command. Finally, to maximize echo cancellation, you enabled the nonlinear feature, which suppresses all incoming waveforms from the phone until the volume is loud enough to be interpreted as speech. Note that this nonlinear feature can lead to "clipping" when the other party begins to speak. You can enter the nonlinear feature with the **non-linear** voice-port configuration-mode command.

An FXO port connects to a phone switch (for example, a CO switch or PBX). Therefore, an FXO port acts like a phone. Typical parameters that you can configure on an FXO port are signaling (which must match the signaling type of the phone switch to which you are connecting), dial type (that is, DTMF or pulse), and the number of incoming rings before the FXO port answers (that is, goes off-hook). Consider the following FXO configuration example.

FXO Port Configuration

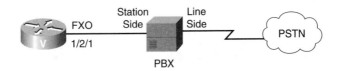

An FXO port acts like a phone. For example, an FXO port
has the capability to dial digits and answer incoming calls.

```
Router(config)#voice-port 1/2/1
Router(config-voiceport)#signal loopstart
Router(config-voiceport)#ring number 3
Router(config-voiceport)#dial-type pulse
```

In this example, voice port 1/2/1 is an FXO port, and you are specifying that it should use loop-start signaling. Also, because the FXO port acts like a phone, you can specify how many rings it receives before it answers. In this case, the FXO port will answer after 3 rings. Also, when the FXO port dials, it is configured to use pulse dialing.

An E&M port typically connects to an existing E&M port on a PBX. Typical parameters that you can configure on an E&M port include the signaling type (for example, wink start), the E&M type (that is, 1, 2, 3, or 5), and the number of wires that are used for the voice path (that is, the "operation"). Consider the following E&M configuration:

```
Router(config)#voice-port 2/1/1
Router(config-voiceport)#type 1
Router(config-voiceport)#operation 4-wire
Router(config-voiceport)#signal wink-start
```

E&M Port Configuration

Some PBXs interconnect using trunks that use E&M ports. You can replace a trunk connection with an IP WAN connection by connecting the PBXs' E&M ports into E&M ports on Cisco voice-enabled routers.

In this example, an E&M port is configured as E&M Type I. In addition, the voice path, which does not use the E&M leads, uses four wires, meaning that both the tip and ring leads have their own return path. The default signaling method of wink start is specified also.

Numerous timing options can be configured for Cisco voice ports. For example, consider the following configuration:

```
Router(config)#voice-port 1/1/1
Router(config-voiceport)#timeouts interdigit 20
Router(config-voiceport)#timeouts initial 20
Router(config-voiceport)#timeouts call-disconnect 20
```

In this example, voice port 1/1/1 is an FXS port. The **interdigit** parameter determines the maximum number of seconds allowed between dialed digits. The **initial** parameter specifies how long the caller can receive a dial tone before he dials the first digit. Finally, the **call-disconnect** parameter indicates how long this port remains in an off-hook condition if the other party disconnects first. All units of measure in this example are seconds.

Digital Voice Ports

Digital voice interfaces, such as T1, E1, and ISDN interfaces, have unique interface-specific configuration parameters. These parameters can include the type of line coding (for example, B8ZS) and framing (for example, ESF) that is used on the digital circuit. Consider the following T1 configuration example, noting that a T1 is configured from controller-configuration mode, as opposed to interface- or voice-port configuration mode.

T1 Controller Configuration

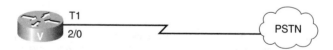

A T1 connection on the Cisco router is a "controller" connection as opposed to a "port." Configure such parameters as "clocking," "line coding," and "framing" in T1 controller configuration mode.

```
Router(config)#controller 2/0
Router(config-controller)#clock source line
Router(config-controller)#framing esf
Router(config-controller)#linecode b8zs
```

In this example, T1 controller 2/0 gets its clocking from the network, as indicated by the **clock source line** command. In addition, the T1 is configured for extended superframing (ESF) and B8ZS line coding.

Sometimes, PBXs use proprietary signaling approaches that a Cisco router cannot interpret. In such a situation, you can configure transparent common channel signaling (T-CCS). With T-CCS, the router allows PBX signaling to flow through the router with no codec manipulation. In controller-configuration mode, you can specify that a T1 is carrying signaling, in the 24th channel, from an external source with the following command:

```
Router(config-controller)#ds0-group 1 timeslots 24 type ext-sig
```

In the next section, you learn about the concept of a *dial peer,* which tells a Cisco router how to send voice packets that are destined for a specific phone number. However, for the sake of completion, a dial-peer configuration-mode command is introduced that is required for the T-CCS configuration. In dial-peer configuration mode, you need to tell the router to transmit the specified signaling channel with no manipulation (for example, from a codec) with the following command:

```
Router(config-dial-peer)#codec clear-channel
```

For verification and troubleshooting purposes, consider the following commands:

- **show voice port**—Displays detailed settings for the voice ports
- **show voice port summary**—Displays a concise view of the installed voice ports
- **show voice dsp**—Displays the codecs that are currently being supported by the router's digital signal processors (DSPs)
- **show controller {T1 | E1}**—Displays the operating parameters for T1 and E1 controllers
- **show isdn status**—Displays Layer 1, 2, and 3 information for an ISDN interface

Various **test** commands are also available for troubleshooting purposes. For example, you can force a voice port to send ringing voltage with the following command:

```
Router#test voice port 1/1 relay ring on
```

You also can play a tone out to an attached phone with the following command:

```
Router#test voice port 1/1 inject-tone local 500hz
```

Note that other frequencies can be specified. You can even cause a gateway to dial a number with the **csim start** *number* command. For example, you could enter the **csim start 5551212** command to cause the router to place a call to a destination phone number of 555-1212. This command is "hidden," meaning that it does not appear in the IOS's context-sensitive help. Cisco also warns that this command occasionally can cause a router to crash. Therefore, use this command with caution.

Configuring Router Dial Peers

Introduction

At this point in the Quick Reference Sheets, you have seen how to configure voice ports on Cisco voice-enabled routers. However, you have not yet trained the routers to reach specific destinations. That is the focus of this section. Specifically, you are going to create dial peers that inform the routers how to reach specific phone numbers. Consider the following topology.

Routers R1 and R2 each have a plain old telephone service (POTS) dial peer that points to their locally attached phone and a VoIP dial peer that points to the IP address of the remote router.

Therefore, when extension 1111 dials extension 2222, router R1 searches for a dial peer that matches a destination pattern of 2222. In this case, R1 has a VoIP dial peer that points to R2's IP address of 10.1.1.2. R1 then forwards the call to R2. Then, R2 receives the incoming call that is destined for extension 2222. R2 searches for a dial peer that matches a destination of 2222, and it finds a POTS dial peer that specifies FXS port 1/1/1. The FXS port then sends ringing voltage out port 1/1/1. Extension 2222 goes off-hook, and the end-to-end call is complete.

Dial Peers and Call Legs

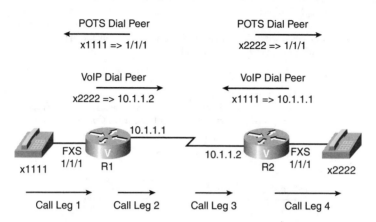

Notice that you have a total of four dial peers that allow a call in the opposite direction. Also, notice that four stages of the call (that is, "call legs") are defined, two call legs from the perspective of each router, as follows:

- **Call Leg #1**—The call comes in to R1 on FXS port 1/1/1.
- **Call Leg #2**—The call is sent from R1 to IP address 10.1.1.2.
- **Call Leg #3**—R2 receives an incoming call that is destined for extension 2222.
- **Call Leg #4**—R2 forwards the call out FXS port 1/1/1.

POTS Dial Peers

When configuring a POTS dial peer, specify the following two parameters:

- The destination-pattern (that is, the phone number)
- The physical port address

Consider the following POTS dial-peer configuration.

POTS Dial Peer

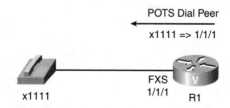

A POTS dial peer associates a phone number
with a physical port. In this instance, a phone
number of 1111 is associated with FXS port 1/1/1.

```
R1(config)#dial-peer voice 1111 pots
R1(config-dial-peer)#destination-pattern 1111
R1(config-dial-peer)#port 1/1/1
```

In this example, an analog phone is attached to FXS port 1/1/1. You entered dial-peer configuration mode for a POTS dial peer with the **dial-peer voice 1111 pots** command. Notice that the 1111 in the **dial-peer** command does not need to match the phone number. The number is merely a locally significant tag. However, to make the configuration more intuitive to interpret, you might want to adopt a practice of using the extension number as the dial-peer tag. The phone's extension number of 1111 is specified with the **destination-pattern 1111** command. The phone's physical location is specified with the **port 1/1/1** command.

VoIP Dial Peers

When configuring a VoIP dial peer, you specify a remote phone number with the same **destination-pattern** command that was used in a POTS dial peer. However, instead of identifying a local port, a VoIP dial peer specifies the voice packets' destination IP address. Consider the following VoIP dial-peer configuration:

VoIP Dial Peer

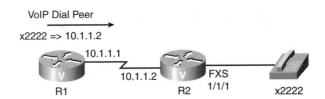

A VoIP dial peer associates a phone number with an IP address. In this instance, a phone number of 2222 is associated with an IP address of 10.1.1.2.

```
R1(config)#dial-peer voice 2222 voip
R1(config-dial-peer)#destination-pattern 2222
R1(config-dial-peer)#session target ipv4:10.1.1.2
```

In this example, router R1 is sending voice packets that are destined for extension 2222 across the IP WAN to IP address 10.1.1.2, as specified with the **session target** command. Note that you must prepend **ipv4:** to the IP address.

At this point, you understand how to establish a dial plan for two phones that are separated by an IP WAN. However, what if you had 1000 extensions on the other side of the WAN? You certainly would not want to create 1000 dial peers. Fortunately, the Cisco IOS allows you to use wildcards to specify a range of addresses. A few of the more frequently used wildcards are as follows:

- T—A T represents a dial string of any length. For example, you could specify a destination pattern of 9T to match any number that begins with a 9, and then you could point any calls matching that pattern out to the PSTN. Because the T can be any number of digits, the router forwards the call, by default, after no digits have been dialed for 10 seconds (by default) or after the caller presses the # key.
- .—A period indicates any single digit. For example, you could specify extension numbers in the range 7000–7999 with the 7... destination pattern.
- []—Brackets can specify a range of numbers. For example, a 123[4-6] destination pattern identifies a four-digit number of 1234, 1235, or 1236.

Destination Patterns

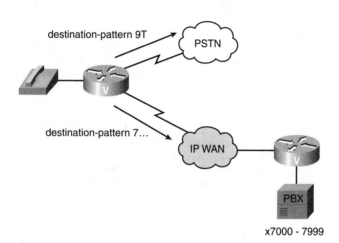

At this point, you have learned about using the **destination-pattern** and **port** commands to match dial peers.

However, a couple of additional options exist for matching inbound dial peers, **incoming called-number** and **answer-address**. To illustrate, consider that all calls destined for a call center are sent out the same trunk, but when the calls reach the call center, they might need to go to different locations (for example, to different customer service agents). You can configure this type of behavior with the **incoming called-number** command.

You can use the **answer-address** command instead of the **destination-pattern** command. For example, if you operate a call center that supports international customers, you can use the **answer-address** *number* command to match a calling number, using caller ID information, to direct the call to an appropriate customer service agent.

You can have a configuration in which multiple destination patterns match a dialed number. The logical question is "Which destination pattern do you use?" The "most specific" destination pattern is used when multiple destination patterns match a called number. Consider the following configuration:

```
Router(config)#dial-peer voice 1 voip
Router(config-dial-peer)#destination-pattern 2468
Router(config-dial-peer)#session target ipv4:192.168.1.1
Router(config-dial-peer)#dial-peer voice 2 voip
Router(config-dial-peer)#destination-pattern 2...
Router(config-dial-peer)#session target ipv4:192.168.2.2
Router(config)#dial-peer voice 3 voip
Router(config-dial-peer)#destination-pattern 2T
Router(config-dial-peer)#session target ipv4:192.168.3.3
```

In this configuration, a dialed number of 2468 is matched by all three dial peers. However, dial peer 1 is the most specific dial peer, matching the pattern exactly without the use of wildcards used to forward the call.

You might want to have multiple dial peers that match specific numbers, for redundancy reasons. For example, you might want to send calls that are destined for extension 4444 across the IP

WAN. However, if the WAN is not available, you want to place the call through the PSTN. To accomplish this, you can have two dial peers: a VoIP dial peer that points across the IP WAN and a POTS dial peer that points to a physical port attached to a PBX or the PSTN. You then can indicate that you prefer to use the VoIP dial peer by assigning "preference" values to the dial peers with the **preference** *number* command.

For example, in dial-peer configuration mode for the VoIP dial peer, you could enter the **preference 0** command. Similarly, you could use the **preference 1** command for the POTS dial peer. Because lower preference values are preferred, the VoIP dial peer is used, if it is available. If the VoIP dial peer is not available, the call would fail over to the POTS dial peer. Note that the valid range of preference values is 0–10.

Digit Forwarding

When the router is connected to a PBX or the PSTN, you need to understand how the router forwards digits. By default, digits that are matched explicitly by the **destination-pattern** command in a POTS dial peer are not forwarded. For example, consider a destination pattern of 123...., which matches the dialed digits 1235555. By default, the router forwards the digits 5555 only to the attached equipment, because explicitly matched digits are stripped. To prevent this behavior, you can use the **no digit-strip command** in dial-peer configuration mode.

In addition to forwarding dialed digits, you also might want to forward additional digits. For example, you might want to prepend a dialed number with a 9 before forwarding the number to a PBX. You can prepend digits to a dialed number with the **prefix** *number* command.

As opposed to using the **no digit-strip** command, you can specify exactly how many digits to forward by using the **forward-digits** *number* command. For example, you could use the dial-peer configuration-mode command **forward-digits 5** to forward the five right-most digits in the dialed number.

You can even instruct the router to replace one dialed number with another. For example, you might have a telecommuter whose home phone number is 555-1234. However, all employees at the headquarters location have four-digit extension numbers. To make the telecommuter's phone appear as a local extension, you can use the **num-exp** *dialed_number translated_number* command. In this example, if you wanted to represent the telecommuter's home phone with a four-digit extension number of 2020, you could enter the **num-exp 2020 5551234** command in global-configuration mode.

Connection Types

Recall the operation of a PLAR connection, as described in a previous section, "Introduction." A PLAR connection automatically dials a predetermined number when a phone goes off-hook. In the following example, when extension 1111 goes off-hook, router R1 automatically dials extension 2222.

PLAR

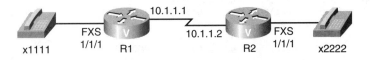

With a Private Line Automatic Ringdown (PLAR) call, when a phone goes off-hook, the attached router automatically places a call to a preconfigured destination. In this instance, when x1111 goes off-hook, router R1 automatically places a call to x2222.

```
R1(config)#dial-peer voice 2222 voip
R1(config-dial-peer)#destination-pattern 2222
R1(config-dial-peer)#session target ipv4:10.1.1.2
R1(config-dial-peer)#voice-port 1/1/1
R1(config-voiceport)#connection plar 2222
```

PLAR Off-Premise Extension (PLAR-OPX) is similar to PLAR. However, with PLAR-OPX, instead of a router answering an incoming call from a PBX—in which case the PBX would consider the call complete—the call is not answered until the destination phone goes off-hook. As a result, an unanswered call can be rerouted to voice mail by the PBX.

In the following PLAR-OPX example, when extension 1111 dials extension 2222, the PBX forwards the call to router R1. Router R1 then places a call to extension 2222. However, because of the PLAR-OPX configuration, R1 (and therefore the PBX) does not consider the call complete until extension 2222 goes off-hook.

PLAR-OPX

With a Private Line Automatic Ringdown Off-Premise Extension (PLAR-OPX)
call, a router connected to a PBX does not indicate to the PBX that the call is complete
until the destination phone goes off-hook. As a result, the PBX might be able to reroute
the call to another location, such as to a voice mail system. In this instance, when x1111 dials
x2222, router R1 does not indicate to the PBX that the call is complete until x2222 goes off-hook.

```
Router(config)#dial-peer voice 2222 voip
Router(config-dial-peer)#destination-pattern 2222
Router(config-dial-peer)#session target ipv4:10.1.1.2
Router(config-dial-peer)#voice-port 1/1/1
Router(config-voiceport)#connection plar-opx 2222
```

Dial Plans

Dial plans organize a group of phone numbers in a hierarchical fashion. Consider the North American dialing plan, which consists of ten digits, as follows:

> 859-555-1212

The first three digits (that is, 859) indicate an area code, which is typically associated with a geographical location within North America. The following three digits (that is, 555) are the central office code (that is, the NXX code), which identifies a central office location within the area that is specified by the area code. The final four digits (that is, 1212) point the local central office to a specific local loop that goes out to a subscriber's physical location.

When designing a dial plan for a customer, consider the following items:

- Where is the dial plan logic located (for example, in a gateway [GW] or in a CCM)?
- Will digit translation be required?
- Can the numbers in the dial plan be reached by multiple paths, for fault-tolerant purposes?
- Should you use digit translations to give dial plans a consistent feel?
- Does an attached voice-mail system require a different number of digits than an extension?
- When do area codes need to be dialed?
- How can the dial plan support different countries, which can have country codes of varying lengths?

Voice over IP Design Considerations

Introduction

In the previous section, you learned about the configuration of a basic VoIP network. However, additional considerations are required. In this section, you examine various VoIP design considerations and are introduced to two additional voice-over-data technologies: Voice over Frame Relay (VoFR) and Voice over ATM (VoATM).

RTP

Consider the characteristics of IP networks. They are considered to be "connectionless," meaning that the IP protocol by itself does not provide guaranteed packet delivery. Also, thanks to various routing protocols, IP networks can support multiple paths between a source and destination; this provides load balancing and fault tolerance.

Voice packets use a Layer 4 protocol, called the Real-Time Transport Protocol (RTP). RTP is encapsulated within the User Datagram Protocol (UDP), another Layer 4 protocol that is connectionless. Because these RTP packets travel over an IP network, with multiple paths, the packets can arrive at different times. Fortunately, RTP provides sequence number information so that the far side of a VoIP call can reorder voice packets.

However, other quality issues must be addressed on a VoIP network. The three main quality challenges are as follows:

- **Delay**—Delay is the time that is required for a packet to travel from its source to its destination. You might have witnessed delay on the evening news, when the news anchor is talking through a satellite to a foreign news correspondent. Because of the satellite delay, the conversation might have seemed unnatural.

- **Jitter**—Jitter is the uneven arrival of packets. For example, consider that in a Voice over IP (VoIP) conversation, packet 1 arrives. Then, 20 ms later, packet 2 arrives. After another 70 ms, packet 3 arrives, and then packet 4 arrives 20 ms behind packet 3. This variation in arrival times (that is, *variable delay*) is not dropping packets, but this jitter can be interpreted by the listener as dropped packets.

- **Drops**—Packet drops occur when a link is congested and a buffer overflows. Some types of traffic, such as UDP traffic (for example, voice), are not retransmitted if packets are dropped.

In the section "Ensuring Voice Quality," later in these Quick Reference Sheets, a variety of the Cisco quality of service (QoS) solutions address these quality issues.

VoFR and VoATM

In addition to Voice over IP, you can encounter a Voice over Frame Relay (VoFR) or Voice over ATM (VoATM) network. Whereas VoIP networks forward voice traffic based on Layer 3 information (that is, an IP address), VoFR and VoATM networks forward voice traffic at Layer 2. Specifically, instead of having the **session target** command specify a remote IP address, VoFR uses the **session target** command to point to a local Data Link Connection Identifier (DLCI). In a similar fashion, VoATM uses the **session target** command to forward voice traffic to a local virtual path identifier/virtual channel identifier (VPI/VCI).

Although forwarding voice traffic at Layer 2 offers the advantage of eliminating Layer 3 overhead (that is, IP header, UDP header, and RTP header), VoFR and VoATM networks do not offer the ability to load-share across multiple paths, as VoIP networks do. Also, you can lose some redundancy in your design, because VoFR and VoATM do not use multiple paths.

Although bandwidth requirements are due in large part to the codec that you select, bandwidth demands also vary based on the transport (for example, FR or ATM) that you use. You can use the following formula to calculate per-call bandwidth requirements for a VoFR circuit:

$$\text{Per\_Call\_Bandwidth} = \text{Codec\_Bandwidth} * (\text{Payload} + \text{Overhead}) / \text{Payload}$$

The units of measure for Codec_Bandwidth are bps, whereas the Payload and Overhead parameters are measured in bytes. Note that the default payload size that is used by G.729 on a VoFR network is 30 bytes.

Cisco provides a web-based Voice Bandwidth Calculator to calculate bandwidth requirements for VoFR, VoATM, and VoIP calls. The calculator, which requires a Cisco.com login, is available at http://tools.cisco.com/Support/VBC/do/CodecCalc1.do.

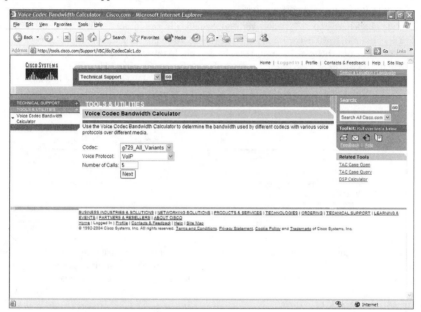

Each asynchronous Transfer Mode (ATM) cells is 53 bytes in size: 48 bytes of payload and 5 bytes of header. If your voice payload does not consume all 48 payload bytes in a cell, the remainder of those 48 bytes is filled with "padding," which can lead to inefficient bandwidth usage. The following formula is used to calculate the per-call bandwidth requirements for a VoATM circuit:

$$\text{Per\_Call\_Bandwidth} = \text{Codec\_Bandwidth} * (\text{Number\_of\_Cells} * 53) / \text{Payload}$$

Note that whereas the G.711 codec requires six ATM cells to send a single voice sample, the G.729 codec requires only one cell per voice sample.

Gateway Considerations

When selecting a gateway (GW) for a VoIP network, consider the following items:

- Do you need an analog or digital gateway?
- What specific ports are required on the gateway?
- What signaling protocol does the gateway need to support?
- Does the gateway need to support Survivable Remote Site Telephony (SRST)?

Voice Protocols

Gateway protocols that you should be familiar with include H.323, the Media Gateway Control Protocol (MGCP), and the Session Initiation Protocol (SIP). Session protocols map to Layer 5 (that is, the session layer) of the OSI model. The session layer is responsible for the setup and teardown of sessions. In the voice environment, you can use these gateway control protocols to set up and tear down voice sessions. In the next section, you learn about each of these protocols.

Voice packets are transmitted using the Real-time Transport Protocol (RTP). A companion protocol, called the Real-Time Transport Control Protocol (RTCP), can monitor the quality of an RTP stream. Both RTP and RTCP operate at Layer 4 and are encapsulated in UDP. UDP ports 16,384 to 32,767 are used by RTP and RTCP. However, RTP uses the even port numbers in that range, whereas RTCP uses the odd port numbers.

One of the challenges with RTP is its overhead. Specifically, the combined IP, UDP, and RTP headers are approximately 40 bytes in size, and the typical voice payload size on a VoIP network is only 20 bytes, which includes 20 ms of voice by default. In this case, the header is twice the size of the payload. Fortunately, Cisco supports RTP Header Compression (cRTP), which can reduce the 40-byte header to 2 or 4 bytes in size (depending on whether UDP checksums are in use).

RTP Header Compression

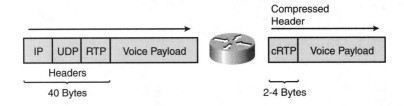

Because cRTP requires router processor resources, you should not enable it in every instance. Specifically, Cisco recommends that you enable cRTP on slow link speeds (that is, speeds of less than 2 Mbps) or when you need to optimize your bandwidth usage on a WAN interface.

Bandwidth Considerations

In the section "Digitizing the Spoken Voice," earlier in these Quick Reference Sheets, you reviewed the codec bandwidth requirements for the G.711 and G.729 codecs, as follows:

- G.711 (64 kbps of bandwidth required for voice payload)
- G.729 (8 kbps of bandwidth required for voice payload)

However, other factors impact the overall bandwidth requirements for voice traffic. For example, the decision of whether to use cRTP can impact the overall bandwidth requirements dramatically. Layer 2 header sizes can vary also. For example, whereas Ethernet has an 18-byte Layer 2 header, both Multilink PPP (MLP) and Frame Relay require only 6 bytes for their Layer 2 header.

In a tunneling environment, you might need to consider the overhead of such protocols as IP Security (IPSec) (50- to 57-byte overhead) and Layer 2 Tunneling Protocol/generic Routing encapsulation (L2TP/GRE) (24-byte overhead). Also, in a service provider environment, you can use Multiprotocol Label Switching (MPLS), which has 4 bytes of overhead.

When you read about the G.729b codec, the concept of voice activity detection (VAD) was introduced. When you have multiple simultaneous conversations (that is, approximately 24 or more), you can benefit from the economies of scale that are offered by VAD to reduce the overall bandwidth consumption. Although you should not use this number for design purposes because VAD's benefit varies with speech patterns, you can enjoy bandwidth savings on the order of a 35 percent reduction when using VAD.

Security Considerations

As another design consideration, you must ensure that your VoIP solution can function in the presence of an enterprise's existing security infrastructure. The Cisco model for security design is called SAFE (Secure Architecture For Enterprise). The main goal of the SAFE blueprint is to provide best-practice information for designing and implementing secure networks. Specifically, the SAFE blueprint seeks to detect and defend against intrusions into the network, to control which traffic can enter and leave the network, and to protect data as it travels through the network. For more information on the Cisco SAFE blueprint, consult http://www.cisco.com/go/safe.

An enterprise network might already have a firewall and a Virtual Private Network (VPN) concentrator in place when you decide to overlay voice traffic on that network. A firewall maintains a set of rules that specify which protocols you can use to communicate from specific outside devices to specific inside devices, and vice versa. The challenge with establishing a voice call through a firewall is that the UDP port that is negotiated for the voice stream varies from session to session. Specifically, voice streams can use any even-numbered UDP port in the range 16,384 to 32,767. Therefore, a "stateful" firewall is required to monitor this negotiation and to open the appropriate port. The Cisco PIX firewall product is an example of a stateful firewall.

The Need for a Stateful Firewall

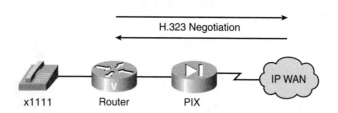

When an H.323 connection is negotiated through a firewall,
the firewall should be able to determine which UDP port has been
negotiated to carry the RTP stream. This is a feature of a "stateful" firewall.

One way to protect voice packets from eavesdropping is to send them through a VPN connection. A VPN is a tunnel over which you can send encrypted packets. As a result, if the voice packets were intercepted, they would be worthless to anyone who intercepted the packets, because the packets are encrypted.

Various VPN mechanisms exist. For example, you can use Layer 2 Tunneling Protocol (L2TP) at Layer 2 or IPSec at Layer 3. Because various VPN technologies have different header sizes, your overall voice bandwidth requirements vary with the VPN technology that you select. However, as a rule, you typically add 30 to 60 bytes of overhead per VoIP packet when you transmit the packet over a VPN.

Gateway Protocols

Introduction

In this section, you learn about the theory and configuration of the following gateway control protocols: H.323, SIP, and MGCP. The discussion begins with a generic overview of gateway protocols.

Gateway Protocol Theory

The ultimate goal of call control is to allow RTP streams to flow directly between endpoints. Therefore, during the call setup process, each endpoint (for example, IP phone) needs to learn the IP address and UDP port to use to get a phone call to the other end.

In addition to setting up a call, you might want to perform call administration and accounting features. These features can keep track of bandwidth usage on the WAN and maintain call records, which you can use for billing or planning purposes. You also might need a way to obtain status information about a current call.

Although your local gateway might know how to reach local phones, the gateway might need to contact an external database of addresses to resolve the location of a remote phone. This external database can learn about remote phones by having the gateway that is used by those remote phones register those phone numbers with the database. By having this central repository of phone number–to–IP address mappings, less configuration needs to be performed on each of the local gateways.

In the Cisco IP telephony environment, the Cisco CallManager (CCM) acts as a database that can direct a gateway (for example, a Cisco voice-enabled router) to a remote gateway that is connected to the destination phone. If all the CCMs are in a single location, that deployment model is called *centralized call control*.

Centralized Deployment Model

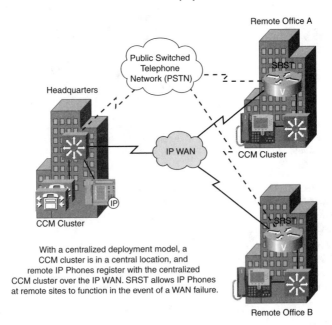

With a centralized deployment model, a CCM cluster is in a central location, and remote IP Phones register with the centralized CCM cluster over the IP WAN. SRST allows IP Phones at remote sites to function in the event of a WAN failure.

However, if CCMs are scattered across all your remote office locations, that deployment model is referred to as *distributed call control*. You can incur additional costs with a distributed call control model, because of the extra equipment and administration required. However, you enjoy greater scalability with the distributed call control model.

Distributed Deployment Model

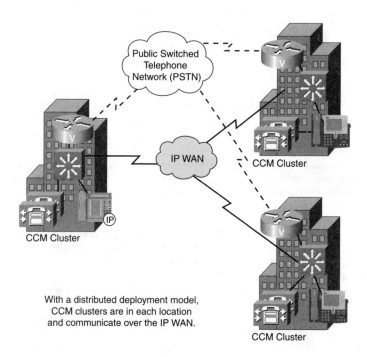

With a distributed deployment model,
CCM clusters are in each location
and communicate over the IP WAN.

Consider the following pros and cons of each approach:

- Centralized call control

  Pros:

  — Less expensive

  — Easier to maintain

  Cons:

  — Single point of failure

  — Less scalable

  — Uses WAN bandwidth for call setup

- Distributed call control

  Pros:

  — More fault tolerant

  — Does not consume WAN bandwidth for call setup

  — More scalable

  Cons:

  — Requires additional equipment

  — Requires more work to perform updates

H.323 Theory and Configuration

H.323 is not a single protocol. Rather, it is a suite of protocols. This suite specifies such things as audio/video codecs and call signaling.

You should be aware of the following two major protocols:

- **H.225**—Performs call setup and Registration, Admission, and Status (RAS) functions
- **H.245**—Performs call control, including a capabilities exchange

In addition to various protocols, H.323 identifies the physical components of a IP telephony network, as follows:

- **Terminals**—An H.323 terminal is an end-user device that communicates with another end-user device. By definition, an H.323 terminal must support the G.711 codec.
- **Gateways**—A gateway (GW) converts between different audio formats/signaling. For example, on one side of the GW, you might use H.225 and H.245 signaling, and the other side of the GW might use E&M wink-start signaling.
- **IP-to-IP gateways**—These gateways allow different VoIP networks to interconnect. For example, if two companies had their own internal VoIP network with their own service provider, an IP-to-IP gateway could allow the two companies to join their VoIP networks. This solution requires no extension-number overlapping between the two companies.
- **Gatekeepers**—To prevent voice calls from oversubscribing the WAN bandwidth, groups of routers, called *zones*, can be identified. Then, a gatekeeper (GK) can keep track of the number of calls made from one zone to another, or calls made within a zone. Based on the available bandwidth within or between zones, a GK can permit or deny a call attempt. The gatekeeper also can perform centralized E.164 number resolution.
- **Multipoint Control Units (MCUs)**—An MCU supports conference calling by adding and removing participants from a call and by mixing voice streams together.

Gatekeepers are optional components, because you can have an H.323 GW directly communicate with another H.323 GW. However, this approach has scalability limitations. If you introduce GKs into the network, GWs communicate with GKs using the RAS channel. In larger topologies, you can have multiple GKs, and those GKs communicate with each other using the RAS channel.

Consider how a call is completed in the following H.323 networks:

- **GW-to-GW calls**—This topology does not require a GK. Specifically, both GWs communicate directly with each other. First, H.225 performs the call setup, followed by H.245 performing a capabilities exchange. However, this negotiation requires numerous packet exchanges between the GWs. Another option is to use H.323 Fast Connect, which performs call setup and does a capabilities exchange in a single exchange of messages between the two GWs.

H.323 Call Setup Without a GK

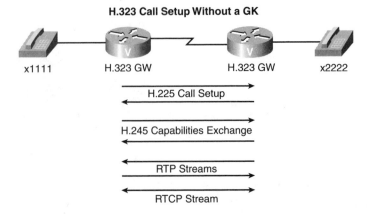

- **GW-to-GK-to-GW calls**—With a GK in your topology, the originating GW requests permission from the GK to place a call using an admission request (ARQ) message, after which the GK can send an admission confirm (ACF) or admission reject (ARJ) message. If permission is granted, the call setup proceeds. The destination GW also sends an ARQ to the GK. If permission is granted, the call setup proceeds as usual, using H.225 and H.245, after which RTP is used to stream audio directly between the GWs.

H.323 Call Setup with a GK

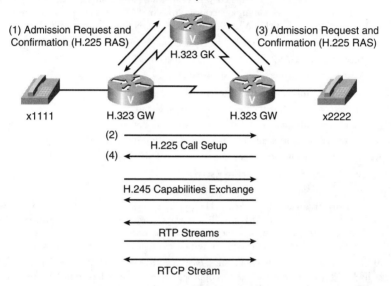

For even larger environments, you can have multiple GKs involved in the call setup. The main difference with such a configuration is that when the first GK gets an admission request, it sends a location request (LRQ) and must receive a location confirm (LCF) from the remote GK before sending an admission confirm (ACF) to the originating GW.

To increase the availability of H.323 networks, you can configure multiple GKs and GWs to service the same phone numbers. You also can use high-availability technologies such as Hot Standby Router Protocol (HSRP) to maintain uptime in an H.323 network.

Numerous options are available to you when configuring H.323 GWs and GKs. For a thorough example, visit http://www.cisco.com/warp/public/788/voip/2zone_gw_gk.pdf.

However, use the following three basic steps to configure an H.323 GW:

Step 1   Enable the GW using the **gateway** command in global-configuration mode.

Step 2   Configure the relationship between the GW and the GK with the **h323-gateway voip id** command in interface-configuration mode.

Step 3   Configure dial peers to point to the GK, with the **session target ras** command.

You can verify and troubleshoot an H.323 configuration with various **show** commands, as follows:

- **show gatekeeper calls**—Displays current phone calls that the GK participated in
- **show call active voice [brief]**—Displays details for current voice calls
- **show call history voice [last *n* | record | brief]**—Displays call record logs

SIP Theory and Configuration

Session Initiation Protocol (SIP) uses the concept of inviting participants into sessions, and those sessions can be advertised by Session Announcement Protocol (SAP). Like H.323, SIP is a peer-to-peer protocol. These peers are called User Agents (UAs). The two types of UAs are as follows:

- **User Agent Clients (UACs)**—Initiate the connection by sending an INVITE message
- **User Agent Servers (UASs)**—Reply to INVITE messages

SIP also leverages the following types of SIP servers:

- **Proxy server**—Performs forwarding for a UAC
- **Registrar server**—Registers the location of current clients
- **Redirect server**—Informs the UA of the next server to contact
- **Location server**—Performs address resolution for SIP proxy and redirect servers

SIP uses clear text for sending messages; the two types of SIP messages are as follows:

- **Request**—A message from a client to a server
- **Response**—A message from a server to a client

A request includes messages such as an INVITE (which requests a participant to join the session) or a BYE (which disconnects the current call). Conversely, a response message uses HTML status messages. For example, you probably have attempted to connect to a website and received a "404 error" or a "500 error." Those same types of responses are used in the SIP environment.

For a SIP client to get the IP address of a SIP server, it has to resolve a SIP address. These addresses are actually URLs that begin with "sip:" as opposed to "http:" which is commonly used in web browsers. SIP addresses can include a variety of information, such as username, password, host name, IP address, and phone number. Following is an example of a SIP address:

> sip:18595551212@ciscopress.com;user=phone

In this example, the **user=phone** argument specifies that the user portion of the URL (that is, 18595551212) is a phone number and not a user ID.

SIP devices can make their addresses known dynamically by registering with a SIP registrar server. When SIP devices have their addresses registered, a SIP client can resolve a SIP address by itself, perhaps through DNS or through a local host table. However, a SIP client can use a SIP proxy server to query a SIP location database to resolve the SIP IP address. Consider a basic SIP call, where one SIP GW communicates directly with another SIP GW, without the use of proxy or redirect servers.

The basic call setup begins when a SIP client sends an INVITE to a SIP server (noting that a SIP IP phone can act as either a client or server, depending on whether it is originating or terminating the call). The destination server (that is, a UAS) responds if it is willing to join the session to which it has been invited. The originating client (that is, a UAC) sends an acknowledgment (that is, and ACK message) to the destination server, and at this point, the RTP streams can flow directly between the SIP GWs.

If you introduce a SIP proxy server into your topology, the call setup procedure is similar to that just discussed. However, the INVITE is sent to the proxy server rather than the destination UAS. The proxy server can consult a location server to learn the IP address of the final endpoint. The destination exchanges call parameters with the proxy server, which responds to the originating UAC. The UAC then forwards an ACK through the proxy server to the destination UAS, after which the RTP stream is established.

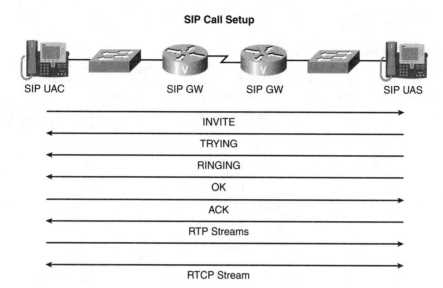

SIP Call Setup

SIP UAC   SIP GW   SIP GW   SIP UAS

INVITE

TRYING

RINGING

OK

ACK

RTP Streams

RTCP Stream

When you use a redirect server, the originating UAC sends an INVITE message to a redirect server, which can consult a location server to determine the path to the destination. The registrar server responds to the UAC with a *moved message,* telling the UAC the IP address of the destination UAS. This operation is much like when you connect to a website and you receive a message saying that the page you are looking for has moved to a new URL; then you are redirected automatically to the new URL. When the UAC learns the location of the destination UAS, a direct connection can be set up between the UAC and UAS. Therefore, the main purpose of a redirect server is essentially to off-load the IP resolution procedure from the UAC.

If one of your SIP servers goes down, the voice network could be rendered unavailable. One way to provide redundancy is to have multiple instances of proxy and redirect servers. Therefore, the UAs can have multiple entries, and if the first server fails, the second server takes over.

Use the following two basic steps to configure SIP on a Cisco router:

Step 1   Enable the UA.

Step 2   Configure dial peers.

Consider the following example:

```
Router(config)#sip-ua
Router(config-sip-ua)#sip-server dns:SERVER1
Router(config-sip-ua)#dial-peer voice 1 voip
Router(config-dial-peer)#destination-pattern 5...
Router(config-dial-peer)#session protocol sipv2
Router(config-dial-peer)#session target sip-server
```

In this example, you enable the SIP UA with the **sip-ua** global-configuration-mode command. Then, you specify the DNS name of your SIP server with the **sip-server** command. When the SIP server has been defined, in VoIP dial-peer configuration mode, you specify that you want the dial peer to use SIP version 2, with the **session protocol sipv2** command. Finally, instead of specifying an IP address as the session target, you use the **session target sip-server** command, which points your dial peer to the SIP server that is defined under sip-ua configuration mode.

In addition to the **show call** commands that you used for H.323 verification, you can also use the **show sip-ua statistics** command to display three different sets of statistics (that is, SIP response statistics, SIP total traffic statistics, and retry statistics).

MGCP Theory and Configuration

Whereas H.323 and SIP were peer-to-peer protocols, MGCP is more of a client–server approach to call control. Specifically, MGCP allows GWs to point to a centralized call agent for processing. In a Cisco environment, this centralized call agent is the Cisco CallManager (CCM).

MGCP Call Setup

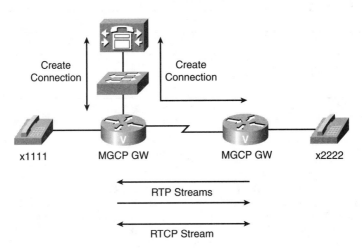

The physical pieces that make up an MGCP network, such as call agents, gateways, and endpoints, are called *components*. However, the logical pieces of an MGCP network, such as calls and connections, are called *concepts*. First, consider the following MGCP components:

- **Endpoints**—An endpoint is where you interface between the VoIP network and the traditional telephony network. For example, an FXS port that connects to a telephone would be considered an endpoint. Endpoint names look much like an e-mail address (for example, circuitID@mgcpgw.ciscopress.com). These names are composed of two parts the locally significant name of the endpoint (before the @ sign) and the DNS name of the MGCP GW (after the @ sign).

- **Gateways**—Gateways are in charge of converting audio between a VoIP network and a circuit-switched network. For example, a residential gateway supports devices that you typically find in residential environments (for example, POTS telephones).

- **Call agents**—A call agent is the intelligence of an MGCP network and controls the gateways and their endpoints. An MGCP gateway can report events to the call agent, and the call agent can, for example, tell the endpoint what type of signaling to send to the phone.

Recall that an MGCP concept is a logical piece of an MGCP network. Consider the following MGCP concepts:

- **Call**—A call is formed when two or more endpoints are interconnected.

- **Events**—An event is what an endpoint has been instructed (by the call agent) to watch for. As an example, an FXS port might notice the event of an attached POTS device going off-hook.

- **Signal**—A call agent instructs an endpoint to send a specific signal when a certain event occurs. For example, after the event of a POTS phone going off-hook, the call agent might instruct the FXS endpoint to send the signal of "dial tone" to the phone.

MGCP groups relevant events and signals into *packages*. For example, a line package contains events and signals that are used on subscriber lines, such as an off-hook event and a dial-tone signal. MGCP GW types are defined by the types of packages that they support. For example, a trunk gateway supports the generic media, DTMF, trunk, and RTP packages.

You do not have to configure an MGCP GW with dial peers for every destination phone number. Instead, the GW can send each dialed digit to the call agent, until a match is made. However, that approach can put a heavy burden on the call agent. An alternate approach is for the gateway to download a *digit map*, which is essentially a copy of the dial plan that is contained in the call agent. When a GW has a digit map, it then has the responsibility of collecting all the dialed digits and finding a pattern match.

To enhance the availability of an MGCP network, survivability strategies such as "MGCP switchover and switchback" and "MGCP gateway fallback" are supported. MGCP switchover and switchback uses two or more CCMs. When a GW sees no MGCP messages from a call agent for a period of time, the GW attempts to establish a connection with a backup CCM. If the primary CCM comes back up, the GW can be configured to switch back to the primary.

MGCP gateway fallback works with SRST to maintain a remote office that connects to a centralized CCM. If the WAN link, which the GW uses to reach the CCM, fails, the GW relies on a fallback H.323 configuration that provides basic functionality for attached IP phones.

MGCP is enabled in global-configuration mode with the **mgcp** command. The IP address of the call agent then is specified with the **mgcp call-agent** *ip_address* command. When MGCP is enabled, you specify which packages the GW expects the call agent to use when communicating with the GW. Consider the following configuration example, where you are specifying that a router is acting as an MGCP GW and that its call agent is located at IP address 10.1.1.1:

```
Router(config)#mgcp
Router(config)#mgcp call-agent 10.1.1.1
```

A POTS dial peer that MGCP uses does not have a **destination-pattern** command. Rather, it uses the **application MGCPAPP** command to indicate that the port specified by the dial peer is controlled by an MGCP call agent. To view information about current MGCP connections on a GW, you can use the **show mgcp connection** command.

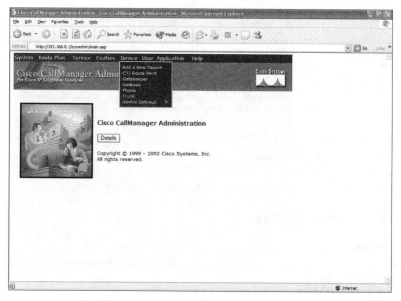

In a Cisco environment, because an MGCP gateway works in conjunction with a Cisco CallManager (CCM), the following items need to be configured on the CCM:

- From the CCM main screen, choose the **Device** menu and select **Gateway**.
- Click the **Add a New Gateway** link.
- Select the **Gateway Type** from the drop-down menu, and click **Next**. (Note that by selecting the appropriate hardware, the CCM automatically determines that you are using MGCP.)
- In the Domain Name field, enter the DNS name of the gateway router.
- Select the appropriate CCM group from the Cisco CallManager Group menu.
- From the Module in Slot 1 drop-down menu, select the appropriate installed module, and click the **Insert** button.
- After the screen refreshes, you see one or more "subunits" listed below the module that you specified. Select the appropriate subunit(s) from the Subunit drop-down menu(s), and click the **Update** button.
- After the screen refreshes, you see one or more "endpoint identifiers" that correspond to physical voice ports on the router. Click an **Endpoint Identifier** link.
- Select the appropriate **Device Pool** from the drop-down menu, and click the **Insert** button.
- For an FXS port, after the screen refreshes, click the **Add DN** link to add a directory number. Enter the directory number (that is, phone number) for the voice port in the Directory Number field, and click the **Insert** button.

At this point, the Cisco MGCP gateway and the CCM (acting as the MGCP call agent) can communicate between themselves using MGCP signaling.

Selecting a Gateway Protocol

When selecting from the three call control protocols (that is, H.323, SIP, and MGCP), consider the following characteristics:

- H.323
  - Mature
  - Uses Abstract Syntax Notation 1 (ASN.1) for call control messages
  - Uses a peer-to-peer model
  - Scales well in an enterprise
- SIP
  - Not as mature as H.323
  - Uses clear text for call control
  - Uses a peer-to-peer model
  - Allows interoperability between diverse vendor equipment
- MGCP
  - Not as mature as H.323
  - Uses clear text for call control
  - Uses a client–server model
  - Ideally positioned for service providers (because of centrally located call agents)

Ensuring V oice Quality

Introduction

In this section, you examine several quality of service (QoS) tools to help you preserve voice quality as voice packets traverse voice-enabled networks. Specifically, you make the following distinctions that affect voice quality:

- Selecting codecs
- Minimizing delay

- Provisioning sufficient bandwidth
- Overcoming jitter

However, you first learn to measure voice quality.

Challenges to Voice Quality

As mentioned earlier in these Quick Reference Sheets, voice quality can be impacted when voice packets are dropped or delayed. Also, variation in the delay (that is, jitter) affects the listener's perception of the voice quality. The *fidelity* of a signal is a measure of the frequency range that is represented by a signal. However, in the voice environment, your main concern is transporting the majority of the frequencies that make up speech patterns, rather than reproducing high-fidelity music, as you would on a home stereo system. Therefore, the G.711 codec samples frequencies up to 4000 Hz, which contains more than 90 percent of the frequencies that are used in human speech patterns.

Earlier, you learned how to measure voice quality using mean opinion score (MOS) or Perceptual Speech Quality Measurement (PSQM). The choice of codecs impacts the score that is given to the voice quality. For example, the G.711 codec has an MOS of 4.1, whereas G.729 has an MOS of 3.92.

Another approach to measuring voice quality is Perceptual Evaluation of Speech Quality (PESQ). Like PSQM, PESQ uses test equipment to measure voice quality, as opposed to a "trained ear." However, PESQ attempts to match MOS rankings. For example, if a codec had an MOS of 3.92, it should have a PESQ score of 3.92. However, the maximum value on the PESQ scale is 4.5, whereas the MOS scale reaches 5.0.

Overcoming Delay

Voice is sent over IP networks in RTP packets, which use UDP for transport. Because UDP is connectionless, the network does not attempt to retransmit a lost packet. Also, because IP networks can load-balance traffic across multiple links, packets can arrive with various interpacket intervals. These characteristics can lead to variable delay, which is called *jitter*. Another example of variable delay is queuing delay, which your queuing strategy can introduce. A queuing strategy determines the order that packets are transmitted out of a queue in the presence of congestion.

Jitter

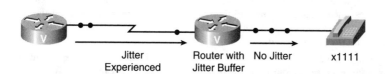

| Jitter | Router with | No Jitter | x1111 |
| Experienced | Jitter Buffer | | |

Jitter occurs when the interpacket gap varies between packets. However, the "jitter buffer" in the destination router can store the packets for a brief period of time and then play the packets out in a smooth and even fashion.

Fortunately, the Cisco voice-enabled routers have a "jitter buffer," which stores packets as they come into a router and then plays the packets out in a smooth fashion. When packets are in the jitter buffer, you can reorder them based on RTP sequence numbers. Although the IOS determines the size of the jitter buffer is automatically, if jitter problems are not eliminated, you can manually configure the jitter buffer with the **playout-delay mode** command. Specifically, the dial-peer configuration-mode command **playout-delay mode adaptive** along with the **playout-delay maximum** *size* command can specify, in milliseconds, the maximum size of the jitter buffer, while allowing the jitter buffer to dynamically adjust its size based on network conditions. Alternatively, you can use the **playout-delay mode** fixed and the **playout-delay nominal** *size* dial-peer configuration-mode commands to specify statically the size of the jitter buffer. You can view current jitter conditions with the **show call active voice** command.

Some delay components, however, are *fixed*, meaning that they do not change during a call. The following are examples of fixed delay:

- **Coder delay**—The amount of time required for a codec to process a voice packet. (For example, a G.729 codec can require 2.5 to 10 ms to do the coding, depending on how many voice calls a DSP is coding. Similarly, the G.723 codec requires 5 to 20 ms for coding.)
- **Serialization delay**—The amount of time required for a packet to exit a serial interface. (For example, a 1500-byte frame requires 214 ms to exit a serial interface running at 56 kbps.)
- **Propagation delay**—The amount of time required for a packet to travel across the network.

Although serialization delay is considered a fixed delay, for the duration of a call, you can minimize the effect of serialization delay by performing Link Fragmentation and Interleaving (LFI). LFI fragments large data payloads and interleaves smaller voice packets among the fragments. On a Voice over IP over PPP circuit, the LFI mechanism that you use is multilink PPP (MLP). However, on a Voice over IP over Frame Relay (VoIPovFR) network, your LFI tool of choice is FRF.12.

The combined fixed and variable delay components create the *delay budget* for a design. However, too much delay adversely affects voice quality. As a design guideline, the ITU G.114 recommendation states that the one-way delay for a voice packet should not exceed 150 ms.

LAN Quality of Service

Normally, quality of service (QoS) technologies are related to the WAN. However, the LAN also needs QoS. For example, you might have multiple Fast Ethernet devices simultaneously communicating to a server that is also connected through Fast Ethernet. Such a situation could lead to "oversubscription" of the bandwidth. Therefore, frames that cannot be sent at the moment can be buffered by a Catalyst switch in a queue. If the queue overflows, all incoming packets are discarded, even high-priority voice packets.

However, if you place voice frames in a different queue from lower-priority data frames, even if the data queue overflows, the voice queue still accepts incoming voice frames.

After frames are queued, the switch's queuing strategy determines in what order frames are emptied from the queues and how bandwidth is made available to those queues. Specifically, many Cisco Catalyst switches support Weighted Round Robin (WRR) queuing, which specifies the "weight" that is given to each queue.

As an example, consider that queue 1 has a weight of 1 and that queue 4 has a weight of 4. In this example, queue 4 receives four times the bandwidth of queue 1 because of its weight.

Catalyst switches such as the 2950 and the 3550 offer four queues where you can place frames. Other switch models can have a different number of queues. However, Cisco recommends a 2Q1T approach, which specifies that you are using two queues, where each of the queues has one threshold. Having a single threshold causes a queue to delay discarding frames until the queue fills to capacity.

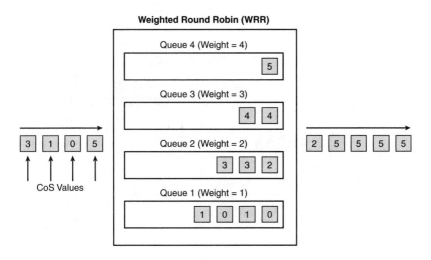

Weighted Round Robin (WRR)

Queue 4 (Weight = 4)

| | 5 |

Queue 3 (Weight = 3)

| | 4 | 4 |

CoS Values

| 3 | 1 | 0 | 5 |

Queue 2 (Weight = 2)

| | 3 | 3 | 2 |

| 2 | 5 | 5 | 5 | 5 |

Queue 1 (Weight = 1)

| | 1 | 0 | 1 | 0 |

WRR "weights" queues to determine the relative amount
of bandwidth available to each queue. In this example,
Queue 4 has twice the available bandwidth of Queue 2.

WAN Quality of Service

Two broad categories of QoS tools exist: Integrated Services (IntServ) and Differentiated Services (DiffServ). Integrated Services provides QoS by guaranteeing treatment to a particular traffic flow. A commonly used IntServ tool is the Resource Reservation Protocol (RSVP).

As the name suggests, Differentiated Services differentiates among different types of traffic and provides different levels of service based on those distinctions. Instead of forcing every network device to classify traffic, DiffServ can mark packets with a particular priority marking that other network devices can reference.

A common type of packet marking is Differentiated Services Code Point (DSCP). DSCP uses the 6 left-most bits in an IPv4 header's type of service (ToS) byte. With 6 bits at its disposal, up to 64 DSCP values (0 to 63) can be assigned to various classes of traffic.

Another type of marking that uses the IPv4 ToS byte is IP Precedence, which uses the 3 left-most bits in the ToS byte. Because it uses 3 bits, IP Precedence has values in the range 0 to 7. However, Cisco recommends that IP Precedence values of 6 or 7 never be used, because they are reserved for network and Internet use. Just marking a packet does not change its operation, unless QoS tools are enabled that can reference that marking. Fortunately, multiple QoS tools exist that can make decisions based on these markings.

Type of Service (ToS) Byte

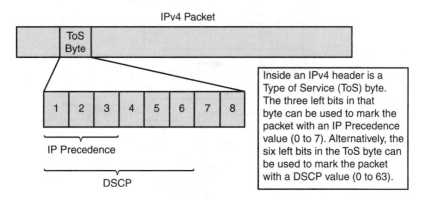

IPv4 Packet

Inside an IPv4 header is a Type of Service (ToS) byte. The three left bits in that byte can be used to mark the packet with an IP Precedence value (0 to 7). Alternatively, the six left bits in the ToS byte can be used to mark the packet with a DSCP value (0 to 63).

You can place most QoS tools in one of the following areas:

- Classification and marking
- Congestion avoidance
- Congestion management
- Traffic conditioning
- Signaling
- Link efficiency mechanisms

Classification and Marking

When configuring QoS, decide which devices in the network you "trust" to make markings. These devices should be as close to the source as possible. For example, you can select a Cisco IP phone as the trust boundary.

When you decide on a trust boundary, configure your edge devices to classify traffic into classes. For example, you could have a Voice over IP (VoIP) class, a database class, an FTP class, a video class, and a default class.

When the traffic is categorized into traffic classes, mark the various traffic classes with DSCP markings. This prevents other devices in the network from having to reclassify the traffic. Instead, these other devices can reference the DSCP markings. However, as mentioned earlier, marking by itself does not alter the behavior of traffic.

Congestion Avoidance

The purpose of congestion avoidance is to prevent an interface's output queue from filling to capacity, because if a queue is full, all newly arriving packets are discarded. Some of those packets can be high priority, and some can be low priority. However, if the queue is full, no room exists for a packet.

With a congestion-avoidance tool, drop thresholds are defined for various markings (for example, DSCP markings). Therefore, as a queue begins to fill, lower-priority packets are dropped more aggressively than higher-priority packets, thus preventing the queue from ever filling to capacity. The Cisco congestion-avoidance tool of choice is Weighted Random Early Detection (WRED).

Weighted Random Early Detection (WRED)

As an output queue fills beyond the Minimum Threshold, WRED begins to discard packets. Those packets are discarded more aggressively as the queue depth increases. When the queue depth exceeds the maximum threshold, all packets are discarded. Minimum and Maximum Thresholds might be defined for each IP Precedence or DSCP value.

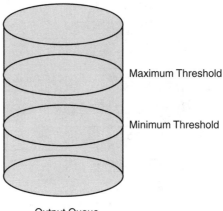

Maximum Threshold

Minimum Threshold

Output Queue

Congestion Management

Congestion-management tools are queuing tools. These queuing tools decide how packets are placed in an interface's output queues and how the packets are forwarded out of the queues. Several queuing tools are available in the IOS. However, modern queuing approaches include the following:

- **Low Latency Queuing (LLQ)**—The preferred queuing method for voice and video traffic, where traffic can be classified in up to 64 different classes, with different amounts of bandwidth given to each class. This method includes the ability to give priority treatment to one or more classes.

- **Class-Based Weighted Fair Queuing (CB-WFQ)**—Similar to LLQ, with the exception of having no priority-queuing mechanism.

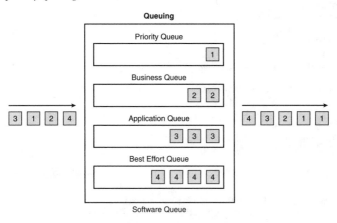

Queuing mechanisms determine in what order and in what quantity specific packets are emptied from a queue.

Many of the Cisco QoS mechanisms are configured using a three-step configuration process called Modular QoS CLI (MQC).

Modular QoS CLI (MQC)

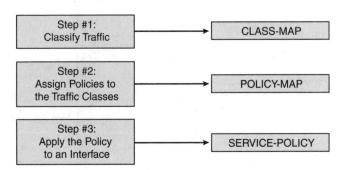

Following is an MQC example where you are classifying various types of e-mail traffic (for example, SMTP, IMAP, and POP3) into one class-map. The KaZaa protocol, which is frequently used for music downloads, is placed in another class-map. Voice over IP (VoIP) traffic is placed in yet another class-map. Then, the policy-map assigns bandwidth allocations or limitations to these traffic types. The code is as follows:

```
Router(config)#class-map match-any EMAIL
Router(config-cmap)#match protocol pop3
Router(config-cmap)#match protocol imap
Router(config-cmap)#match protocol smtp
Router(config-cmap)#exit
Router(config)#class-map MUSIC
Router(config-cmap)#match protocol kazaa2
Router(config-cmap)#exit
Router(config)#class-map VOICE
Router(config-cmap)#match protocol rtp
Router(config-cmap)#exit
Router(config)#policy-map CVOICE
Router(config-pmap)#class EMAIL
Router(config-pmap-c)#bandwidth 128
Router(config-pmap-c)#exit
Router(config-pmap)#class MUSIC
Router(config-pmap-c)#police 32000
Router(config-pmap-c)#exit
Router(config-pmap)#class-map VOICE
Router(config-pmap-c)#priority 256
Router(config-pmap-c)#exit
Router(config-pmap)#exit
Router(config)#interface serial 0/1
Router(config-if)#service-policy output CVOICE
```

Notice that the **CVOICE** policy-map makes 128 kbps of bandwidth available to e-mail traffic. However, KaZaa version 2 traffic has its bandwidth limited to 32 kbps. Voice packets not only have access to 256 kbps of bandwidth, but they also receive "priority" treatment, meaning that they are sent first (that is, ahead of other traffic), up to the 256-kbps limit.

The next logical question is this: What happens to all the traffic that you did not classify? Interestingly, Cisco created a class-map named class-default, which categorizes any traffic that is not matched by one of the defined class-maps. Finally, in the previous example, the policy-map is applied in the outbound direction on the Serial 0/1 interface.

Traffic Conditioning

Although some of the congestion-management techniques can guarantee bandwidth amounts, in some situations, you might want to limit bandwidth usage. For example, you might want to prevent oversubscription of a link. The two categories of traffic conditioning are as follows:

- **Policing**—Limits traffic rates, with excess traffic being dropped
- **Shaping**—Limits traffic rates, with excess traffic being delayed

Shaping buffers excess traffic, while policing drops excess traffic. These characteristics suggest that policing is more appropriate on high-speed interfaces, whereas shaping is more appropriate on low-speed interfaces.

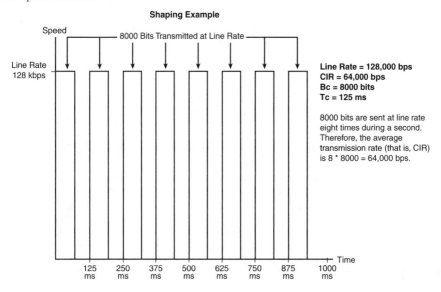

Signaling

The IntServ model uses signaling to allow an application to reserve bandwidth for the duration of the application. RSVP is the primary QoS signaling protocol. One of the main characteristics of signaling is that signaling is performed *end to end,* meaning that all routers along the path from the source to the destination must be configured to support the IntServ mechanism (for example, RSVP). Also, note that when the Cisco voice-enabled routers are configured to reserve bandwidth using RSVP, reservations are made in both directions.

Link Efficiency Mechanisms

Link efficiency mechanisms help make the most of the limited bandwidth that is available on WAN links. Two link efficiency mechanisms are as follows:

- **Link Fragmentation and Interleaving (LFI)**—Takes large payloads, fragments them, and interleaves smaller packets among the fragments to reduce serialization delay for latency-sensitive traffic (for use on link speeds of less than 768 kbps)
- **RTP Header Compression (cRTP)**—Takes a 40-byte VoIP header and compresses it to 2 or 4 bytes (for use on link speeds of less than 2 Mbps)

Link Efficiency Mechanisms

Compressed Header

| IP | UDP | RTP | Voice Payload |

Headers

40 Bytes

| cRTP | Voice Payload |

2 - 4 Bytes

Header Compression

| V | V | V | V | D |

| V | D | V | D | V | D | V | D |

Link Fragmentation and Interleaving (LFI)

AutoQoS

Optimizing a QoS configuration for VoIP can be a daunting task. Fortunately, Cisco added a feature called AutoQoS to many of its router and switch platforms. AutoQos automatically generates router-based or switch-based VoIP QoS configurations.

On a router platform, the following command enables AutoQoS from either interface-configuration mode or from DLCI-configuration mode, if you have a Frame Relay circuit:

```
Router(config-if)#auto qos voip
```

After you enter this command, the IOS automatically executes a series of QoS configuration commands that depend on the configured interface bandwidth. For example, on a PPP interface running at less than 768 kbps, the AutoQoS feature automatically configures LLQ, cRTP, MLP, and even an SNMP configuration, where quality issues can be reported to an SNMP network management server.

Preventing WAN Oversubscription

Consider a scenario in which you have 50 kbps of bandwidth on an IP WAN, and perhaps a single voice call requires 25 kbps of bandwidth. After two voice calls are placed across the IP WAN, no more bandwidth is available. Therefore, if a third phone call is set up across the IP WAN, you have oversubscribed the bandwidth; this leads to poor quality for all three calls. To prevent such an occurrence, you can configure one or more Call Admission Control (CAC) mechanisms to prevent this oversubscription. CAC mechanisms fall in one of the following three categories:

- **Local CAC mechanisms**—Make admission-control decisions based on information known to the local router (for example, the number of connections placed using a particular dial peer).

- **Measurement-based CAC mechanisms**—Send Service Assurance Agent (SAA) probes out into the network to determine network conditions. A request to place a phone call across the IP WAN is then permitted or denied based on the probes' results.

- **Resource-based CAC mechanisms**—Determine how much bandwidth has been used between different network locations. For example, a gatekeeper can keep track of the amount of bandwidth that is used between two defined zones.

Cisco also supports CAC features for the following call control protocols, which were discussed earlier:

- **H.323**—CAC can permit or deny a call attempt based on a router's available resources (for example, CPU and memory).
- **SIP**—CAC can send SAA probes into the network to determine whether a call attempt should be permitted.
- **MGCP**—CAC can make admission-control decisions based on available router resources, SAA probes, and available network bandwidth.

Bandwidth Provisioning

The essence of bandwidth provisioning for voice networks is to determine how many calls that you might need to support during peak periods. You can obtain current call volumes from various sources, such as your telephony service provider or your PBX's Station Message Detail Recorder (SMDR) records.

As a designer, you must determine an acceptable grade of service (GoS), which is the probability that a call will be blocked because of bandwidth oversubscription. Typically, you use a GoS of P(.01), which specifies a 1 percent probability of a blocked call during the busiest hour.

With the GoS determined, you next need to determine the number of Erlangs that you need to support during your busiest hour. An Erlang is defined as 1 hour of conversation. For example, two phone calls that lasted 30 minutes each would equal one Erlang.

As a design best practice, you can calculate the number of Erlangs that you need to support with the following formula:

$$\text{Erlangs} = \text{Hours\_of\_phone\_use\_in\_a\_month} / 22 * 0.15 * 1.10$$

The 22 represents the number of business days per month. The 0.15 indicates that approximately 15 percent of your phone system usage occurs during the busiest hour. Finally, the 1.10 adds 10 percent for call-processing overhead.

With the number of required Erlangs and the GoS value, you can determine the number of required trunks using an Erlang table or calculator, such as the one found at http://www.erlang.com/calculator/erlb.

When you have the number of trunks that you need, you can translate that number into the amount of bandwidth that you require by determining how much bandwidth is needed for a single voice call and then multiplying that amount by the number of trunks that you need. As a reminder, you can use the Cisco voice bandwidth calculator for this purpose. You can find this calculator at http://tools.cisco.com/Support/VBC/do/CodecCalc1.do.

Note that a Cisco.com login is required for the bandwidth calculator.

PART III CIPT

Section 1
The Cisco CallManager

Section 2
IP Telephony Components

Section 3
Dial Plans

Section 4
IP Telephony Options

Section 5
IP Telephony Applications

Section 6
Administrative Utilities

Section 7
Cisco CallManager 4.x Enhancements

CIPT Quick Reference Sheets

CIPT Section 1
The Cisco CallManager

IP telephony networks allow you to consolidate voice, video, and data traffic on the same network. You can enjoy significant cost savings from such a converged network. In a Cisco IP Telephony network, the central component is the Cisco CallManager (CCM).

The flash cards in this section review the Cisco model for converged networking (that is, AVVID) and how the CCM plays a role in the AVVID model. Because the CCM is software, you must select an appropriate hardware platform on which to install the software. You are challenged to distinguish between various platforms and design options. Also, these flash cards verify your knowledge of installation and upgrade considerations for the CCM.

Question 1

Define Architecture for Voice, Video, and Integrated Data (AVVID), as it relates to IP telephony.

Question 2

Routers and switches are categorized under which layer of the AVVID model?

Question 3

Explain the function of the Cisco CallManager (CCM) in an IP telephony network.

Question 1 Answer

The Cisco AVVID solution brings voice, video, and data communication technologies together under a common umbrella. Specifically, the Cisco AVVID model for voice technologies contains the following four layers: Client, Application, Call-Processing, and Infrastructure.

Question 2 Answer

The Infrastructure layer of the AVVID model is the underlying data network, which includes such components as routers and switches.

Question 3 Answer

The Cisco CallManager (CCM) is a software component that runs on Cisco-approved server platforms. The CCM makes call-forwarding decisions, controls IP phones, and can support other optional features (for example, automatic route selection and call transfer).

Question 4

Which protocol do Cisco IP Phones use when communicating with the Cisco CallManager?

Question 5

How many IP phones can the Cisco MCS-7815-1000 support?

Question 6

What is a device unit?

Question 4 Answer

Cisco IP Phones use the proprietary Skinny protocol to communicate with the CCM. The CCM then assists the IP phone in setting up a call.

Question 5 Answer

The Cisco MCS-7815-1000 can support up to 200 IP phones. Also, note that the Cisco MCS-7815-1000 is not directly rack mountable; it comes in a tower case. However, a rack-mount kit is available as an extra purchase.

Question 6 Answer

The amount of "work" that a CCM can do is measured in *device units*. Each device that registers with the CCM requires one or more of these device units, but the number of device units supported can vary depending on the number of calls that the CCM is supporting simultaneously. This call load is called the Busy Hour Call Attempts (BHCAs), which is the maximum number of simultaneous calls during the busiest hour of the day.

Question 7

How many CCM servers in a CCM cluster can function as a publisher?

Question 8

What is the term for CCM servers in a cluster that have a read-only copy of the SQL database?

Question 9

What type of messages does a Cisco IP Phone send to its backup CCM server?

Question 7 Answer

One CCM server in a cluster is designated as a "publisher," and that CCM replicates its database information to subscribers.

Question 8 Answer

Only one CCM server in a cluster has a writable copy of the SQL database. That server is called the *publisher*. All other CCM servers in a cluster have a read-only copy of the SQL database. Those servers are called *subscribers*.

Question 9 Answer

The IP phone sends keepalive messages to the primary CCM server and a Transport Control Protocol (TCP) connect message to its backup CCM server (that is, secondary CCM server).

Question 10

A Cisco IP Phone can have a list of how many CCM servers, for redundancy purposes?

Question 11

How many CCM servers does Cisco recommend for supporting 2000 IP phones?

Question 12

How many CCM servers does Cisco recommend for supporting 8000 device units in a 2:1 redundancy model, assuming that you are using MCS-7835 servers?

Question 10 Answer

A Cisco IP Phone can have a prioritized list of three CCM servers, for redundancy. If the primary CCM server fails, the IP phone establishes a connection with the secondary (that is, backup) CCM server and sends a TCP connect message to the tertiary server in the CCM list.

Question 11 Answer

Regardless of whether you are using a 1:1 or 2:1 redundancy model, Cisco recommends that you have three CCM servers in a cluster to support up to 2500 IP phones. One CCM server acts as a publisher and Trivial File Transfer Protocol (TFTP) server (for 1000 phones or more). The second CCM acts as a primary CCM server, and the third CCM acts as a backup CCM server.

Question 12 Answer

In a 2:1 redundancy model, Cisco recommends using four CCM servers for supporting 5001 through 10,000 device units. In this cluster, one CCM acts as a publisher and TFTP server, two CCMs act as primary CCM servers, and the remaining CCM acts as a backup server for the two primary CCM servers.

Question 13

Where are CCM servers located in a centralized call-processing model?

Question 14

How many sites can a distributed call-processing model support?

Question 15

List two tasks that you should perform after installing a CCM server.

Question 13 Answer

In a centralized call-processing model, the CCM cluster is located at the central site. IP phones at remote locations register over the IP WAN, with the CCM cluster located at the central site.

Question 14 Answer

CCM clusters are located at each site in a distributed call-processing model. These clusters can be interconnected through the use of intercluster trunks, allowing the distributed call-processing model to scale to hundreds of sites.

Question 15 Answer

Because the administrative password is reset during the CCM installation, you should reset the administrative passwords on all CCM servers in the cluster. Also, because the CCM software runs on a Windows 2000 server platform, you should disable unnecessary services, for performance and security reasons.

CIPT Section 2
IP Telephony Components

The primary interface that a user has into a Cisco IP Telephony network is the IP phone. The flash cards in this section review various characteristics of IP phones and how to configure the Cisco CallManager (CCM) to support IP phones. In addition, the IP phones need power to operate, and many Cisco Catalyst switches can provide "inline" power, over the wires in the Cat 5 cable that is connected to the IP phone. These flash cards challenge you with the syntax that is required to configure inline power.

For quality of service (QoS) purposes, you often want voice traffic to reside in a different VLAN from data traffic. Therefore, Cisco allows you to configure a Catalyst switch to place voice traffic in a separate VLAN. These flash cards confirm your ability to configure this separate VLAN on a Catalyst switch. Finally, because IP phones must use a gateway to communicate off the IP telephony network, these flash cards ask you to distinguish among gateway control protocols.

Question 1

How many 10-Mbps Ethernet ports are on a Cisco 7905 IP phone?

Question 2

Which Cisco IP phone is designed for conference room applications?

Question 3

Why does a Dynamic Host Configuration Protocol (DHCP) server return the address of a Trivial File Transfer Protocol (TFTP) server to an IP phone?

Question 1 Answer

Unlike higher-end IP phones, such as the Cisco 7910+SW, 7940, and 7960 IP phones, the Cisco 7905 IP Phone has only one Ethernet port, which connects the IP phone to a switch. Therefore, you cannot daisy chain a PC through a Cisco 7905 IP Phone.

Question 2 Answer

The Cisco 7935 IP Phone is a conference station. It is actually a Polycom conference room speakerphone that has been converted into an IP phone and Cisco branded.

Question 3 Answer

The IP phone needs the address of a TFTP server to download the IP phone's configuration, which includes a list of up to three prioritized CCMs.

Question 4

How much bandwidth is required for voice payload when using the G.729 codec?

Question 5

Under which menu option would you remove an IP phone's dependence on Domain Name System (DNS)?

Question 6

Which menu option would you select to add a phone button template?

Question 4 Answer

The G.729 codec requires 8 kbps of bandwidth for voice payload. Therefore, the G.729 codec provides a significant bandwidth savings over the G.711 codec, which requires 64 kbps of bandwidth for voice payload.

Question 5 Answer

By default, the CCM is known by its DNS name, as opposed to its IP address. To remove the CCM server's dependence on DNS, from the Cisco CallManager Administration page, select **System, Server menu** and click the CCM that you are interested in. In the DNS/IP Address field, enter the CCM's IP address and click the **Update** button.

Question 6 Answer

To add a phone button template, select **Device, Device Settings, Phone Button Template** and click the **Add New Phone Button Template** button.

You can select a phone button template from the drop-down menu and click the **Copy** button. At that point, you can rename the copy of the template to an intuitive name. Select which buttons are speed-dial buttons and which buttons are line appearances. You can also assign a label for each button.

Question 7

How does a port that is configured for inline power determine whether it is attached to an IP phone?

Question 8

Which pins on a Cat 5 cable provide power when a Catalyst switch is providing inline power to an attached Cisco IP Phone?

Question 9

Which pins on a Cat 5 cable provide power when an external patch panel is providing inline power to an attached Cisco IP Phone?

Question 7 Answer

Inline power allows the switch port (or router port) that connects to an IP phone to detect the presence of the IP phone by sending a Fast Link Pulse (FLP). If an IP phone is attached to the switch port in an unpowered condition, a relay inside the IP phone allows the FLP to flow through the IP phone and back to the switch port. When the Catalyst switch port sees the FLP returning from the IP phone, the switch realizes that an unpowered IP phone is indeed attached, and the switch can then apply inline power across the Ethernet leads.

Question 8 Answer

A Catalyst switch uses the Ethernet pins (that is, pins 1, 2, 3, and 6) for inline power.

Question 9 Answer

When an IP phone is using an external patch panel for inline power, the Ethernet leads still need to connect to a switch, for basic network connectivity. Therefore, when an external patch panel is being used for inline power, pins 4, 5, 7, and 8 (that is, the non-Ethernet pins) are used for inline power.

Question 10

How many IP phones does the Cisco Inline Power Patch Panel support?

Question 11

Which command would you issue to enable inline power on port 3/10 on a Catalyst 6500, running the Catalyst Operating System (Cat OS)?

Question 12

Which Cat OS command specifies the amount of power to allocate to an inline-powered phone?

Question 10 Answer

The Cisco Inline Power Patch Panel supports up to 48 IP phones. Note that the external patch panel uses the non-Ethernet leads for powering attached IP phones.

Question 11 Answer

The Cat OS command that enables inline power for a port is **set port inlinepower** *<mod/port>* **<auto | never>**. Therefore, to enable inline power on port 3/10, you would use the command **set port inlinepower 3/10 auto**.

Question 12 Answer

On a Cat OS platform, the **set port inlinepower defaultallocation** *power* command defines how much power to make available to an attached IP phone. The *power* unit of measure is milliwatts.

Question 13

What is the default inline power allocation for a Catalyst 6500 Series switch?

Question 14

Which command enables inline power for an interface on a Catalyst platform running the Native IOS?

Question 15

What is a VVID, as it relates to IP telephony?

Question 13 Answer

By default, a Catalyst 6500 Series switch allocates 7 watts per port for inline power.

Question 14 Answer

To enable inline power for an interface on a Native IOS–based Catalyst switch, use the power inline <auto | never> command.

Question 15 Answer

A VVID is the Voice VLAN ID. Specifically, the VVID defines the number of the auxiliary VLAN that is dedicated to carrying voice traffic from an IP phone to a Catalyst switch. Recall that an IEEE 802.1Q trunk is formed between the IP phone and the Catalyst switch. If the IP phone has a PC attached, the IP phone forwards the PC's data traffic in the trunk's Native VLAN, which is known by the Port VLAN ID (PVID).

Question 16

Which command would you use on a Cat OS switch to specify an auxiliary VLAN of 100 on port 3/3?

Question 17

Which class of service (CoS) marking does an IP phone assign, by default, to voice frames?

Question 18

Which CoS marking does an IP phone assign, by default, to frames that are coming from an attached PC?

Question 16 Answer

The **set port auxiliaryvlan <mod/port> <*vlan* | untagged | dot1p | none>** command specifies auxiliary VLAN information for a port on a Catalyst platform that is running the Cat OS. In this example, you would issue the **set port auxiliaryvlan 3/3 100** command.

Question 17 Answer

An IP phone can mark the CoS priority level of a frame that it sends to a switch. The valid range of values for CoS markings are 0 to 7. However, Cisco recommends that you never use 6 or 7, because those values are reserved for network use. The Cisco IP phone, by default, marks voice frames with a CoS value of 5.

Question 18 Answer

To give voice frames that are coming from the IP phone priority over data frames that are coming from a PC that is attached to the IP phone, the Cisco IP Phone assigns a CoS marking of 0 (that is, the lowest priority value) to data frames that are coming from an attached PC.

Question 19

Which Cat OS command syntax would you use to assign a specific CoS marking to frames that are coming into an IP phone's extra Ethernet port (that is, where a PC could attach)?

Question 20

Which Cat OS command syntax can you use to indicate whether you will trust a CoS marking that is coming from an IP phone's downstream device?

Question 21

Which Native IOS command syntax can you use to indicate whether an IP phone should trust the CoS marking of an attached device (for example, another IP phone or a PC)?

Question 19 Answer

To assign a specific CoS value to frames that are coming from a Cisco IP Phone's downstream device (for example, an attached PC), use the following Cat OS command:

```
Switch>(enable)set port qos <mod/port> cos-ext <cos_value>
```

Question 20 Answer

To indicate whether the CoS value of a downstream device is trusted, issue the following command in the Cat OS:

```
Switch>(enable)set port qos <mod/port> trust-ext <untrusted | trust-cos>
```

Question 21 Answer

In a Native IOS environment, you can use the following interface-configuration mode command to specify a CoS value for frames that are coming from a device that is attached to an IP phone, to specify that CoS values from an attached device are not trusted, or to specify that CoS values from an attached device are trusted:

```
switchport priority extend {cos_value | none | trust}
```

Question 22

Where does the call-forwarding intelligence reside for an H.323 gateway?

Question 22 Answer

An H.323 gateway has call-forwarding intelligence locally configured on the gateway. MGCP (Media Gateway Control Protocol), however, points to an external call agent (for example, the Cisco CallManager) for call-forwarding intelligence.

CIPT Section 3
Dial Plans

One of the primary responsibilities of the Cisco CallManager (CCM) is to route calls based on dialed digits. However, you might also need to restrict certain phones (for example, lobby phones) from calling certain destinations (for example, international numbers). You might need to manipulate the dialed digits, based on whether the call is going to be placed over the IP WAN or over a Public Switched Telephone Network (PSTN) gateway. For example, you might need to add an area code and an office code to dialed digits, if the CCM decides to forward those dialed digits over the PSTN.

These flash cards challenge you to recall the architecture of route plans, the types of available gateways, the use of wildcards in a route pattern, and approaches to manipulating dialed digits. You also should be able to distinguish between partitions and calling search spaces, define how locations can prevent oversubscription of bandwidth on the IP WAN, and describe how Survivable Remote Site Telephony (SRST) can provide redundancy for a centralized CCM deployment.

Question 1

How are "on-cluster" calls different from "off-cluster" calls?

Question 2

List the elements in a route plan's hierarchy.

Question 3

When creating a route plan, which of the following components should you create first?

- Route list
- Device
- Route pattern
- Route group

Question 1 Answer

On-cluster calls are calls made within the CCM cluster; therefore, they do not require much configuration. Off-cluster calls have a destination that is not a member of the local cluster. Therefore, these call types require external route patterns.

Question 2 Answer

The elements in a route plan's hierarchy are as follows:

- **Route pattern**—Matches a dialed number and points to a route list
- **Route list**—Is a prioritized list of one or more route groups
- **Route group**—Points to devices, such as routers acting as gateways
- **Devices**—Forward calls, typically either over the IP WAN or out to the PSTN

Question 3 Answer

When configuring a route plan, you create devices first. Then you add the devices to a route group. You add a prioritized list of route groups is added to a route list, and a route pattern matches dialed digits and points to a route list.

Question 4

What is the purpose of an intercluster trunk?

Question 5

A route pattern can point directly to which two of the following?

- Route list
- Device
- Route pattern
- Route group

Question 6

Under which Cisco CallManager Administration menu option do you find the Gateway menu selection?

Question 4 Answer

An intercluster trunk joins two CCM clusters, thus allowing communication between devices that are registered with different clusters.

Question 5 Answer

A route pattern can directly point to a route list or to a device. However, if multiple paths exist to reach a destination number, you typically create a route plan hierarchy, in which a route pattern points to a route list. In smaller environments, where perhaps you can use only a single gateway to reach a destination phone number, you can point the route pattern directly to a device.

Question 6 Answer

You can find the Cisco CallManager Administration Gateway menu selection under the Device main menu option.

Question 7

You have a Catalyst 6500 Series switch (running the Cat OS) with a WS-6608-T1 module. This module can function as what type of gateway?

Question 8

What does a route group contain?

Question 9

What does the "X" wildcard represent in a route pattern?

Question 7 Answer

The WS-6608-T1 module can function as an MGCP (Media Gateway Control Protocol) gateway. However, because the gateway is not running the Native IOS, it is referred to as a non-IOS MGCP gateway.

Question 8 Answer

A route group contains a prioritized list of gateways.

Question 9 Answer

You can use the "X" wildcard in a route pattern to represent a single dialed digit, specifically digits 0 to 9. For example, a route pattern of 41XX matches numbers in the range of 4100 through 4199.

Question 10

What does the "@" wildcard represent in a route pattern?

Question 11

What does the "^" character represent in the 123[^123] route pattern?

Question 12

The 555X route pattern matches what range of dialed numbers?

Question 10 Answer

You can use the "@" wildcard in a route pattern to represent the North American Numbering Plan. This plan includes all phone number patterns that you can dial from North America, such as 911, 411, long-distance numbers, and even international numbers.

Question 11 Answer

The caret symbol (^) in brackets indicates all dialed digits except the digits, or range of digits, within the brackets. In this example, the route pattern matches four-digit numbers that end with any digit except 1, 2, or 3.

Question 12 Answer

The "X" wildcard represents a single dialed digit. Therefore, the 555X route pattern matches numbers in the range of 5550 through 5559.

Question 13

The 123[4-68] route pattern matches what numbers?

Question 14

The 9.!# route pattern allows a user to dial a 9 to call off the IP telephony network. The user can then dial any number of digits. What key on a telephone keypad can a user press to indicate that he is finished dialing?

Question 15

What does a caller hear if she dials a number that no route pattern matches?

Question 13 Answer

The "[4-68]" in the route pattern matches dialed digits of 4 through 6 and 8. Therefore, the 123[4-68] route pattern matches the following numbers:

1234

1235

1236

1238

Question 14 Answer

A user can press the "#" key (that is, the pound or octothorp key) can be used to indicate the end of the dialed digits. Alternatively, the caller could wait until the T302 timer expires, after which the call is placed.

Question 15 Answer

If a caller dials a number that is not matched by a route pattern, she hears a fast busy signal.

Question 16

A caller dials the number 555-2468. The following route patterns match the dialed number:

- 55524XX
- 55524[6-8]8

Which of these route patterns is used?

Question 17

What is the purpose of a route filter?

Question 18

What does the "==" (that is, double equal sign) route filter operator indicate?

Question 16 Answer

When more than one route pattern matches a dialed number, the route pattern that matches the fewest number of numbers is used. The 55524XX route pattern matches 100 numbers, in the range 5552400 to 5552499. The 55524[6-8]8 route pattern matches only three numbers: 5552468, 5552478, and 5552488. Therefore, the 55524[6-8]8 route pattern is matched, because it is the most specific route pattern.

Question 17 Answer

A route filter limits the patterns that are matched by a route pattern. For example, you could use a route filter to filter out 911 calls from the North American Numbering Plan route pattern.

Question 18 Answer

You can use the double equal sign route filter operator to match a specific value. For example, you can match an area code of 900 by specifying the AREA CODE == 900 route filter option.

Question 19

You apply a "PreDot" discard instruction to the 91606.@ route pattern. Which digits are discarded by the PreDot discard instruction?

Question 20

What is the purpose of the "10-10-Dialing" discard instruction?

Question 21

What type of transformation mask changes the caller ID information that the called party sees on the PSTN?

Question 19 Answer

The PreDot discard instruction indicates that everything before the period (that is, the dot) in the route pattern should be discarded. Therefore, in this example, the 91606 digits are discarded. In North America, the PreDot discard instruction often is used with the 9.@ route pattern, which strips off the 9 before sending digits to the PSTN.

Question 20 Answer

In North America, callers often can select their long-distance carrier by dialing 10-10-*XXX*, where *XXX* are carrier-specific digits. To control the long-distance carrier that is selected, regardless of the 10-10-*XXX* code that the caller dials, you can use a 10-10-Dialing discard instruction.

Question 21 Answer

Caller ID information that sees the called party on the PSTN can be manipulated by using a calling party transformation mask.

Question 22

An internal phone has a directory number of 12345, and that extension places a call to a phone on the PSTN. However, before forwarding the caller ID information to the PSTN, a calling party transformation mask of 800555X000 is applied. What caller ID information does the called party see on the PSTN?

Question 23

A called number transformation mask of XXXXXXX is applied to a dialed number of 8595551234. What number is forwarded to the PSTN?

Question 24

From what Cisco CallManager Administration menu option can you create or modify a translation pattern?

Question 22 Answer

The caller ID information that the called party sees on the PSTN is 8005552000. Note that the caller ID information is determined by letting the digit positions in the original caller ID that correspond to the X positions in the transformation mask flow through the mask. In this example, the fourth position from the right in the calling party transformation mask has an X. Therefore, the fourth position from the right in the original caller ID information, which is a 2 in this example, flows through the mask, yielding the caller ID information 8005552000.

Question 23 Answer

In this example, the seven Xs in the called number transformation mask allow the 7 right-most digits in the dialed number to flow through the mask. As a result, the number that is forwarded to the PSTN is 5551234, which is the originally dialed number without the area code.

Question 24 Answer

You configure a translation pattern from the **Route Plan, Translation Pattern** menu option.

Question 25

Define a *partition,* in the CCM context.

Question 26

Define a calling search space.

Question 27

Under what Cisco CallManager Administration menu option do you create or modify a partition?

Question 25 Answer

A *partition* defines a grouping of numbers and typically contains route patterns or directory numbers.

Question 26 Answer

A *calling search space* is a list of partitions in which a device (for example, an IP phone) is allowed to look when matching dialed digits.

Question 27 Answer

You can modify or create a partition under the **Route Plan, Partition** menu option.

Question 28

Under which Cisco CallManager Administration menu option do you create or modify a calling search space?

Question 29

Which Cisco software product synchronizes a CCM cluster's phone database with the 911 Public Safety Answering Point (PSAP)?

Question 30

Which H.323 message does a CCM send to an H.323 gatekeeper when the CCM wants permission to place a call across the IP WAN?

Question 28 Answer

You can modify or create a calling search space under the **Route Plan, Calling Search Space** menu option.

Question 29 Answer

The Cisco Emergency Responder (Cisco ER) software synchronizes a CCM cluster's phone database with the 911 PSAP, which can identify the caller's approximate physical location.

Question 30 Answer

The CCM can request permission to send a call across the IP WAN by sending an admission request (ARQ) message to an H.323 gatekeeper. The gatekeeper can respond with either an admission confirm (ACF) or an admission reject (ARJ) message.

Question 31

Which H.323 message can a CCM send to an H.323 gatekeeper to request a different amount of bandwidth for an existing H.323 session?

Question 32

What is the purpose of a CCM "location?"

Question 33

Which Cisco CallManager Administration menu option can you use to create or modify a location?

Question 31 Answer

The CCM can send a bandwidth request (BRQ) to the GK to request a different amount of bandwidth for an existing H.323 session, and the GK can respond with either a bandwidth confirm (BCF) or a bandwidth reject (BRJ) message.

Question 32 Answer

The CCM can use a location to prevent oversubscription of the IP WAN in a centralized deployment model. Specifically, you can define a location and configure the bandwidth amount available between the remote site that is associated with the location and the central site. IP phones at the remote site can be assigned to the location. Then, when an IP phone at the remote site calls back to the central site, the centralized CCM cluster determines, based on available bandwidth and the codec selection, whether to permit the call.

Question 33 Answer

You can modify or create a location under the **System, Location** menu option.

Question 34

What is the purpose of Survivable Remote Site Telephony (SRST)?

Question 35

What global configuration IOS command can you use to enter the configuration mode for SRST?

Question 36

Which SRST configuration command specifies the IP address that a router uses when communicating with IP phones through the Skinny protocol?

Question 34 Answer

Centralized IP deployment models have the disadvantage of remote IP phones being rendered unusable if the IP WAN goes down, because the remote IP phones no longer have a path back to the centralized CCM cluster. To prevent such an occurrence, you can use SRST, which allows an IOS router at the remote site to provide limited support for those phones. Although SRST supports basic IP phone features (for example, hold, transfer, PSTN dialing, internal dialing, and so on), it does not provide higher-end features, such as conference calling and music on hold.

Question 35 Answer

You can use the **call-manager-fallback** global-configuration mode IOS command to enter the "cm-fallback" configuration mode, from which you can configure SRST.

Question 36 Answer

You use the **ip source-address** *ip_address* IOS command in cm-fallback configuration mode to specify the IP address that a router uses to communicate with IP phones, through the Skinny protocol, when the router is functioning in a CallManager fallback condition.

Question 37

Which SRST configuration command specifies the maximum number of IP phones that can register with the SRST router?

Question 38

Which Cisco CallManager Administration menu option can you use to configure SRST?

Question 37 Answer

The **max-ephones** *number* IOS command specifies the maximum number of IP phones that can register with the SRST router.

Question 38 Answer

You can configure SRST using the **System, SRST** menu option.

CIPT Section 4
IP Telephony Options

The Cisco CallManager (CCM) offers many more features than just placing phone calls. You can perform conference calling, hear music on hold, convert from one codec type to another, and many other such features. Some of these features, however, require resources (for example, digital signal processors).

These flash cards confirm your understanding of various media resources and how they are configured. These media resources can be made available to your devices (for example, IP phones) through media resource group lists (MRGLs). You are challenged to explain configuration steps that are involved in configuring these MRGLs. A variety of CCM features are reviewed, and you should understand how users can log in to a web interface to configure many of their own features (for example, speed-dial information).

Question 1

Which type of media resource is required for transcoding?

Question 2

Distinguish between "ad-hoc" and "meet-me" conferences.

Question 3

Acting as a software media resource, how many users can the CCM server support on a single conference call?

Question 1 Answer

Transcoding requires a hardware media resource, specifically, digital signal processor (DSP) resources. You can use the DSP resources that are installed in certain Cisco routers or switches for this function.

Question 2 Answer

An ad-hoc conference call occurs when a user dials one or more users into an existing call. A meet-me conference call occurs when all users dial a specific number at a specific time to join a conference.

Question 3 Answer

A CCM server acting as a software media resource can support 48 users in a single conference, or up to 16 users in each of three simultaneous conferences.

Question 4

Identify the Catalyst 6000/6500 module that has eight T1 ports and can serve as a DSP resource.

Question 5

Which Cisco CallManager Administration menu option can you use to configure a conference calling bridge?

Question 6

Which type of media resource can you use as a media termination point (MTP)?

Question 4 Answer

The WS-X6608-T1 module has eight T1 ports, which you can use as part of a non-IOS Media Gateway Control Protocol (MGCP) gateway configuration. However, this module also contains many DSPs, which you can use as hardware media resources.

Question 5 Answer

You can configure conference calling bridge using the **Service, Media Resource, Conference Bridge** menu option.

Question 6 Answer

The CCM server provides the software media resource that an MTP uses. The MTP essentially holds onto a call while functions such as hold, transfer, and conferencing are being initiated.

Question 7

Define transcoding.

Question 8

What are the only two codecs that you can transcode between using a Catalyst 4000 WS-X4604-GWY module?

Question 9

What is the difference between "user hold" and "network hold"?

Question 7 Answer

Transcoding is the conversion of a high-bandwidth codec sample to a low-bandwidth codec sample, and vice versa. For example, you could do transcoding to convert a G.729 voice stream into a G.711 voice stream. However, to convert between two low-bandwidth codecs (for example, G.729 and G.723), you perform transcoding twice (for example, G.729 to G.711 and then G.711 to G.723).

Question 8 Answer

The Catalyst 4000 WS-X4604-GWY module supports transcoding only between the G.729 and G.711 codecs. Therefore, if you need transcoding support for the G.723 codec (used by first-generation Cisco IP phones), you might require the Catalyst 6000 WS-X6608-T1/E1 module.

Question 9 Answer

User hold occurs when a user presses the Hold button on a phone. Network hold occurs when the network places a party on hold, because the user pressed a key to perform an action such as transfer, conference, or call park.

Question 10

What is the maximum number of unicast music on hold (MOH) streams that you can send simultaneously from a single server?

Question 11

Which Windows 2000 Control Panel icon can you use to view the preferred sound recording device for configuring a fixed MOH source?

Question 12

Describe how an IP phone obtains a media resource from the media resource manager.

Question 10 Answer

You can send a maximum of 500 unicast MOH streams or a maximum of 204 multicast MOH streams from a single server. Realize, however, that a single multicast MOH stream could potentially service thousands of IP phones.

Question 11 Answer

You can view the preferred sound recording device that Windows 2000 server uses by opening the Sounds and Multimedia Control Panel icon and selecting the **Audio** tab.

Question 12 Answer

The following steps describe how an IP phone gains access to a media resource:

Step 1 A device (for example, an IP phone) requests a resource (for example, an MOH resource) from a media resource manager.

Step 2 The media resource manager points to a media resource group list (MRGL), which is a prioritized listing of media resource groups (MRGs).

Step 3 The MRGs point to specific resources.

Question 13

Which Cisco CallManager Administration menu option can you use to configure an MRG?

Question 14

You have an IP phone that is configured with an MRGL. However, the IP phone's device pool is configured with a different MRGL. Which MRGL does the IP phone use?

Question 15

Define softkeys.

Question 13 Answer

To create an MRG, select the **Service, Media Resource, Media Resource Group** menu option and click the **Add a New Media Resource Group** link. You then name the MRG and select which of the available resources you want to be part of the MRG.

Question 14 Answer

An MRGL that is assigned to an IP phone takes precedence over an MRGL that is assigned to the IP phone's device pool. Therefore, in this example, the IP phone uses only the MRGL that is assigned to the phone.

Question 15 Answer

Softkeys are buttons on an IP phone that have different functions under different circumstances. For example, while an IP phone is on-hook, perhaps one of the softkeys (for example, one of the buttons below the LCD on a Cisco 7940 or 7960 IP phone) is labeled "Redial," while that same softkey can be labeled "Hold" during a call.

Question 16

List the three standard softkey templates.

Question 17

What is the purpose of a "speed-dial" button?

Question 18

Describe the purpose of the "auto answer" feature.

Question 16 Answer

By default, the CCM gives you the following standard templates:

- Standard IPMA Assistant
- Standard IPMA Manager
- Standard User

Question 17 Answer

A speed-dial button, which an administrator or a user can configure, associates a speed-dial button with a configured phone number and label. The user can then dial the preconfigured number with a single press of the speed-dial button.

Question 18 Answer

The auto answer feature allows a phone to answer a call as soon as it comes in. This type of feature can be useful for customer service agents who are wearing headsets. The auto answer feature is enabled through a drop-down menu in the Directory Number Configuration screen, where you can choose between the Auto Answer Off, Auto Answer with Headset, and Auto Answer with Speakerphone options.

Question 19

Which type of line feature is required to support the "barge" feature?

Question 20

Which menu option configures the "call pickup" feature?

Question 21

What is the purpose of the "call park" feature?

Question 19 Answer

The barge feature, which allows a phone to join an existing phone call, requires a shared line appearance.

Question 20 Answer

To configure call pickup, you need to define a directory number that the call pickup feature is to use. You do that by selecting the **Feature, Call Pickup** menu option and clicking the **Add a New Call Pickup Number** link. After you define the call pickup directory number, assign the number to a specific line, using the Directory Number Configuration screen for an IP phone.

Question 21 Answer

The call park feature allows a user to place a call (that is, "park" a call) in a location that a number identifies. You then can retrieve that parked call from the parked location from another phone. Configure call park from the **Feature, Call Park** menu option.

Question 22

How is the "callback" feature added to a user's phone?

Question 23

List the three call-forwarding behaviors that you can assign to a directory number.

Question 24

Which menu option accesses the Cisco IP Manager Assistant (IPMA) Configuration Wizard?

Question 22 Answer

The callback feature can alert a caller when a number, which was previously busy, becomes available. To add the callback feature to a user's phone, you assign the callback feature to a softkey, through a softkey template, on the user's phone.

Question 23 Answer

You can configure a directory number in the following ways:

- Always forward calls
- Forward calls when the line is busy
- Forward calls after a certain number of rings

Question 24 Answer

You can run the Cisco IPMA Configuration Wizard by selecting the **Service, Cisco IPMA Configuration Wizard** menu option. Note that you can run this wizard only once.

Question 25

What is the purpose of the "shared-line appearance" feature?

Question 26

Which programming language provides applications such as stock quotes and weather reports to the display of a Cisco 7960 Phone?

Question 27

Which menu option allows you to add a new user?

Question 25 Answer

The shared-line appearance feature allows you to have a directory number on more than one phone. Typically, the first phone to answer an incoming call has control of the line, and other phones with that line appearance cannot access that line for the duration of the call. However, you can allow another phone to access the line, even if it is in use, if you have the barge feature enabled.

Question 26 Answer

Several Cisco IP Phones, including the 7960, can leverage the Extensible Markup Language (XML) to provide applications to the phone's LCD.

Question 27 Answer

You can add a new user through the **User, Add a New User** menu option. After you add a user, you can associate a device with that user. Note that you can have more than one device (for example, a Cisco 7940 and a Cisco IP SoftPhone) associated with a user. After you create the user account and associate it with one or more devices, you can allow the user to log in to a web page and configure his own settings.

Question 28

Which URL can users use to log in and configure their own phone settings?

Question 29

List at least three settings that a user can configure on his own phone, through a web page.

Question 30

A user might be able to configure the "locale" of his web interface and IP phone. What does the locale determine?

Question 28 Answer

Instead of configuring every option on each user's phone (for example, speed-dial settings), you should probably give users the ability to configure many of their own options. After you create an account for a user, she can log in to the following URL to manipulate her phone's settings:

```
http://CCM_name_or_IP/ccmuser
```

Question 29 Answer

Users can personalize features on their own phones through a web page. Examples of the user-configurable features, which you can allow or disallow, include the following:

- Services (for example, weather information)
- Speed-dial numbers
- Call forwarding
- Personal address book
- Message-waiting indicator
- Locale

Question 30 Answer

The locale of a user's IP phone customization web page or an IP phone determines the language that is used in the web interface or on the IP phone.

CIPT Section 5
IP Telephony Applications

Although the Cisco CallManager (CCM) is certainly the primary Cisco IP Telephony application, you can add other Cisco applications to enhance the users' experience. For example, you can replace the traditional Private Branch Exchange (PBX) receptionist's console with the Cisco Attendant Console. Mobile users can benefit from the "extension mobility" feature, and users can participate in an IP telephony network with a Cisco IP SoftPhone.

The flash cards in this section verify your understanding of such features as the Cisco Attendant Console, extension mobility, and the Cisco IP SoftPhone. Also, you are challenged to recall the features of various applications, including Unity, IP IVR, Personal Assistant, IP Auto Attendant, CRS, IP ICD, Conference Connection, and IPCC.

Question 1

For redundancy, you can configure the Cisco Attendant Console to point to how many CCM servers?

Question 2

The Attendant Console feature requires several components working together. Which component, running on a CCM server, supports the Attendant Console feature?

Question 3

How many Attendant Console clients are supported in a single CCM cluster?

Question 1 Answer

Although you can configure a Cisco IP Phone to point to three CCM servers, you can configure the Cisco Attendant Console to point to only two CCM servers.

Question 2 Answer

The Attendant Console's server application is called the Telephony Call Dispatcher (TCD).

Question 3 Answer

A maximum of 96 Attendant Console clients are supported per CCM cluster.

Question 4

What is a "pilot number" used for?

Question 5

What is a hunt group?

Question 6

How many hunt groups are supported by a single CCM cluster?

Question 4 Answer

A pilot number is a phone number that points to a hunt group, which could contain one or more phone numbers.

Question 5 Answer

A *hunt group* is a list of specific directory numbers that incoming calls can be distributed across. These directory numbers are called *hunt group members*. Outside callers, however, dial a common number (that is, the pilot number) to reach this internally defined hunt group.

Question 6 Answer

A single CCM cluster supports 32 hunt groups.

Question 7

A hunt group can contain a maximum of how many members?

Question 8

Which Cisco application can you use to overcome the CCM's hunt group scalability limitations?

Question 9

List the three steps for configuring a CCM server to support the Attendant Console application.

Question 7 Answer

A hunt group can contain a maximum of 16 members.

Question 8 Answer

The CCM's hunt group scalability limitations might be too restrictive for large call center environments. However, you can overcome this limitation by deploying the Cisco IP Contact Center (IPCC) application. Note that CallManager 4.0 can overcome hunt group scalability issues if queuing is not required.

Question 9 Answer

The three steps to configure a CCM server to support the Attendant Console are as follows:

Step 1   Add users for the Attendant Console.

Step 2   Add a pilot number.

Step 3   Add a hunt group.

Question 10

Which Cisco CallManager Administration menu option can you use to create an Attendant Console user?

Question 11

Which Cisco CallManager Administration menu option creates a "pilot point"?

Question 12

Which Cisco CallManager Administration menu option can you use to create a "hunt group"?

Question 10 Answer

You can select the **Service, Cisco CM Attendant Console, Cisco CM Attendant Console User** menu option and click the **Add a New Attendant Console User** link to add an Attendant Console user.

Question 11 Answer

A *pilot point* is a number that outside callers dial. Internally, this pilot point directs incoming calls to a member of a hunt group. You can select the **Service, Cisco CM Attendant Console, Pilot Point** menu option and click the **Add a New Pilot Point** link to create a pilot point.

Question 12 Answer

You can create a hunt group by selecting the **Service, Cisco CM Attendant Console, Hunt Group** menu option. Then select a pilot point from the left pane and click the **Add Member** button to add the specific directory numbers that comprise the hunt group.

Question 13

You want to install the Attendant Console application on a user's PC. From which Cisco CallManager Administration menu option can you download this application?

Question 14

Define the Cisco IP SoftPhone.

Question 15

Which requires more device units, a Cisco IP Phone or a Cisco IP SoftPhone?

Question 13 Answer

You can download the Attendant Console application from a CCM server's Cisco CallManager Administration web page by selecting the **Application, Install Plugins** menu option and clicking the **Cisco CallManager Attendant Console** icon.

Question 14 Answer

The Cisco IP SoftPhone is software that emulates the function of an IP phone. Because the IP SoftPhone runs on a PC, it can leverage a Lightweight Directory Access Protocol (LDAP) directory to locate user information. The IP SoftPhone is not free, however. There is a licensing fee.

Question 15 Answer

The resources (that is, device units) that are consumed by the Cisco IP SoftPhone are more than the resources that are consumed by a Cisco IP Phone. In CCM version 3.2, under low call-volume conditions, the Cisco IP SoftPhone consumed 20 device units whereas the Cisco IP Phone consumed only 1. This ratio is much improved in CCM version 3.3, in which a Cisco IP SoftPhone consumes only 2 device units under low call-volume conditions.

Question 16

Which type of port must you create to support a Cisco IP SoftPhone?

Question 17

Which User Configuration screen check box must you select to permit the user to use a Cisco IP SoftPhone?

Question 18

How is the ciscotsp001.tsp TAPI Service Provider (TSP) added to a user's system?

Question 16 Answer

To configure support for a Cisco IP SoftPhone, you first create a computer technology integration (CTI) port for each of your SoftPhones. You do this by selecting the **Device, Phone** menu option and clicking the **Add a New Phone** link. From the Phone type drop-down menu, select **CTI Port**. Finally, enter the device name, select the appropriate device pool, and click the **Insert** button.

Question 17 Answer

A Cisco IP SoftPhone uses a CTI port. To enable a user to use a Cisco IP SoftPhone, in the User Configuration screen, select the **Enable CTI Application Use** check box and then click the **Update** button (or the **Insert** button for a new user).

Question 18 Answer

The ciscotsp001.tsp TSP is installed as part of the Cisco IP SoftPhone installation.

Question 19

What is the benefit of the "extension mobility" feature?

Question 20

When configuring the extension mobility feature, you create a new service. What URL do you enter in the Service URL field of the Cisco IP Phone Services screen?

Question 21

When you are configuring the extension mobility feature, what does the "Auto Logout" feature do?

Question 19 Answer

With the extension mobility feature, a user can log in to a phone, and the Device Profile that is assigned to the user is applied to the phone. Therefore, a user can receive, for example, his speed-dial and softkey settings on different phones throughout an enterprise. Specifically, a user can press the **Services** button on an IP phone to log in to the phone, which can then retrieve his profile.

Question 20 Answer

When configuring extension mobility, you create a new service. In the Service URL field of the Cisco IP Phone Services screen, you enter http://*CCM_IP_address*/emapp/EMAppServlet?device=#DEVICENAME#.

Question 21 Answer

The Auto Logout feature allows a user to log in to a phone while automatically logging her out of a phone that she was logged in to previously.

Question 22

When using extension mobility, when is the default device profile used?

Question 23

Which Cisco application offers a converged messaging solution?

Question 24

What is the purpose of the Cisco IP Interactive Voice Response (IP IVR) application?

Question 22 Answer

Extension mobility allows users to log in to a phone, after which the phone takes on the properties that are associated with the user's profile. However, if a user is not logged in to the phone, the phone uses its default device profile.

Question 23 Answer

The Cisco Unity product provides a converged messaging solution. Specifically, Cisco Unity allows e-mail messages, fax messages, and voice-mail messages to reside in a single location. You can then, for example, retrieve your fax messages through e-mail or your e-mail messages through a phone call, thanks to Cisco Unity's text-to-speech conversion capabilities.

Question 24 Answer

The Cisco IVR application supports the integration of database information with the IP telephony system. For example, when you call into your automated banking system and provide your PIN to receive your account balance, you are using an IVR system.

Question 25

Describe the features of the Cisco Personal Assistant application.

Question 26

Identify the feature provided by the Cisco IP Auto Attendant application.

Question 27

What is the purpose of the Cisco Response Solution (CRS) application?

Question 25 Answer

The Cisco Personal Assistant application offers you tremendous control over incoming and outgoing calls. For example, if your children call, you might want the call to be transferred to your cell phone. If your phone rings between 5 p.m. and 8 p.m., you might want the call to be transferred to your home phone. The Cisco Personal Assistant can accommodate such requirements.

Question 26 Answer

The Cisco IP Auto Attendant allows a caller to navigate through a menu to reach a particular extension or department. This feature can reduce receptionist staffing expenses.

Question 27 Answer

The CRS version 3.0 software supports other applications, such as IVR applications. Essentially, simple applications (for example, weather reports or stock quotes on a phone's display) use XML, whereas more complex applications (for example, contact center applications) rely on the CRS.

Question 28

For which environment is the Cisco IP Integrated Contact Distribution (ICD) application best suited for?

Question 29

Which Cisco application overcomes the CCM's software and hardware conference bridge scalability limitations for meet-me conferences?

Question 30

Which Cisco application is most appropriate for large call center environments?

Question 28 Answer

You can use the Cisco IP ICD application for smaller call center environments. It has the ability to route calls intelligently.

Question 29 Answer

The Cisco Conference Connection supports larger meet-me conference calls than you could accommodate with either a CCM software conference bridge or a DSP-enabled hardware conference bridge.

Question 30 Answer

The Cisco IP Contact Center (IPCC) Enterprise product is a more robust solution than ICD for routing calls intelligently. Specifically, the Cisco IPCC is appropriate for large contact centers. You could even have a "virtual call center," where customer service agents work from home.

CIPT Section 6
Administrative Utilities

Cisco offers various tools for streamlining the process of adding users, phones, and devices into the CCM database. These tools alleviate the burden of manually configuring each CCM database entry. These flash cards verify your knowledge of these tools.

To troubleshoot CCM issues, you have an arsenal of GUI and command-line tools at your disposal. Some of these tools are Cisco utilities, whereas others are Microsoft utilities. These flash cards also challenge your understanding of these tools.

Question 1

What is the purpose of the Cisco Bulk Administration Tool (BAT) utility?

Question 2

Explain how the Cisco Tool for Auto-Registered Phone Support (TAPS) utility can expedite the installation of phones into a CCM database.

Question 3

From where do you download the BAT utility?

Question 1 Answer

The BAT utility allows you to import numerous devices, users, lines, or gateways into the CCM database. This can save the time that would be required to make each addition manually.

Question 2 Answer

You use the TAPS utility in conjunction with the BAT utility. Specifically, you can add a group of phones configured with a "dummy" MAC address using BAT. Then, if the Auto Registration feature is enabled, you or your users can dial a TAPS directory number to download the phone's configuration and to update the CCM database with the phone's correct MAC address.

Question 3 Answer

You can download and install the BAT utility from the Cisco CallManager Administration's **Application, Install Plugins** menu option. Note that you can install BAT only on a CallManager server.

Question 4

To assist you with creating BAT templates, the BAT installation includes templates that you can modify for your use. What Microsoft application were these templates created in?

Question 5

Into what directory does the BAT installation place its BAT templates?

Question 6

When you add phones, users, and so on using BAT, you use a BAT template and a Comma Separated Values (.CSV) file. How does the information that is contained in these files differ?

Question 4 Answer

Microsoft Excel templates are included as part of the BAT installation.

Question 5 Answer

As part of the BAT installation, templates are copied to the C:\CiscoWebs\BAT\Excel\Templates directory. You can use these templates for bulk phone, gateway, line, or user configurations.

Question 6 Answer

The BAT template defines generic values (for example, calling search space and device pool), whereas the .CSV file contains specific values (for example, usernames, passwords, and department information).

Question 7

List three requirements for installing the TAPS application.

Question 8

From the SQL Server Enterprise Manager utility, you can determine whether a server is acting as a publisher or a subscriber. Which folders indicate whether a server is a publisher or a subscriber?

Question 9

If a publisher goes down, can you recover by upgrading a subscriber to a publisher?

Question 7 Answer

Following are the requirements to install the TAPS application:

- The installer must have access to the CCM publisher's database.

- The Cisco Customer Response Solution (CRS) application must be installed.

- BAT must be installed on the CCM publisher prior to the TAPS utility installation.

Question 8 Answer

If a CCM server is a publisher, the SQL Server Enterprise Manager shows a Publications folder for that server. Alternatively, you see a Pull Subscriptions folder on a subscriber.

Question 9 Answer

You cannot upgrade a subscriber to a publisher. Rather, you have to rebuild the publisher and restore the database information from a backup.

Question 10

How do you recover from a subscriber failure?

Question 11

What is the purpose of the show db tables command?

Question 12

What is the purpose of the netstat command?

Question 10 Answer

If a subscriber fails, you can rebuild the subscriber CCM, and after it is back up, you can "pull" the current database from the publisher. So, when recovering from a subscriber failure, you do not need to worry about restoring the database from a backup copy.

Question 11 Answer

The **show db tables** command can interrogate database information from the command line.

Question 12 Answer

You can use the **netstat** command to display current sessions. As part of the output, you can see which ports are in use for the active sessions.

Question 13

What Cisco CallManager Serviceability menu option can you use to start services, stop services, and view their current status?

Question 14

What is the purpose of the Real-Time Monitoring Tool (RTMT) utility?

Question 13 Answer

On the Cisco CallManager Serviceability page, you can access the Control Center menu option, from which you can start and stop services and view their current status.

Question 14 Answer

The RTMT can provide real-time information about what is happening within a CCM cluster. For example, you can see the active calls and phones that have registered, which could be valuable in forecasting expansion needs.

CIPT Section 7
Cisco CallManager 4.x Enhancements

Version 4.*x* of the Cisco CallManager (CCM) does not radically alter the architecture that is found in CCM 3.3. For example, many of the scalability limitations are the same, and the route group, route list, and route plan hierarchy remain the same. Cisco did, however, enhance many of the existing features and added a few new ones.

These flash cards test your knowledge of some of the most significant CCM enhancements. These enhancements include security, call control, and troubleshooting features for the administrator. The user also benefits from features such as Abbreviated Dialing and privacy.

Question 1

When CCM 4.*x* was released, what was the only Cisco IP Phone to include a factory-installed certificate, for authentication purposes?

Question 2

What is the purpose of the Certificate Authority Proxy Function (CAPF) service?

Question 3

What are the three security modes in which a Cisco IP Phone can operate?

Question 1 Answer

When CCM 4.*x* was introduced, only the Cisco 7970 IP Phone included a factory-installed certificate.

Question 2 Answer

The Cisco 7940 and 7960 IP Phones can use the CAPF service for certificates, because these phones do not have factory-installed certificates. These certificates are used for authorization.

Question 3 Answer

An IP phone can operate in the nonsecure, authenticated, or encrypted mode. Therefore, it can use the authentication feature without necessarily encrypting voice packets.

Question 4

What Session Initiation Protocol (SIP) functionality is introduced in CCM 4.x?

Question 5

Describe the purpose of the Dialed Number Analyzer (DNA) utility.

Question 6

How many buttons must a user press to use the Abbreviated Dialing feature?

Question 4 Answer

CCM 4.*x* supports SIP trunks, which allow the CCM environment to communicate with SIP networks.

Question 5 Answer

The DNA utility allows administrators to view detailed call setup information. For example, an administrator could see which route pattern matched and which transformation mask was applied to a dialed number.

Question 6 Answer

Abbreviated Dialing allows a user to dial a number by pressing only three buttons. Specifically, the user presses the AbbrDial button, followed by two digits. A total of 99 abbreviated dialing entries are supported. A user can configure his abbreviated dial settings through http://*CCM_IP_address*/CCMUser/speeddial.asp.

Question 7

A user has a shared-line appearance. Which button can that user press to prevent someone from joining a call through the barge feature?

Question 8

Identify the purpose of the Malicious Call ID (MCID) softkey.

Question 9

When a user presses the iDivert softkey, where is a call diverted?

Question 7 Answer

If her phone is configured with a Privacy line button, a user can prevent someone from joining a call using the barge feature. The privacy feature also can suppress the displaying of incoming call information on another phone with the same shared-line appearance.

Question 8 Answer

A user can press the MCID softkey when he receives, for example, a threatening or harassing call. The MCID can mark a call as "malicious" in the CCM call detail records, send a network management trap, and even notify the local central office of the malicious call. Such a feature can dramatically expedite the apprehension of an offender.

Question 9 Answer

The iDivert softkey diverts a call to voice mail.

Question 10

What call types, other than an incoming call, can you divert using the Immediate Divert feature?

Question 10 Answer

The Immediate Divert feature can divert active calls and calls on hold, in addition to incoming calls.

CIPT Quick Reference Sheets

The Cisco CallManager

Introduction

In years past, voice, video, and data traffic resided on their own physical networks. However, the vision for the future, and today, is for voice, video, and data to reside on the same network. Having such a "converged" solution provides numerous economic benefits, including lower administrative costs. However, connectivity between converged networks and legacy Private Branch Exchanges (PBXs) and the Public Switched Telephony Network (PSTN) is a necessity in your design.

In this section, you examine a central component in your IP telephony network: the Cisco CallManager (CCM). You examine how the CCM fits into Cisco's Architecture for Voice, Video, and Integrated Data (AVVID) strategy. CCM hardware platforms and deployment models are also examined, in addition to CCM installation and upgrading procedures.

AVIDD

Cisco's AVVID solution brings voice, video, and data communication technologies under a common umbrella. Specifically, Cisco's AVVID model contains the following four layers, as it relates to voice:

- **Client**—The client layer encompasses the devices that interface with the network. For example, IP phones, PCs, and Cisco IP SoftPhones fall under this layer.
- **Application**—The application layer includes applications that enhance the services that are available to the converged network. For example, Cisco's Unity application provides converged messaging solutions and would be categorized under the application layer.
- **Call-processing**—The call-processing layer performs the call setup functions, such as those that traditionally are performed by the PBX. The Cisco CallManager, for example, resides at the call-processing layer.
- **Infrastructure**—The infrastructure layer is the underlying data network, which includes components such as routers and switches.

The primary focus of these quick reference sheets is the Cisco CallManager.

Cisco CallManager

The Cisco CallManager (CCM) is a software component that runs on approved server platforms. The CCM makes call-forwarding decisions, controls IP phones, and can support other optional features (for example, automatic route selection and call transfer).

Consider the following scenario. A Cisco IP Phone goes off-hook and communicates with a CCM using the Skinny protocol. The IP phone dials digits, which the CCM interprets. The CCM then signals to the destination IP phone that the phone is receiving a call. After the destination phone goes off-hook, a Real-Time Transport Protocol (RTP) stream is set up directly between the IP phones.

Call Setup

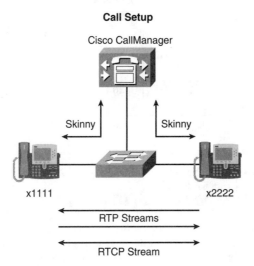

The CCM is administered through the Cisco CallManager Administration web interface. If you know the IP address or domain name of a CCM server, you can access the CCM administration interface at the http://server_IP_or_name/ccmadmin.

Throughout these quick reference sheets, you should spend quite a bit of time exploring the menus that are available under this interface, including the System, Route Plan, Service, Feature, Device, and User menus.

As mentioned earlier, the CCM is software. Therefore, it needs to run on a server. Specifically, version 3.3 of the CCM software runs on a Windows 2000 server. The CCM needs to maintain database information to store information such as IP phone registrations. Instead of trying to create its own proprietary database, Cisco decided to use a well-established database application, Microsoft SQL Server 2000.

User information is stored in a *directory*. You could use the DC Directory that comes with the CCM software. Alternatively, you could leverage Microsoft Active Directory Service. For disaster recovery, you also need some backup application. As an example, you can use the Spirian Technologies Inc. (STI) Backup utility to back up the CCM database.

IP Telephony Design Considerations

The cost savings that an IP telephony environment offers are numerous. For example, an IP telephony solution usually lends itself to reduced staffing expenses, reduced wiring costs, and reduced administrative costs for functions such as moves, adds, and changes. In addition to cost savings, IP telephony solutions also enhance the functionality of your overall telephony solution by providing value-added feature such as extension mobility and a consolidated messaging system.

Although the CCM 3.3 software is an application that runs on a Windows 2000 server, the server hardware must be a specific platform that identifies Cisco. Although many of these approved servers are Cisco branded, the hardware often is manufactured by IBM or Compaq. The following table details several characteristics for comparison.

Server Model	RAM (MB)	Hard Drive(s)	Number of IP Phones Supported	Rack Mount Information
Cisco ICS SPE 310	512	One 20.4-GB HD	Up to 500	N/A (The server is a module that installs in an ICS 7750.)
Cisco MCS 7815-1000	512	One 20.4-GB HD	Up to 200	Tower case with rack-mount kit available.
Cisco MCS 7825-1133	1024	One 40-GB HD	Up to 1000	1 RU (Rack Unit).
Cisco MCS 7835-1266	1024	Dual 18.2-GB HDs with hardware RAID	Up to 2500	2 RUs.
Cisco MCS 7845-1400	2048	Four 72-MB HDs with hardware RAID	Up to 7500	2 RUs.

The amount of "work" that a CCM can do is measured in *device units*. Each device that registers with the CCM requires one or more of these device units, but the number of device units supported can vary depending on the number of calls that the CCM must support simultaneously. This call load is referred to as Busy Hour Call Attempts (BHCAs), which is the maximum number of active calls during the busiest hour of the day.

To achieve the level of availability that is found in a PBX environment, you need to have more than one CCM at your disposal. Groupings of CCMs are called *clusters*. One CCM in a cluster is designated as a *Publisher,* and that CCM replicates its database information to *Subscribers*. This database replication includes information such as registration and data logging.

When a configuration change is made, the change is written to the Publisher. You still can access the CCM web interface, even if the Publisher is down. However, you cannot write changes to the database. When a Publisher is again available, it immediately sends configuration changes to Subscribers.

The Publisher's database is replicated to Subscribers periodically, but under normal operation, the Subscribers still retrieve information from the Publisher's database. If the Publisher becomes unavailable, Subscribers use their local copy of the database.

The CCMs in a cluster also communicate run-time data directly to each other, using a logical full-mesh topology. This run-time data includes information such as calls in progress, gateway and IP phone registration, and information about digital signal processor (DSP) resources.

As an example of run-time data, consider an IP phone that is registering with a CCM. The CCM lets all other CCMs in the cluster know about the registration. Then, the IP phone sends a keep-alive message to its primary CCM, which it registered with, every 30 seconds. For redundancy, the IP phone also sends a TCP "connect" message to a backup CCM so that the IP phone can fail over to the backup CCM. The IP phone also can be configured with a third (that is, tertiary) CCM, to which it can fall back if both the primary and backup CCMs fail.

IP Telephony Design Options

When you create your cluster, you need to identify the roles that the various CCMs play. For example, because the Publisher plays such a vital role, you probably do not want IP phones registering with the Publisher. Also, the IP phones' configuration files are stored on a Trivial File Transfer Protocol (TFTP) server, and you might want to use the Publisher for that function. Finally, you might want to designate which CCMs are going to be backup CCMs for primary CCMs.

Also, you need to select your redundancy design approach, either 1:1 redundancy or 2:1 redundancy. With 1:1 redundancy, each primary CCM has a dedicated backup CCM to take over in the event of a primary CCM failure. To reduce costs, however, you can opt for a 2:1 redundancy model, where you have one backup CCM for every two primary CCMs. Although this provides cost savings, you sacrifice an extra layer of redundancy.

Redundancy Design Options

1:1 Redundancy Design   2:1 Redundancy Design

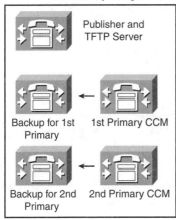

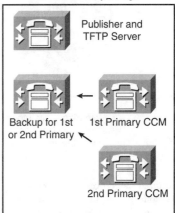

The following table, which is specific to the MCS-7835 server, indicates the number of CCM servers that Cisco recommends to support a specific number of IP phones.

IP Phones	1:1 Redundancy	2:1 Redundancy
Up to 2500 (5000 device units)	3 CCM servers: • 1 Publisher and TFTP server (for 1000 or more IP phones) • 1 primary CCM • 1 backup CCM	3 CCM servers: • 1 Publisher and TFTP server (for 1000 or more IP phones) • 1 primary CCM • 1 backup CCM
Up to 5000 (10,000 device units)	5 CCM servers: • 1 Publisher and TFTP server • 2 primary CCMs • 2 backup CCMs	4 CCM servers: • 1 Publisher and TFTP server • 2 primary CCMs • 1 backup CCM
Up to 10,000 (20,000 device units)	9 CCM servers: • 1 Publisher and TFTP server • 4 primary CCMs • 4 backup CCMs	7 CCM servers: • 1 Publisher and TFTP server • 4 primary CCMs • 2 backup CCMs

When designing an IP telephony network, select from one of the following four CCM design models:

- **Single-Site**—IP phones and CCMs are located at a single site. This model has the following features:
  - Uses the G.711 codec for all calls.
  - Leverages high-availability features in the network infrastructure.
  - Has a simplified dial plan.

Single-Site Model

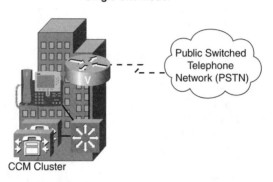

CCM Cluster

With Single-Site Model, all CCMs and IP Phones
reside at a single location. The PSTN is used for all
calls between the campus and the outside world.

- **Centralized Call Processing**—IP phones are at multiple sites, and all CCMs are at a single site. This model has the following features:
  - CCM cluster is located at a central site.
  - IP phones are located at multiple sites.
  - Has lower maintenance costs than the Distributed Call Processing model.
  - Uses Survivable Remote Site Telephony (SRST) for remote site redundancy.
  - Uses WAN bandwidth for call setup.

  Note that the SRST feature allows a Cisco router to step in for the CCM in the event of a WAN failure. The SRST feature is available on a variety of platforms. However, as an example, the Cisco 7200 Series router's SRST feature can support 480 IP phones.

- **Distributed Call Processing**—IP phones and CCMs are at multiple sites. This model has the following features:
  - Can scale to hundreds of sites.
  - Contains multiple sites, each with its own CCM cluster.
  - Local site functionality is not affected by WAN failure.
  - Uses a gatekeeper to prevent WAN bandwidth oversubscription.

Centralized Call Processing Model

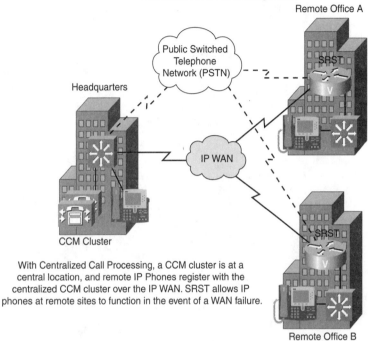

With Centralized Call Processing, a CCM cluster is at a
central location, and remote IP Phones register with the
centralized CCM cluster over the IP WAN. SRST allows IP
phones at remote sites to function in the event of a WAN failure.

Distributed Call Processing Model

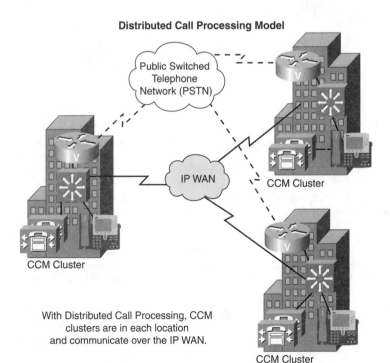

With Distributed Call Processing, CCM
clusters are in each location
and communicate over the IP WAN.

- **Clustering over the WAN**—IP phones and CCMs are at multiple sites, with all CCMs logically assigned to the same cluster. This model has the following features:
  — Cluster is composed of CCMs that are located at multiple sites.
  — Requires 900 kbps of WAN bandwidth for every 10,000 Busy Hour Call Attempts (BHCAs).
  — Requires a maximum round-trip time (RTT) of 40 ms between any two CCMs in the cluster.

Clustering over the WAN Model

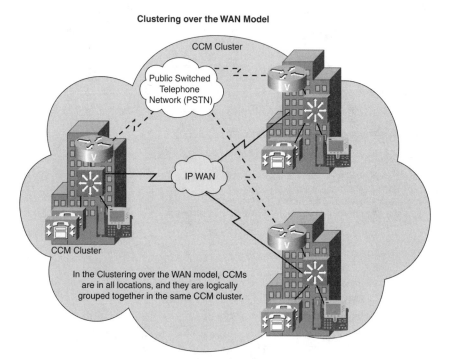

CallManager Installation

You need three CD-ROMs to install the CCM on a Media Convergence Server (MCS). First, you use a hardware-detection CD-ROM to detect the correct platform and to prompt for the correct CDs. Second, you use an operating system CD-ROM that is appropriate for your platform. Finally, you need the CCM 3.3 CD-ROM.

During the installation, you are prompted for various information, such as the Cisco product key (so that you install only the options that you purchased), the TCP/IP properties for the CCM server, and the admin password. Also, you can enable various services on the CCM server, such as the TFTP service, the "messaging interface" service to support legacy voice-mail systems that use the SMDI (Simplified Message Desk Interface) protocol, and the "CDR insert" service to allow the CCM to write call detail records to the SQL database. These types of services also can be enabled after the CCM installation through the CCM Service Activation Page, which is located in the Application menu.

After completing the installation, you should change the passwords on all servers in the CCM cluster. Also, disable unneeded services (for example, the FTP Publishing Service and Remote Desktop Sharing).

To determine which CCM versions you can upgrade to current CCM versions, reference the CCM compatibility matrix, which is located at http://www.cisco.com/univercd/cc/td/doc/product/voice/c_callmg/ccmcomp.htm.

When you upgrade a CCM Publisher, make sure that you back up the Publisher database. You also should reset any hardware to its original configuration, because you need to reimage the system. Cisco also recommends that you take the server out of any Windows domain. Although you do not need to back up the database when updating a Subscriber, you still do a reimage of a Subscriber server when performing an upgrade.

IP Telephony Components

Introduction

In this section, you review the features of several Cisco IP Phone models and examine how to configure a CCM server to support these phones. Because these IP phones typically connect to a Cisco Catalyst switch, examine the Catalyst syntax for setting up inline power and auxiliary VLANs. Finally, review various gateways that can connect your IP telephony network to an existing PBX or to the PSTN.

IP Telephones

Cisco has several models of IP phones. Some have displays, and some support inline power (where the IP phone is powered over the Cat 5 network cable). Most modern Cisco IP Phones support the G.711 and G.729a codecs. Following is a partial listing of Cisco IP Telephones:

- 7910/7910+SW:
  - Support local or inline power.
  - Are entry-level phones that are useful for lobby or lab environments.
  - Support G.711 and G.729a codecs.
  - 7910+SW model has a second 10/100-Mbps Ethernet port for a daisy-chain configuration.
  - Have no XML support.
  - Support Skinny protocol.
- 7905:
  - Supports local or inline power.
  - Is an entry-level phone that is useful for lobby or lab environments.
  - Supports G.711 and G.729a codecs.
  - Has a single 10-Mbps Ethernet port.
  - Offers limited XML support.
  - Supports H.323, MGCP (Media Gateway Control Protocol), or Skinny protocols, with the appropriate firmware.
- 7940/7960
  - Support inline power.
  - Have large display screens with XML support.
  - Are feature-rich phone for employees.
  - Support G.711 and G.729 codecs.
  - Have a second 10/100-Mbps Ethernet port for a daisy-chain configuration.
  - Support MGCP, Session Initiation Protocol (SIP), and Skinny protocol with appropriate firmware.
  - The 7940 has a two line-appearance/speed-dial buttons, and the 7960 has a six line-appearance/speed-dial buttons.

A few other Cisco VoIP devices are as follows:

- **7935 Conference Station**—An IP phone that uses Polycom's speakerphone technology.
- **IP SoftPhone**—A software application that lets you use a PC and a headset as an IP phone.
- **ATA 188**—The Cisco Analog Telephone Adapter (ATA) 188 allows a traditional analog phone to connect to your IP telephony network. The ATA 188 also has two 10/100-Mbps Ethernet ports, allowing both an analog phone and a PC to feed into a single switch port.
- **7914 Expansion Module**—Attaches to a Cisco 7960 phone and adds 14 line-appearance/speed-dial buttons, which could be valuable as an office attendant's console.

When you plug your IP phone into a Catalyst switch, assuming that you are using inline power, the switch sends a Fast Link Pulse (FLP) to determine whether an IP phone is attached to a switch port. If the switch detects an IP phone, the switch provides –48 VDC to power the IP phone. The switch then uses Cisco Discovery Protocol (CDP) to inform the IP phone of the phone's voice VLAN.

When the IP phone knows what VLAN it belongs to, it can use Dynamic Host Configuration Protocol (DHCP) to obtain an IP address. In addition to IP address information, the DHCP server informs the IP phone of the IP address of a TFTP server. The IP phone can download its configuration file from this TFTP server. This configuration file contains information such as a list of up to three CCMs that the IP phone can register with. Finally, the IP phone registers with the first CCM in the list.

The Cisco IP phone can code the spoken voice into a binary form using Pulse Code Modulation (PCM). The remote IP phone can decode the PCM information into analog waveforms that a listener can understand. A codec performs this process of coding and decoding. A bandwidth of 64 kbps is required to send just the payload of this encoded voice. The G.711 uses this approach. However, you should probably use less bandwidth per call when sending voice across an IP WAN. Therefore, you can sacrifice some voice quality to achieve bandwidth savings by using other codecs that offer compression. The bandwidth requirements for several codecs are shown in the following table.

Codec	Bandwidth Requirement (kbps)
G.711	64
G.726	16, 24, or 32 (depending on the "difference signal" being used)
G.728	16
G.729	8

When communicating over the IP WAN, Cisco IP phones typically use the G.729a codec. This codec, like the G.729 codec, requires 8 kbps of bandwidth (payload only). However, G.729a requires slightly less processing power than G.729.

Configuring the CCM for IP Phones

Typically, you want IP phones to access a CCM by an IP address, as opposed to the CCM's DNS name. If the CCM was accessible only by its DNS name, DNS would become a potential point of failure in your environment. To remove this dependence on DNS, from the CCMAdmin page, select the **System, Server** menu option and click the CCM that you are interested in. In the **Host Name/IP Address** field, enter the CCM's IP address and click the **Update** button. Alternatively, when specifying a new CCM, you can enter the IP address in the Host Name/IP Address field, as shown in the following figure.

```
System  Route Plan  Service  Feature  Device  User  Application  Help
```

Cisco CallManager Administration
For Cisco IP Telephony Solutions

CISCO SYSTEMS

Server Configuration

Add a New Server
Back to Find/List Servers

Current Server: New
Status: Ready

[Insert]

Host Name/IP Address*

MAC Address

Description

Note: You must update the DNS server when a DNS name is used.
* indicates required item

Instead of configuring all of an IP phone's parameters (for example, Date/Time Group and Softkey Template) for every IP phone, you create *device pools,* assign parameters to the device pools, and then associate IP phones with those device pools. The following sections describe how you can create some of the required properties for your device pools.

Cisco CallManager Group

As mentioned earlier, an IP phone can have a list of up to three CCMs, for redundancy. You can configure this "CCM group" by selecting the **System, Cisco CallManager Group** menu option and clicking either the **Add New Cisco CallManager Group** link or an existing CCM group.

Date/Time Group

Different IP phones and devices can be located in different time zones from the CCM server. You can create different Date/Time groups by selecting the **System, Date/Time Group** menu option and clicking the **Add a New Date/Time Group** link.

Region

To use different codecs when you communicate between different IP phones (perhaps phones that are separated by the IP WAN), you define *regions.* You can specify which codec to use when calling from one region to another, as well as within the region. To create a region, select the **System, Region** menu option and click the **Add a New Region** link.

Softkey Template

The 7940 and 7960 IP phones allow the configuration of *softkeys,* which are the four keys below the LCD. You can add a softkey template by selecting the **Device, Device Settings, Softkey Template** menu option and clicking the **Add a New Softkey Template** link.

When you have configured a CCM group, a Date/Time group, Region, and Softkey Template, you can (on some CCM 3.3 revisions) specify these parameters in a new device pool by selecting the **System, Device Pool** menu option and clicking the **Add a New Device Pool** link.

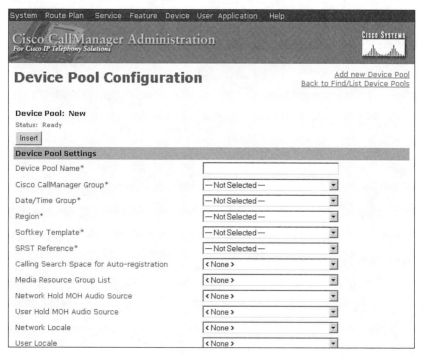

On the 7960, you can find six buttons, located on the right of the display; they can act as line-appearance or speed-dial buttons. By default, two line-appearance buttons and four speed-dial buttons are on a 7960 IP phone. However, you should have templates for any combination of line-appearance and speed-dial buttons (that is, 1 to 6 line-appearance buttons), noting that at least one button must be defined as a line-appearance.

To add a phone button template, select the **Device, Device Settings, Phone Button Template** menu option and click the **Add New Phone Button Template** link.

You can select a phone button template from the drop-down menu, and click the **Copy** button. At that point, you can rename the copy of the template to an intuitive name. Select which buttons are speed-dial buttons and which buttons are line-appearances. You also can assign a label for each button.

If you manually add an IP phone to a CCM, you specify the phone's Media Access Control (MAC) address as the IP phone's unique identifier. The MAC address is typically on a bar-code sticker that is found on the back of the IP phone and also on the box that the IP phone was shipped in. To add a phone, select the **Device, Phone** menu and click the **Add a New Phone** link.

You then select the IP phone's model and click the Next button. At that point, you specify the MAC address of the IP phone and select the appropriate device pool. Other optional parameters also can be configured.

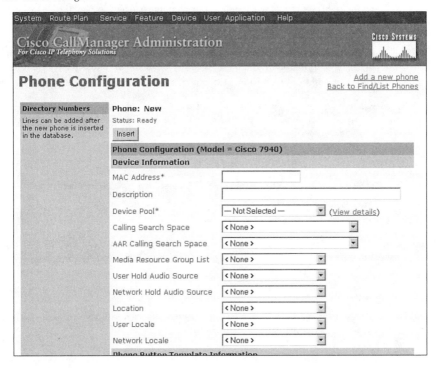

Alternatively, IP phones can "auto register," which means they automatically receive a directory number from a specified range. The CCM then can automatically write the MAC address and associated directory number (DN) to the SQL database. To configure this auto-registration option, select the **System, Cisco CallManager** menu option, click the Find button to list the known CCMs, click the CCM that you are interested in, and deselect the **Auto-registration Disabled on this Cisco CallManager** check box. You then specify the starting and ending DN and click the **Update** button.

The devices (for example, IP phones) that are auto-registered use default settings that you can manipulate from the **System, Device Defaults** menu option. For example, you can use this window to specify the default device pool for a 7960 IP phone.

Configuring Cisco Catalyst Switches for IP Phones

Typically, you should connect your Cisco IP phones to Catalyst switches that support inline power. These switches also can form an IEEE 802.1Q trunk with the IP phone so that the IP phone can place voice traffic in one VLAN, place data traffic (for example, traffic from a connected PC) in a separate VLAN, and assign different priority markings to frames in the different VLANs.

Some of the switches that support inline power include Catalyst 3524-PWR XL, 4000 Series, 6000 Series, and 6500 Series switches. Routers such as the 2600, 3600, and 3700 Series that can accept the 16-Port 10/100 Ethernet Switch Module also can support inline power.

Inline power allows the switch port (or router port) that connects to the IP phone to detect the presence of an IP phone (by sending Fast Link Pulses) and apply power (that is, –48 VDC) over the same pins that are used for Ethernet communication (that is, pins 1, 2, 3, and 6). Alternatively, if you do not have switch or router hardware that supports inline power, you can use an external patch panel. This patch panel can power the attached IP phone over the non-Ethernet pins (that is, pins 4, 5, 7, and 8). In this scenario, the IP phones connect to the patch panel, and the patch panel connects to the switch. An external patch panel supports 48 IP phones. Therefore, the Cisco IP phone can be powered over the Ethernet or the non-Ethernet pins.

The configuration for inline power varies based on your switch platform (for example, Cat OS or Native IOS). In the Cat OS environment, use the following command to enable inline power:

```
Switch>(enable)set port inlinepower <mod/port> <auto | off>
```

Note that you cannot set the inline power to "on," because you would not want to apply power inadvertently to the Ethernet leads of a device that is not equipped for inline power. Also, in a Cat OS environment, you can specify the amount of power (in milliwatts) to allocate to an inline powered port with the following command:

```
Switch>(enable)set port inlinepower defaultallocation power
```

The default power allocation on a Cat OS platform is 7 watts (that is, 7000 milliwatts).

In a Native IOS environment, enable inline power with the following command:

```
Switch(config-if)#power inline <auto | never>
```

The Catalyst switch can detect an attached IP phone and then dynamically create an IEEE 802.1Q trunk between the switch and the phone. This trunk carries traffic from the following two VLANs:

- **Auxiliary VLAN**—Identified by the Voice VLAN ID (VVID), the auxiliary VLAN carries the voice traffic.
- **Native VLAN**—Identified by the Port VLAN ID (PVID), the native VLAN carries the traffic from an upstream device attached to the IP phone (for example, a PC).

This VLAN information is communicated to the phone using the Cisco Discovery Protocol (CDP). In the Cat OS environment, you specify the auxiliary VLAN with the following command:

```
Switch>(enable)set port auxiliaryvlan <mod/port> <vlan | untagged | dot1p | none>
```

For example, to specify an auxiliary VLAN of 100 for port 3/2 on a Catalyst 6500 running the Cat OS, you would enter the command **set port auxiliaryvlan 3/2 100**. Note that the **untagged** option instructs the IP phone not to tag the voice traffic with a different VLAN ID. The **dot1p** option instructs the IP phone to mark the voice traffic with a CoS priority marking but not to send the voice traffic in a VLAN that is separate from the data traffic. Finally, the **none** option disables the auxiliary VLAN feature for a particular port.

In the Native IOS environment, you can configure an interface as a trunk interface using the **dot1q** encapsulation and issue the **switchport voice vlan vlan_id** command to specify the auxiliary VLAN.

To verify your auxiliary VLAN configuration, use the **show port auxiliaryvlan vlan_id** command with the Cat OS or the **show interface interface_id switchport** command with the Native IOS. Also, note that when you are assigning IP address space to these auxiliary VLANs, many administrators prefer to use private IP address space (for example, the 10.X.X.X address space) for IP address preservation and for an added layer of security.

By default, Cisco IP Phones mark voice packets with a class of service (CoS) priority marking of 5. Traffic that is coming from an attached PC typically is marked with a CoS value of 0. Alternatively, you could specify a CoS value that the IP phone should assign to traffic that is coming from an attached PC. However, consider a situation in which you have one IP phone plugged into another IP phone, in a daisy-chain configuration. In that example, you should probably trust the CoS markings that are coming from that daisy-chained IP phone and not have the other IP phone rewrite those CoS markings to a 0 value. To trust the daisy-chained IP phone, you can configure your IP phone with an "extended trust," meaning that it trusts and does not remark incoming CoS values. Note, however, that Cisco does not support the daisy-chaining of IP phones.

Extended Trust

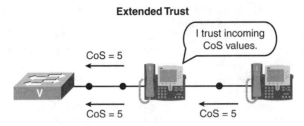

An IP phone can trust CoS markings from an attached device (for example, another IP phone) or assign a specific CoS value to frames coming from an attached device.

To assign a specific CoS value for traffic that is coming into an IP phone from a downstream device (for example, a PC or another IP phone), use the following command in the Cat OS:

```
Switch>(enable)set port qos <mod/port> cos-ext <cos_value>
```

Similarly, to indicate whether the CoS value of a downstream device is trusted or is not trusted, issue the following command in the Cat OS:

```
Switch>(enable)set port qos <mod/port> trust-ext <untrusted | trust-cos>
```

You also can configure CoS trust relationships in the Native IOS with the following command:

```
Switch(config-if)#switchport priority extend {cos_value | none | trust}
```

Connecting to the PSTN

A *gateway* moves traffic between the IP telephony environment and the PSTN or PBX. The two main types of gateways are *analog* and *digital* gateways. Analog gateways have port types such as Foreign Exchange Station (FXS), Foreign Exchange Office (FXO), and E&M. Digital gateways include port types such as T1, E1, and ISDN. (See the CVOICE quick reference sheets for more information on these port types.)

Typically, these gateways run either the H.323 or MGCP call control protocol. With H.323, call-forwarding intelligence is configured in the gateway. However, with an MGCP gateway, the gateway points to an external call agent (for example, a Cisco CallManager) for call-forwarding information. Although most Cisco MGCP gateways are IOS based, you can have a switch module, such as a module in the Catalyst 6500 running the Cat OS, acting as an MGCP gateway. Such a gateway is referred to as a *non-IOS MGCP gateway*. Most IOS gateways (for example, the 2600, 3600, 3700, and 7200 Series routers) can function as either an H.323 or an MGCP gateway. Look for the following four primary requirements in a gateway:

- **DTMF relay**—You want to send dual-tone multifrequency (DTMF) tones through the gateway without having those tones processed by a codec (which could degrade the tones to the point that they are unrecognizable).
- **CCM redundancy**—You want the gateway to fail over to a backup CCM if the primary CCM fails.
- **Supplementary services**—A gateway should be able to support services such as transfer, hold, and multiparty calling.
- **Call survivability**—A voice call should not be terminated if a CCM fails.

Dial Plans

Introduction

A dial plan, or a "route plan," in a PBX environment involves creating rules that dictate which phones can, for example, call long distance and which trunks should be used to place a particular call. You also must create route plans in the CCM environment. In addition, your CCM configuration allows you to limit calls. For example, perhaps you do not want employees making long-distance calls. You can restrict those types of calls using partitions and calling search spaces.

Designing Route Plans

Dial plans in the PBX environment were concerned primarily with accessing the PSTN. However, with your CCM, you need to support calls over the IP WAN and accommodate those calls that fall back to the PSTN if the IP WAN becomes unavailable. Such a fallback scenario might require you to add numbers to the originally dialed number (for example, area code and office code) prior to sending the dialed digits to the PSTN.

Specifically, the IP telephony network has the following types of calls:

- **On-cluster calls**—Calls that are made within the CCM cluster and do not require much configuration.
- **Off-cluster calls**—Calls that have a destination that is not a member of the local cluster. Therefore, these call types require external route patterns.

A CCM route plan typically uses a hierarchical approach. Following are the steps of the hierarchy:

Step 1 The user dials a number, and a route pattern matches that number.

Step 2 The route pattern points to a route list, which is a prioritized list of one or more route groups.

Step 3 The route groups point to the devices (for example, routers) that get the call to the destination, perhaps through the IP WAN or through the PSTN.

Route Plan Hierarchy

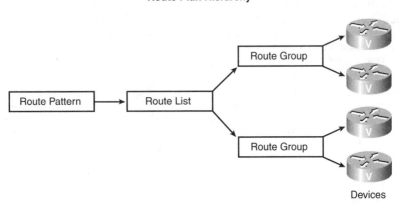

Devices

To configure these route patterns, start from the ground up, beginning with defining your gateways. Some gateways can go to the PSTN, whereas other gateways use the IP WAN. Therefore, create route groups that group common gateway types (for example, gateways that connect to the PSTN).

Next, define route lists, which are prioritized lists of route groups. For example, the route list can determine whether you prefer to use the PSTN or the IP WAN gateways as your first choice.

Finally, identify the route pattern, which matches the dialed digits and points to a route list. Consider each of these configuration steps, beginning with the gateway configuration.

Typically, you can select from the following types of gateways: intercluster trunk, non-IOS MGCP, MGCP, and H.323.

Note that an intercluster trunk is not technically a gateway. Rather, you can configure an intercluster trunk to join two CCM clusters. Therefore, when you place a call from one CCM cluster to another, rather than forwarding the call to a gateway, you forward the call across an intercluster trunk. To configure an intercluster trunk, select the **Device, Trunk** menu option and click the **Add a New Trunk** link.

To configure an H.323 gateway, select the **Device, Gateway** menu option and click the **Add a New Gateway** link. Then select H.323 as the gateway type. Note that H.323 gateways have call-forwarding intelligence locally configured on the gateway.

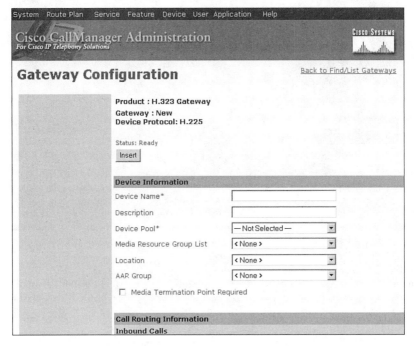

Unlike H.323, MGCP gateways point to an external call agent (for example, a CCM) for call-forwarding intelligence. To add an MGCP gateway, select the **Device, Gateway** menu option and click the **Add a New Gateway** link. Then, select the MGCP gateway's hardware platform from the drop-down menu.

The final gateway type is a non-IOS MGCP gateway, which runs the MGCP call control protocol on a device that is not running the Cisco IOS, such as a module in a Catalyst 6500 that is running the Cat OS. To add a new non-IOS MGCP gateway, select the **Device, Gateway** menu option and click the **Add a New Gateway** link. Again, select the appropriate MGCP gateway hardware platform.

When you have the appropriate gateways configured, create a route group, which is a prioritized listing of your gateways. To create a route group, select the **Route Plan, Route Group** menu option and click the **Add a New Route Group** link. Then name the route group and add the specific gateways that you want to be members of the route group, remembering that the order in which the gateways are listed determines the order in which the gateways are selected.

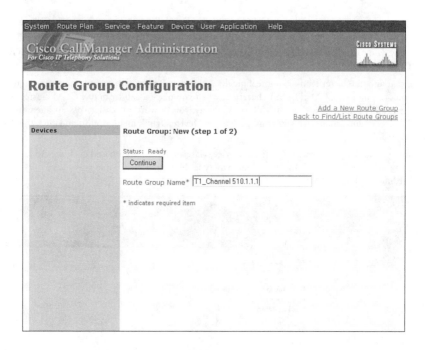

When the route groups are configured, define route lists, which are prioritized listings of route groups. For example, a route list could point first to a route group that forwards calls to the IP WAN. However, if no devices in that route group are available, the route list could point to a route group that forwards calls to the PSTN. To create a route list, select the **Route Plan, Route List** menu option and click the **Add a New Route List** link. Then, name the route list and select the route groups in the order that you want the route groups to be used. During this step, various "translation" options appear. These options are discussed later in these quick reference sheets.

Finally, create appropriate route patterns to match potential dial strings. These route patterns point to a route list, which is an ordered list of route groups. However, you do not want to create a route pattern for every possible dial string that a caller can dial. Therefore, you leverage the power of wildcard characters in the route pattern. Consider the following wildcard characters:

- **X**—This character represents a single dialed digit in the range 0 to 9.
- **@**—This symbol represents the North American Numbering Plan.
- **[x–y]**—Numbers in brackets identify a range of numbers, or specific numbers, that can match a single dialed digit. If a dash exists between the numbers, all numbers in that range of numbers are included.
- **[^x–y]**—Placing the caret character before numbers in brackets matches all numbers except those numbers that are defined in the brackets.
- **!**—This symbol represents one or more digits in the range 0 to 9. This wildcard is useful for international dialing, where the country code lengths can vary. To indicate to the CCM that the dialing is complete, a caller either can press the # key or wait for the interdigit timeout to expire.
- **.**—The period character indicates the end of an access code, such as the 9 key.
- **#**—This character indicates that a caller can press the pound key to end a dial string when matching a variable-length dial string (that is, a dial string with the ! wildcard).

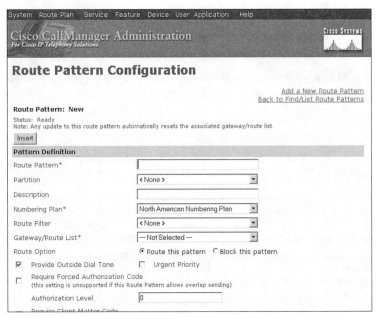

To reinforce these wildcards, consider the examples in the following table.

Numbers to Match	Route Pattern
2200–2299	22XX
2200–2499	2[2–4]XX
2200–2299 and 2400–2699	2[24–6]XX

To create a new route pattern, select the **Route Plan, Route Pattern** menu option and click the **Add a New Route Pattern** link. In the Route Pattern field, enter the numbers and wildcards that you are matching.

Understanding how a CCM matches dialed digits to a route pattern can help troubleshoot your route plans. The CCM looks at each digit individually and starts narrowing down the route patterns to ones that are potential matches. However, the caller receives a busy signal if the CCM determines that no matches are available.

After all the digits are dialed, if the CCM has more than one route pattern that matches all the digits, the CCM uses the most specific route pattern. For example, consider the following scenario:

> Dialed number: 555-1234

> CCM route pattern matches: 555-12XX, 555-12[2–4]X

In this example, the CCM uses the 555-12[2–4]X route pattern, because 100 potential matches exist for the 555-12XX route pattern whereas only 30 potential matches exist for the 555-12[2–4]X route pattern. Therefore, the 555-12[2–4]X route pattern is deemed to be more specific.

You can use a *route filter* to limit the patterns that are matched by the route pattern. For example, you probably do not want to match every dial string that is matched by the @ route pattern (that is, the North American Numbering Plan). With a route filter, used in conjunction with a route pattern, you can, for example, block 900 numbers, block calls to the local operator, and block calls to 411 information services.

The following four primary operators are used when configuring route filters:

- **==:** You can use the double equal sign operator to match a specific value.
- **NOT-SELECTED:** You can use this operator to indicate that the route filter does not apply to a specific parameter, such as an area code.
- **EXISTS:** You can use this operator to match a condition where a parameter, such as an area code, exists.
- **DOES-NOT-EXIST:** You can use this operator to match a condition where a parameter, such as an area code, does not exist.

As an example, you could filter calls to 900 numbers with the following route filter:

> AREA CODE == 900

You also might need to convert (that is, transform) a dialed number. For example, if callers have to dial a 9 to get an outside line before they dial the actual phone number, you probably do not want to forward the 9 to the PSTN. Therefore, you can use a *digit discard instruction,* telling the CCM not to forward the 9. In this example, if you had a route pattern of 9.@, you could use a "PreDot" digit discard instruction to instruct the CCM not to forward digits before the dot, which in this case is the 9. Another popular digit discard instruction is "10-10-Dialing," which instructs the CCM to discard the 1010XXX digits that callers can dial to select a specific long-distance carrier. You can even use multiple digit discard instructions in tandem.

Another powerful approach to manipulating dialed digits is to use a *transformation mask.* A calling party transformation mask can change caller ID information. For example, if you ran a tele-marketing firm, you could alter what appears on the caller ID display of the phones that your firm calls. Consider the example that is shown in the following table.

Directory number	12345
External phone number mask	859555XXXX
Result	8595552345
Calling party transformation mask	800555X000
Result	8005552000

In this example, notice that you are manipulating caller ID information with both an external phone number mask and with a calling party transformation mask. The external phone number mask is used for internal extensions. So, in this example, when extension 12345 dials another internal number, its caller ID information is transformed to 8595552345.

The calling party transformation mask determines what the caller ID information looks like when an external phone receives the call. In this example, the calling party transformation mask transforms caller ID information to 8005552000. Note that numbers flow through the mask positions that have an X, and the numbers are transformed when the corresponding mask position is set to a number.

You also can apply a called party transformation mask, which transforms the number that is actually being dialed. Consider the example that is shown in the following table.

Dialed number	8595551234
Called number transformation mask	XXXXXXX
Result	5551234

In this example, you are using a called party transformation mask to strip the area code from the dialed number. You can configure transformation masks from the Route Pattern Configuration or the Route List Configuration screens. If you configure the translation pattern within the Route Pattern Configuration screen, the number is transformed as it is dialed. However, if you configure the translation pattern within the Route List Configuration screen, you only transform the number if it is sent out of a gateway.

Besides transformation masks, you also can change dialed digits using a *translation pattern*. Consider that the range of numbers inside your company is 5000 to 5999. However, when outside users dial into your company, the last four digits of the DID (Direct Inward Dialing) numbers are 6000 to 6999. In this example, you could use a translation pattern to transform incoming 6XXX numbers to the internal 5XXX numbers. You can create or modify translation pattern from the **Route Plan, Translation Pattern** menu option.

System   Route Plan   Service   Feature   Device   User   Application   Help

Cisco CallManager Administration
For Cisco IP Telephony Solutions

CISCO SYSTEMS

Translation Pattern Configuration

Add a New Translation Pattern
Back to Find/List Translation Patterns

Translation Pattern: New
Status: Ready

Insert

Pattern Definition

Translation Pattern	
Partition	< None >
Description	
Numbering Plan*	North American Numbering Plan
Route Filter	< None >
Calling Search Space	< None >
Route Option	⊙ Route this pattern ○ Block this pattern
☑ Provide Outside Dial Tone	☑ Urgent Priority

Calling Party Transformations

☐ Use Calling Party's External Phone Number Mask

Calling Party Transform Mask

Route plans certainly can become complex. Therefore, Cisco offers a tool to let you view a comprehensive route plan report. Select the **Route Plan, Route Plan Report** menu option to enter the Route Plan Report utility. When you are in the utility, click the **View In File** link to open or save a .CSV-formatted route plan report.

Restricting Calls

PBXs use class of service definitions that dictate where a phone can call. For example, a class of service for a lobby phone might restrict that phone from placing international calls. In a similar fashion, you can use partitions and calling search spaces in a CCM environment to restrict calls. These terms are described as follows:

- **Partition**—A partition defines a grouping of numbers and typically contains route patterns or directory numbers. For example, phones that can reach one route pattern within a partition can reach all route patterns within the partition.
- **Calling search space**—A calling search space is a list of partitions in which a device (for example, an IP phone) is allowed to look when matching dialed digits.

Partitions and calling search spaces offer several advantages, including the ability to route calls by the geographic location of a phone (for example, to help prevent a 911 call from being routed to an incorrect location), the ability to assign different classes of users with different permissions, and the ability to assign different classes of "tenants" within a building (for example, where one tenant might be paying a monthly fee for long-distance service while the other tenant only wants to make local calls).

To create a partition, select the **Route Plan, Partition** menu option and click the **Add a New Partition** link. A window appears with a large text box where you can enter your partition names and optionally enter a description of the partition, using the format *Partition_Name, Description*.

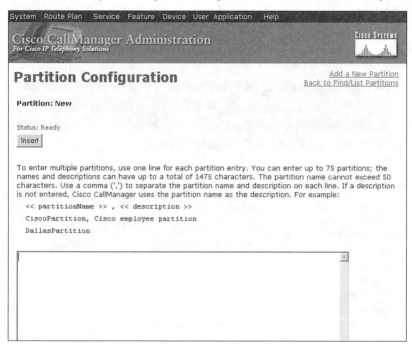

Again, calling search spaces (CSSs) list partitions (for example, directory numbers and route patterns) that can be reached. Then, the CSSs are assigned to devices, such as an IP phone, to define which partitions the devices can reach. To configure CSSs, select the **Route Plan, Calling Search Space** menu option and click the **Add a New Calling Search Space** link. Here, define the CSS name and define which partitions belong to the CSS. As a final step, configure a device (for example, an IP phone) to use a specific CSS. This final step associates your restrictions to the device.

Partitions and CSSs also can help route 911 calls. Note, however, that these quick reference sheets do not cover 911 call routing in the depth that is required to implement a 911 solution.

Consider a centralized CCM deployment, where IP phones at remote sites pointed back to a centralized CCM cluster. If an IP phone in Kentucky dialed 911, and the CCM that the IP phone was registered with was located in Florida, a 911 operator in Florida could answer the call and send emergency vehicles to the Florida location, instead of the Kentucky location. Therefore, you would want your CCM environment to be configured so that when an IP phone in Kentucky placed a 911 call, that call would be routed to the local PSTN.

For larger environments, you also might want to implement the Cisco Emergency Responder (CER) software. The CER software synchronizes the CCM cluster's phone database with the 911 Public Safety Answering Point (PSAP), which can identify the caller's approximate physical location.

One of the major benefits of IP phones is the ability to move those phones from location to location. However, if you move a phone to another location, you still need the CER software to know where the phone is located. Cisco's endpoint location technologies can use CDP, or a switch's CAM table, to identify the switch that a specific IP phone is connected to. Because the switch's location does not change, the CER software can use the switch location information to approximate the location for the IP phones.

Preventing WAN Bandwidth Oversubscription

A finite amount of bandwidth is available over the IP WAN, and if too many voice calls are placed across the IP WAN, the voice quality of all voice calls suffers. Therefore, you use Call Admission Control (CAC) mechanisms to prevent the oversubscription of WAN bandwidth.

One such CAC mechanism uses a gatekeeper (GK) to keep track of the number of calls and the codec used for those calls across the IP WAN. You can configure your CCM statically with a GK. After the CCM knows the location of a GK, the CCM registers with the GK using a registration request (RRQ) message. After the CCM registers with the GK, the CCM can request permission to place a call across the IP WAN using an admission request (ARQ) message, and the GK can respond with either an admission confirm (ACF) or admission reject (ARJ) message, based on available IP WAN bandwidth resources. Either the CCM or the GK can disconnect the call with a disengage request (DRQ) message. Also, if the CCM wants to change the codec during the call, the CCM can send a bandwidth request (BRQ) to the GK, and the GK can respond with either a bandwidth confirm (BCF) or bandwidth reject (BRJ) message.

Call Setup with GK

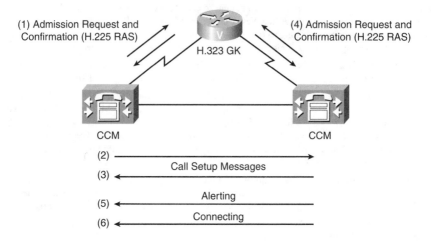

(1) Admission Request and Confirmation (H.225 RAS)

(4) Admission Request and Confirmation (H.225 RAS)

H.323 GK

CCM   CCM

(2) ——————————————→

Call Setup Messages

(3) ←——————————————

Alerting

(5) ←——————————————

Connecting

(6) ←——————————————

You can point to a GK by selecting the **Device, Gatekeeper** menu option and clicking the **Add a New Gatekeeper** link. After adding your GKs, you can trunk to those GKs by selecting the **Device, Trunk** menu option and clicking the **Add a New Trunk** link. The trunk type that you specify is an Inter-Cluster Trunk (Gatekeeper Controlled).

However, in a centralized CCM deployment model, you do not use a GK. Instead, you define a "location" for each site and specify how much bandwidth is available between that site and the central site, where the CCM cluster is located. Then, a CCM can make the decision as to whether a call should be permitted over the IP WAN, based on the codec in use and the number of concurrent calls over the IP WAN.

To configure a location, select the **System, Location** menu option and click the **Add a New Location** link. Then, simply name the location, specify the bandwidth that is available between this location and the central site, and click the **Insert** button.

Fault Tolerance

Centralized IP deployment models have the disadvantage of remote IP phones being rendered unusable if the IP WAN goes down, because the remote IP phones no longer have a path back to the centralized CCM cluster. To prevent such an occurrence, you can use Survivable Remote Site Telephony (SRST), which allows an IOS router at the remote site to provide limited support for those phones. Although SRST supports the basic IP phone features (for example, hold, transfer, PSTN dialing, internal dialing, and so on), higher-end features, such as conference calling and music on hold, are not provided.

You use four basic commands to configure SRST on an IOS router. The following configuration specifies that the IOS router uses an IP address of 10.1.1.1 when communicating with IP phones, using the Skinny protocol. Also, the maximum number of IP phones that can register with the SRST router is 10, and the maximum number of directory numbers configured on the SRST router is 10. The commands are as follows:

```
Router(config)#call-manager-fallback
Router(config-cm-fallback)#ip source-address 10.1.1.1
Router(config-cm-fallback)#max-ephones 10
Router(config-cm-fallback)#max-dn 10
```

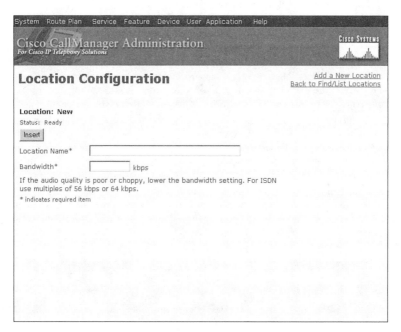

CCM version 3.3 allows you to point IP phones to another SRST router, other than the IP phone's default gateway. You enable SRST for your IP phones by creating an *SRST reference*. To create an SRST reference, select the **System, SRST** menu option and click the **Add a New SRST Reference** link. You can add multiple SRST references and then assign the SRST references to an IP phone's device pool.

IP Telephony Options

Introduction

Now that your route plans are configured, turn your attention to a few additional features that you can enable in your IP telephony network. Specifically, this section of the quick reference sheets discusses how to share your media resources among devices in a CCM cluster, how to manipulate an IP phone's softkeys, what features are available on the Cisco IP phones, and how to create user accounts.

Assigning CCM Media Resources

A CCM environment has two basic types of media resources: hardware media resources and software media resources. Hardware resources can use digital signal processors (DSPs) in a Catalyst 6500 switch, for example, to provide such features as transcoding or conference-calling resources. You also need media resources to provide a media termination point (MTP) and a music on hold (MOH) resource.

To activate your software media resources, use the CCM's Service Activation screen by selecting the **Application, Cisco CallManager Serviceability** menu option and then selecting the **Tools, Service Activation** menu option from the Cisco CallManager Serviceability screen. Select the services that you want to add (for example, Cisco IP Voice Media Streaming App), and click the **Update** button.

As mentioned earlier, you need media resources to support features such as a conference call. Following are two basic types of conference calls:

- **Ad hoc**—Occurs when a user dials one or more users into an existing call
- **Meet-me**—Occurs when all users dial a specific number at a specific time to join a conference

The size of a conference call depends on the resources that are dedicated to that conference call. For example, a CCM server that is acting as a software media resource can support 48 users in a single conference call or up to 16 users in each of three simultaneous conference calls.

You can add modules, such as the WS-X6608-T1/E1 for a Catalyst 6X00 switch or the WS-X4604-GWY for a Catalyst 4000 switch, to those specific Catalyst switches to provide hardware-conferencing resources. However, the WS-X4604-GWY module only supports the G.711 codec and a total of 24 conference resources, whereas the WS-X6608-T1/E1 module supports additional codecs (for example, G.729 and G.723) and up to 32 conferencing resources per port.

To set up a conference bridge, select the **Service, Media Resource, Conference Bridge** menu option and select the **Add a New Conference Bridge** link. Then, select the type of bridge (for example, hardware, software, or IOS bridge) and provide the required information. For example, for a hardware conference bridge, you might need to provide the MAC address for a specific port on the module that contains the DSPs.

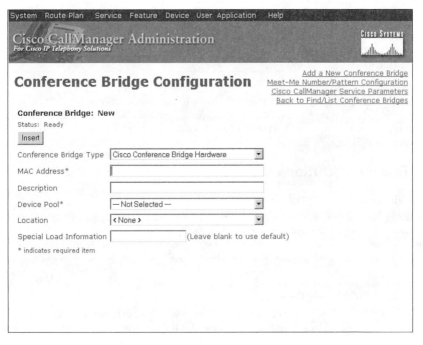

When a caller puts a call on hold, transfers a call, parks a call, or holds an ad hoc conference, he needs to terminate the original call temporarily while he, for example, dials in another participant for the call. To support these types of services, you need a media termination point (MTP), which the CCM provides. Specifically, the CCM supports 64 MTP resources.

To add an MTP, select the **Service, Media Resource, Media Termination Point** menu option and click the **Add a New Media Termination Point** link. You then enter some basic information about the MTP, including the host server, MTP name, and device pool.

Transcoding is the process of converting from a high-bandwidth codec to low-bandwidth codec, and vice versa. However, the CCM cannot perform transcoding. Hardware resources are required. The WS-X6608-T1/E1 module for the Catalyst 6000 Series switches supports transcoding for a variety of codecs and provides up to 24 transcoding resources per port. However, the WS-X4604-GWY module for the Catalyst 4000 Series switches supports transcoding only between the G.729 and G.711 codecs and a maximum of 16 conferencing resources per module.

When creating a transcoding resource, select the **Service, Media Resource, Transcoder** menu option and click the **Add a New Transcoder** link.

The CCM environment allows you to have live or recorded music on hold (MOH) for your users. You can assign an MOH audio source for the following types of holds:

- **User hold**—Occurs when a user presses the Hold button on a phone
- **Network hold**—Occurs when the network places a party on hold because the user pressed a key to perform an action, such as transfer, conference, or call park

MOH can be sent through unicast or multicast, which can offer significant bandwidth savings. Specifically, you can have a maximum of 500 unicast MOH streams or a maximum of 204 multicast MOH streams. Realize, however, that a single multicast MOH stream could service thousands of IP phones. To add an MOH audio source file to your CCM environment, you can drop an audio file (for example, an MP3 file) in the following directory on one of your CCM servers:

C:\Program Files\Cisco\MOH\DropMOHAudioSourceFilesHere

Then, the audio file is converted automatically to formats for use by the CCM and deleted from its original location.

After your MOH audio source files are converted for MOH use, you can view them from your Music On Hold (MOH) Audio Source Configuration screen by selecting the **Service, Media Resource, Music on Hold Audio Source** menu option. From this screen, select the **Play continuously (repeat)** check box to make your audio files loop. On this screen, you also can enable the multicast of MOH by selecting the **Allow Multicasting** check box.

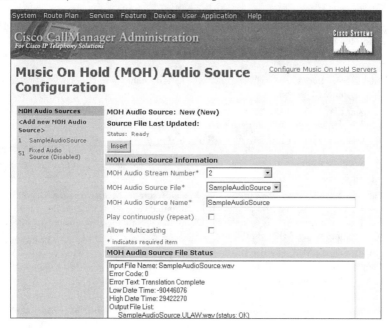

Instead of playing recorded music as your MOH, you also have the option of using an external music source. This external source connects to one of your CCM server's sound cards. You need to know the exact name of the preferred sound-recording device that is known to the CCM server. You can obtain this device name by opening the Sounds and Multimedia Control Panel icon and selecting the Audio tab.

You need the exact name of the audio source from the Control Panel because you need to specify the audio source in the Music On Hold (MOH) Fixed Audio Source Configuration screen. Access this screen by selecting the **Service, Media Resource, Music On Hold Audio Source** menu selection and clicking the **Fixed Audio Source** link in the **MOH Audio Sources** sidebar. Note that this will always be Audio Source #51.

In this screen, enter the audio source name and the audio source device. You also can specify whether you want to allow multicasting, and then finish by clicking the Update button. Now that the sources are defined, you can assign them to actual devices, using the user or network hold options.

You can share media resources such as MTPs, MOH, and transcoding devices by using media resource groups (MRGs) and media resource group lists (MRGLs). For example, you can create an ordered list of MTP resources, and if the first MTP resource is unavailable, you can use the next MTP resource. However, you probably do not want to use an MOH resource that is located across the IP WAN. So, you need to be careful in assigning these resources.

Media resources are configured in a hierarchical fashion, much like route plans. Consider how an IP phone gains access to a media resource. The following steps occur:

Step 1   A device (for example, an IP phone) requests a resource (for example, an MOH resource) from a media resource manager.

Step 2   The media resource manager points to a media resource group list (MRGL), which is a prioritized listing of media resource groups (MRGs).

Step 3   The MRGs point to specific resources.

Consider the following example. You have your CCM cluster spanning two geographical locations: Lexington and Louisville. You create a Lexington MRG, which points to media resources that are located in Lexington, and you create a Louisville MRG, which points to media resources that are located in Louisville. Then, you create an MRGL to be used by each location. For the Lexington location, the MRGL points first to the Lexington MRG and then points to the Louisville MRG as a backup. Conversely, the Louisville MRGL points to the Louisville MRG first and to the Lexington MRG second.

Now consider how to configure MRGs and MRGLs. First, understand that there is a default MRG, and by default, every IP phone in the cluster has access to that group. Therefore, you need to create unique MRGs and MRGLs and then point your IP phones and device pools to specific MRGLs. To create an MRG, select the **Service, Media Resource, Group** menu option and click the **Add a New Media Resource Group** link. Then, name the MRG and select the available resources that you want to be part of the MRG.

You create the MRGL by selecting the **Service, Media Resource, Media Resource Group List** menu option and clicking the **Add a New Media Resource Group List** link. At that point, name the list and associate your MRGs with the MRGL. Remember that the order is important, because this list determines which MRG is used first.

Then, you can assign MRGLs to an IP phone or a device pool. However, what would happen if you assigned one MRGL to an IP phone's device pool and another MRGL to the IP phone? Which MRGL would the IP phone use?

An MRGL that is assigned to an IP phone takes precedence over an MRGL that is assigned to the IP phone's device pool. Therefore, in this example, the IP phone uses only the MRGL that is assigned to the phone.

Media Resource Group Lists

Lexington_MRGL

Lexington_MRG

Conf_HW_Lex

MOH_Lex

Transcode_Lex

Louisville_MRG

Conf_HW_Lou

MOH_Lou

Transcode_Lou

Louisville_MRGL

Louisville_MRG

Conf_HW_Lou

MOH_Lou

Transcode_Lou

Lexington_MRG

Conf_HW_Lex

MOH_Lex

Transcode_Lex

Configuring Softkeys

Softkeys are buttons on an IP phone that have different functions in different circumstances. For example, while an IP phone is on-hook, one of the softkeys (for example, the buttons that are below the LCD on a Cisco 7940 or 7960 IP phone) is labeled "Redial," while that same softkey can be labeled "Hold" during a call. You can influence what these keys do by using either standard or nonstandard softkey templates.

By default, the CCM gives you the Standard IPMA Assistant, Standard IPMA Manager, and Standard User softkey templates. To create a new softkey template, make a copy of an existing template and make modifications to that copy. Access the Softkey Template Configuration screen by selecting the **Device, Device Settings, Softkey Template** menu option. Then, click the **Find** button to display the existing templates. Click the template that you want to copy, and click the **Copy** button.

After assigning a new name to your copy, click the **Configure Softkey Layout** link to specify the softkey functions under various conditions (for example, connected, on-hook, off-hook, and ring in). If you do not want certain IP phones to have access to some of the features that the softkeys provide (for example, conference calling), use this screen to remove those features from the softkey template that you will associate with the IP phones.

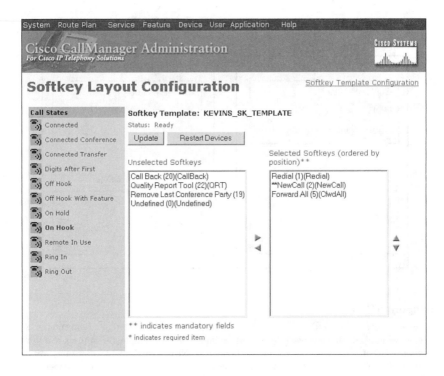

When the softkey template is defined, apply it to a device pool, a specific device (for example, an IP phone), or a user device profile (discussed later in these quick reference sheets). Be aware that after assigning a softkey template to a device pool, device, or user device profile, you must remove that assignment before you are allowed to delete a softkey template.

IP Phone Features Overview

Cisco IP Phones have a vast array of features for your users (for example, conference calling, transfer, and speed dial). Consider some of the more commonly used features. First, consider how to change an IP phone's speed-dial configuration.

Speed Dial

Administrators usually prefer to have users change their own speed-dial settings. For example, you might not want to change someone's speed-dial configuration every time that he gets a new girlfriend. As discussed later in these quick reference sheets, you can delegate such a task to the user. However, you do have the option of specifying the number and label that are associated with a specific IP phone's speed-dial configuration by clicking the **Add/Update Speed Dials** link in the Phone Configuration page.

Auto Answer

The "auto answer" feature allows a phone to answer a call as soon as it comes in. This type of feature can be useful for customer service agents who are wearing headsets. The auto answer feature is enabled through a drop-down menu in the Directory Number Configuration screen, where you can select between the Auto Answer Off, Auto Answer with Headset, and Auto Answer with Speakerphone options.

Barge

You might have called into a company's customer service department and heard a message similar to "This call might be monitored for quality assurance." The message is letting you know that another party can be added to the conversation. You can permit this in your CCM environment by enabling the "barge" feature (also known as "barge-in"). For the barge feature to work, however, the line in use must be a *shared line appearance,* meaning that the line appearance is present on more than one phone. You enable the barge feature on a cluster by selecting the True value for the Barge Enabled Flag parameter that is available on the Service Parameters Configuration screen.

Call Park

The "call park" feature allows a user to place a call (that is, "park" a call) in a location that is identified by a number. Then, the user can retrieve that parked call from the parked location from another phone. Call park can be configured from the **Feature, Call Park** menu option.

Call Pickup/Group Call Pickup

You can allow a phone, with a single key press, to pick up a call that currently is ringing on another phone within a defined group. If the phone is in the same defined group that your phone is a member of, you can do a "call pickup." However, if the phone is in a different group, you can press a group call pickup key and specify a group of the phone that is ringing. To configure call pickup, you need to define a directory number to be used by the call pickup feature. You do that by selecting the **Feature, Call Pickup** menu option and clicking the **Add a New Call Pickup Number** link. After you define the call pickup directory number, you can assign it to a specific line by using the Directory Number Configuration page for an IP phone.

Callback

If you call a number that is currently busy, you can use the "callback" feature to alert you when the originally called line is no longer busy. The callback feature can be assigned to a softkey on the Softkey Layout Configuration screen.

Call Forwarding

You can configure a phone to forward calls to a particular destination (for example, to a voice-mail system) under specific conditions (for example, always forward, forward when a line is busy, or forward when the line has not answered within a certain number of rings). Call forwarding is configured on the Directory Number Configuration page.

Cisco IP Manager Assistant (IPMA)

The IPMA feature improves call handling between managers and assistants. For example, calls coming into a manager's phone could be redirected to an assistant or to voice mail based on con-figured rules. You can set up the IPMA feature using the Cisco IPMA Configuration Wizard, which is available under the **Service, Cisco IPMA Configuration Wizard** menu option.

Shared Line Appearance

The "shared line appearance" feature allows you to have a directory number on more than one phone. Typically, the first phone to answer an incoming call has control of the line, and other phones with that line appearance cannot access that line for the duration of the call. However, as mentioned earlier, you can allow another phone to access the line, even if it is in use, if you have the barge feature enabled.

XML Services

Cisco IP phones, such as the 7940 and 7960, support eXtensible Markup Language (XML). As a result, you can access a variety of information (for example, stock quotes, news headlines, or weather information) through an XML application. You can point your IP phone to a specific URL that has XML content on the Cisco IP Phone Services Configuration page.

User Configuration

Instead of administering all features (for example, speed dial) for all IP phones in your environment, you can permit users to configure many of their own features through a web page. First, create a user account through the **User, Add a New User** menu option.

After you add a user, you can associate a device with that user. Note that you can have more than one device (for example, a Cisco 7940 and a Cisco IP SoftPhone) associated with a user.

After you have created the user account and associated it with one or more devices, you can allow the user to log in and configure her own settings by accessing http://*CCM_name_or_IP*/ccmuser.

After the user logs in, she can select the device for which she want to manipulate settings. For example, she might want to configure her speed-dial buttons, but one of her associated devices is a Cisco 7940 (with only one speed-dial button), and the other associated device is a Cisco 7960 (with a maximum of five speed-dial buttons). From this user interface, a user can configure the following features:

- Services (for example, weather information)
- Speed-dial buttons
- Call forwarding
- Personal address book
- Message-waiting indicator
- Locale (that is, the language that is used on the web interface or on the IP phone)

IP Telephony Applications

Introduction

This section covers add-on IP telephony applications, including the Attendant Console and IP SoftPhone. Also examined are messaging, conferencing, and call center solutions.

Attendant Console

In a PBX environment, a receptionist might need a large, bulky console with an attached 25-pair cable to manage multiple incoming calls for a department. Now, with the CCM Attendant Console, the receptionist can receive and forward a large number of incoming calls using a GUI interface. For redundancy, if a CCM server fails, the Attendant Console can fall back to a backup CCM server.

Several components work together to form the Attendant Console solution. First, the Attendant Console's server application is called the Telephony Call Dispatcher (TCD).

The CCM Attendant Console Client software runs on the client's (for example, the receptionist's) PC. Note that you can have a maximum of 96 CCM Attendant Console clients per CCM cluster. You also must create a user account for the attendant to log in to the Attendant Console.

You can have callers dial a single number (that is, a *pilot number*). However, this pilot number can point to a *hunt group*, which is a list of specific directory numbers that incoming calls can be distributed across. These directory numbers are called *hunt group members*. You can have multiple attendants acting as these hunt group members.

Note that you can have no more than 32 hunt groups per cluster and no more than 16 members in a hunt group. If you require a more scalable solution, the Cisco IP Contact Center (IPCC) is an option.

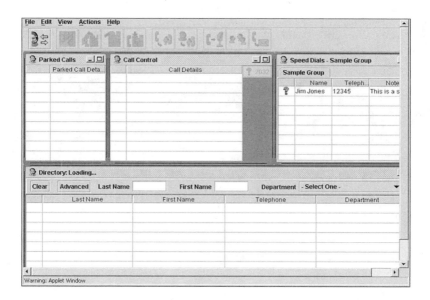

The three steps to configuring a CCM server to support the Attendant Console are as follows:

Step 1   Add users for the Attendant Console.

Step 2   Add a pilot number.

Step 3   Add a hunt group.

Consider each of these steps, beginning with adding users for the Attendant Console. Select the Service, **Cisco CM Attendant Console, Cisco CM Attendant Console User** menu option and click the **Add a New Attendant Console User** link to add an Attendant Console user.

Next, configure the pilot point, which defines the number that outside callers dial. Select the **Service, Cisco CM Attendant Console, Pilot Point** menu option, and click on the **Add a New Pilot Point** link. As part of this configuration, you can choose to route incoming calls to the hunt group member that has been idle the longest or to the first available hunt group member.

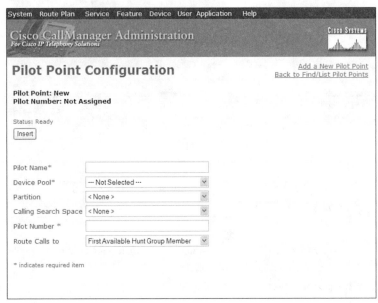

Finally, configure the hunt group by selecting the **Service, Cisco CM Attendant Console, Hunt Group** menu option. Then, select a pilot point from the left pane and click the **Add Member** button to add the specific directory numbers that comprise the hunt group.

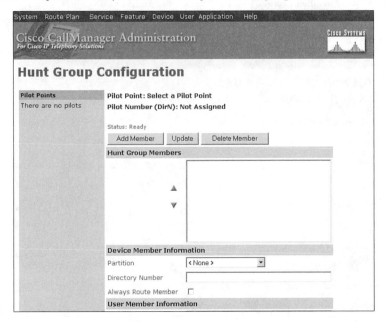

After you set up the CCM side of the Attendant Console, you can go to the client computer and download the Attendant Console client application by selecting the Cisco CallManager Administration's **Application, Install Plugins** menu option and clicking the **Cisco CallManager Attendant Console** icon.

IP SoftPhone

The Cisco IP SoftPhone is software that emulates the function of an IP phone. Because the IP SoftPhone runs on a PC, it can leverage a Lightweight Directory Access Protocol (LDAP) directory to locate user information. The IP SoftPhone is not free, however; you must pay a licensing fee.

You can use the Cisco IP SoftPhone by itself, or use it in conjunction with an actual IP phone. The Cisco IP SoftPhone application provides keyboard shortcuts, which minimize the number of times that a user needs to use a mouse.

Note that the resources (that is, device units) that are consumed by the Cisco IP SoftPhone are greater than the resources that are consumed by a Cisco IP Phone. In CCM version 3.2, under low call-volume conditions, the Cisco IP SoftPhone consumed 20 device units, whereas the Cisco IP Phone consumed only 1. This ratio is much improved in CCM version 3.3. Now, a Cisco IP SoftPhone consumes only two device units under low call-volume conditions.

To configure support for the Cisco IP SoftPhone, first create a CTI port for each of your SoftPhones by selecting the **Device, Phone** menu option and clicking the **Add a New Phone** link. From the Phone type drop-down menu, select **CTI Port**. Finally, enter the device name, select the appropriate device pool, and click the **Insert** button.

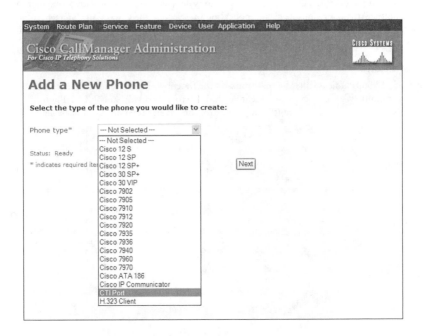

Next, enable a user to use the CTI port. In the User Configuration screen, select the **Enable CTI Application Use** check box and click the **Update** button (or the **Insert** button for a new user). Then, associate the CTI port with a user account. On the User Information page, click the **Device Association** link. You can then search the available devices, check the CTI port that you added, and click the **Update** button.

The Cisco IP SoftPhone software is installed on the user's PC. As part of the setup, you specify the username, password, and one or two CCM servers. When you install the Cisco IP SoftPhone, a TAPI Service Provider (TSP) is added to your system. This TSP (that is, the ciscotsp001.tsp TSP) can be configured from the Phone and Modem Options or the Telephony Control Panel icon if you want to reconfigure these username, password, or CCM server options. When it is first launched, the Cisco IP SoftPhone displays the lines that you can select from. Select your lines and click **OK**.

Configuring Extension Mobility

With the "extension mobility" feature, a user can log in to a phone, and his profile will be applied to the phone. Therefore, a user can receive, for example, his speed-dial and softkey settings on different phones throughout an enterprise. Specifically, a user can press the **Services** button on an IP phone to log in to the phone; this retrieves the user's profile.

The following six basic steps are required to configure extension mobility:

Step 1 Start the extension mobility service on the CCM server. Enter the Cisco CallManager Serviceability application by selecting the **Application, Cisco CallManager Serviceability** menu option. From the Cisco CallManager Serviceability screen, select the **Tools, Service Activation** menu option. Select the **Cisco Extended Functions** and **Cisco Extension Mobility Logout** check boxes, and click the **Update** button.

Step 2   Create a new service to be used by extension mobility. Select the **Feature, Cisco IP Phone Services** menu option, and click the **Add a New IP Phone Service** link. Name the service, and enter the following in the Service URL field:

http://*CCM_IP_address*/emapp/EMAppServlet?device=#DEVICENAME#

Later, you will assign this service to devices that require extension mobility.

Step 3   As a best practice, tweak the service parameters. Select the **Service, Service Parameters** menu option. From the drop-down menus, select the appropriate CCM server and the Cisco Extension Mobility Logout service. Select **True** for the Enforce Maximum Login Time service. Change the Maximum Login Time to 168:00.

In the Multiple Login Behavior field, select Auto Logout, which allows a user to log in to a phone while automatically logging him out of a phone that he had previously logged in to. Choose **True** for the Alphanumeric Userid field. Select **False** for the Remember last user logged in field. Then, click the **Update** button to apply your changes.

Step 4   Create a default device profile for each IP phone. Select the **Device, Device Settings, Device Profile Default** menu option, and click the **Add a New Device Profile Default** link. Select the device type from the Device Type drop-down menu. Select the settings (for example, music on hold, locale, and phone button template) that you want to be applied to an IP phone when no one is logged in to the phone.

Step 5   Create device profiles for the users. Select the **Device, Device Settings, Device Profile** menu option, and click the **Add a New User Device Profile** link. Specify the user device profile name and the associated settings for a particular device type. When finished, click the **Insert** button.

Step 6   Configure the phone to use the extension mobility feature. Select the **Device, Phone** menu option, and click the **Find** button to locate the phone that you want to configure for extension mobility. Click the desired phone, and then click the **Subscribe/Unsubscribe Services** link. Select the service that you created in Step 2. Click the **Continue** button, and then click the **Subscribe** button. On the Phone Configuration page, select the **Enable Extension Mobility Feature** check box. In the Logout Profile drop-down menu, select the **Use Current Device Settings** option. Finally, click the **Update** button.

Add-On Applications

Cisco also offers numerous add-on applications to enhance the functionality of the CCM solution. Following are a few examples of these applications:

- **Unity**—The Cisco Unity product provides a converged messaging solution. Specifically, Cisco Unity allows e-mail messages, fax messages, and voice-mail messages to reside in a single location. You can then, for example, retrieve your fax messages through e-mail or your e-mail messages through a phone call, thanks to Cisco Unity's text-to-speech conversion capabilities.

- **IP IVR**—The Cisco IP Interactive Voice Response (IVR) application supports the integration of database information with the IP telephony system. For example, when you call in to your automated banking system and provide your PIN to receive your account balance, you are using an IVR system.

- **Personal Assistant**—The Cisco Personal Assistant application offers you tremendous control over incoming and outgoing calls. For example, if your children call, you might want the call to be transferred to your cell phone. If your phone rings between 5 p.m. and 8 p.m., you might want the call to be transferred to your home phone. The Cisco Personal Assistant can accommodate such requirements.

- **IP Auto Attendant**—The Cisco IP Auto Attendant allows a caller to navigate a menu to reach a particular extension or department. This feature can reduce receptionist staffing expenses.
- **CRS**—The Cisco Response Solution (CRS) version 3.0 software supports other applications, such as IVR applications. Essentially, simple applications (for example, weather reports or news headlines on a phone's display) use XM, whereas more complex applications (for example, contact center applications) rely on the CRS.
- **IP ICD**—The Cisco IP Integrated Contact Distribution (ICD) application can be used for smaller call center environments and has the ability to route calls intelligently.
- **Conference Connection**—The Cisco Conference Connection supports larger conference calls that you could accommodate with either a CCM software conference bridge or a DSP-enabled hardware conference bridge.
- **IPCC**—The Cisco IP Contact Center (IPCC) is a much more robust solution than ICD for routing calls intelligently. Specifically, Cisco's IPCC is appropriate for large contact centers. You could even have a "virtual call center," in which customer service agents work from home.

Administrative Utilities

Introduction

At this point in these quick reference sheets, you understand how to manually add users, gateways, lines, and phones to a CCM's database. However, you might need to configure many of these devices as you, for example, roll out IP telephony to a new department or location within your company. Fortunately, Cisco offers a tool to help you make bulk changes. This tool, in addition to a collection of troubleshooting tools, is considered in this section of the quick reference sheets.

BAT

The Bulk Administration Tool (BAT) allows you to import many devices, users, lines, and gateways into the CCM database. This can save the time that is required to make each addition manually. You also can use BAT in conjunction with TAPS, the Tool for Auto-Registered Phone Support. Specifically, you can add a group of phones that are configured with a "dummy" MAC address using BAT. Then, if the auto registration feature is enabled, you or your users can dial a TAPS directory number to download the phone's configuration and to update the CCM database with the phone's correct MAC address.

You can download and install the BAT utility from the Cisco CallManager Administration's **Application, Install Plugins** menu option.

You must install the BAT utility on the CCM server that is acting as the SQL Publisher. As part of the installation, Excel templates are copied to the C:\CiscoWebs\BAT\Excel\Templates directory. You can use these templates for bulk phone, gateway, line, or user configurations.

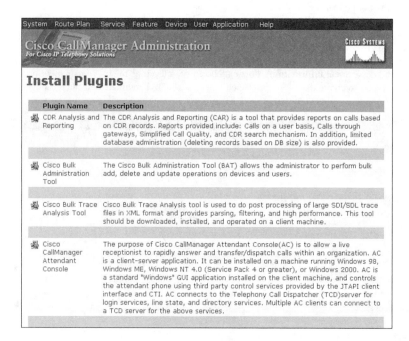

In the BAT utility, you can set up a template for different types of phones. From the screen that is shown in the following figure, you can specify things such as the device type, device pool, calling search space, and music on hold information.

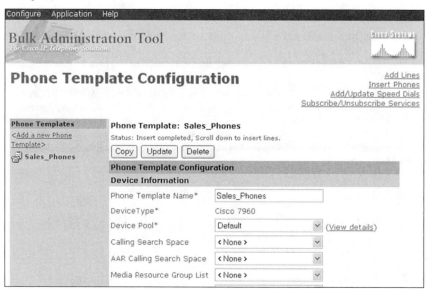

You then specify line-specific information, such as call waiting. Also, you can specify parameters such as partition information for specific lines. At this point, you have created your BAT template and defined generic values for users, devices, and so on. The next piece of the BAT puzzle is to create a .CSV (comma-separated value) file that has specific values (for example, usernames, passwords, and department information). Fortunately, you can leverage the previously mentioned Excel templates to create this .CSV file. When you have the BAT template and the .CSV file, you can, for example, combine the two in the BAT utility to create the actual users.

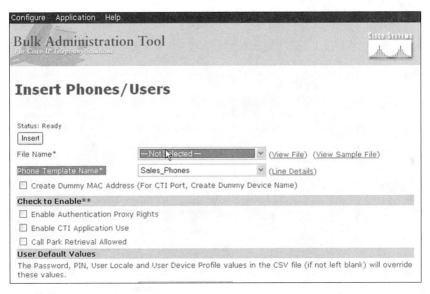

If you are using BAT to add phones to your CCM database, the TAPS utility can help you avoid having to add all of the phones' MAC addresses manually. To install TAPS, you need access to the CCM Publisher's database. You also must install the Cisco Customer Response Solution (CRS) application.

After installing TAPS, you need a CTI route point with a directory number. Specify the call-forwarding behavior for that DN, and create one or more CTI ports and a user who has permission to control the CTI route point and ports. Then, create a partition that restricts auto-registered IP phones to the CTI route point number. At that point you, or preferably your users, can dial this number to download a phone's configuration and to update the CCM database with the phone's correct MAC address information.

Troubleshooting

You can use several Microsoft and Cisco utilities to troubleshoot issues in your CCM environment. For example, because the CCM runs on a Windows 2000 server, you can leverage the Windows Event Viewer to view errors with the CCM application.

After you have installed the CCM on a Windows 2000 server, you can install additional Performance Monitor options. As a best practice, you should use the Performance Monitor to take baseline performance measurements when the CCM environment is operating normally. Then, you can compare that baseline to Performance Monitor data that you collect when you are troubleshooting a CCM issue.

As another best practice, when you change a password on one CCM server in a cluster, you should make cluster-wide password changes. In addition to the Administrator account, which is part of a default Windows 2000 server installation, the Cisco CallManager installation creates user accounts, including "SQLSvc" and "sa." Although the Administrator account password can be different on various CCM servers in a cluster, having unique passwords on different servers could cause confusion when you are using the Cisco CallManager Administration web interface.

Microsoft SQL server has its own tool for monitoring CCM database services. You might leverage this tool, the SQL Server Enterprise Manager, to troubleshoot database replication issues. You also can use this tool to determine whether a particular CCM server is a Publisher or a Subscriber. If a CCM server is a Publisher, the SQL Server Enterprise Manager shows a Publications folder for that server. Alternatively, you see a Pull Subscriptions folder on a Subscriber.

As a reminder, for troubleshooting database-replication issues, the Publisher has the only writable copy of the database. The Publisher then pushes database changes to Subscribers in the CCM cluster. As a result, if the Publisher goes down, you cannot make changes or additions to the CCM cluster. A common point of confusion comes from the misconception that you can recover from such a situation by promoting a Subscriber to a Publisher. Unfortunately, that is not an option. Rather, you have to rebuild the Publisher and restore the database information from a backup.

If a Subscriber fails, you can rebuild the Subscriber CCM, and when it is back up, you can "pull" the current database from the Publisher. So, when recovering from a Subscriber failure, you do not need to worry about restoring the database from a backup copy.

You might be using the Data Connection Directory (DC-Directory) application to maintain your user directory. Various DC-Directory tools are available to repair synchronization issues between servers in the cluster. Also, if you have SQL expertise, you might want to use the SQL Query Analyzer to troubleshoot SQL issues.

When working with the Cisco Technical Assistance Center (TAC), you might need to know the specific versions of CCM components that are running on your system. You can view this information by selecting the **Help, Component Versions** Cisco CallManager Administration menu option. In addition, you can click the Details button in the Cisco CallManager Administration main window to view additional version and database information.

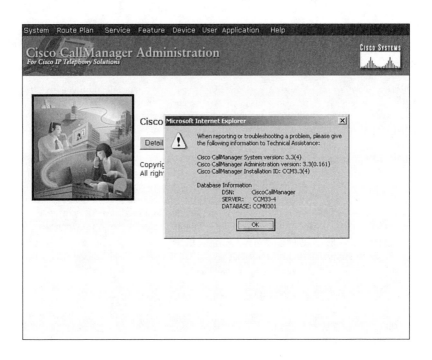

Besides the GUI diagnostic and troubleshooting utilities that are at your disposal, the CCM installation also installs various command-line utilities. For example, the **show db tables** command can interrogate database information from the command line.

The Windows 2000 operating system also provides various command-line tools that are useful in your troubleshooting efforts, including the following:

- **net start**—This command manually starts and stops Windows services.
- **ping**—This command tests connectivity with an IP address.
- **nslookup**—This command can resolve a DNS name to an IP address.
- **netstat**—This command displays current sessions.

From the Cisco CallManager Administration screen's Application menu, launch the Cisco CallManager Serviceability application. From this application, you can configure alarms and trace files. For example, you can configure alarms to send you e-mail when a certain condition (for example, exceeding a specific usage threshold) is met. Also, you can configure trace files to view extremely detailed transaction information.

On the Cisco CallManager Serviceability page, you can access the **Control Center** menu option, from which you can start and stop services and view the current status of services.

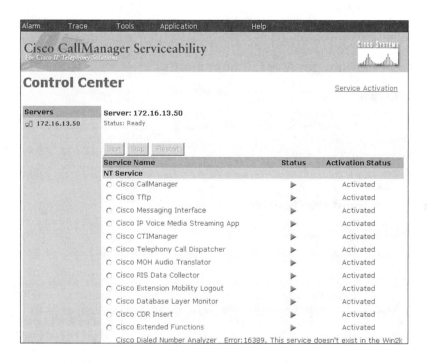

The Real-Time Monitoring Tool (RTMT) can give you real-time information about what is happening within a CCM cluster.

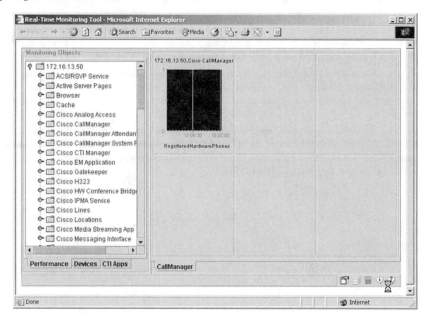

For example, you can see the active calls and phones that have registered, which could be valuable in forecasting expansion needs.

Cisco CallManager 4. *x* Enhancements

Introduction

The primary focus of these quick reference sheets has been on CallManager 3.3, which reflects the content in the CIPT course at the time of publication. In the future, however, readers can face certification questions regarding CCM 4.*x*. Although the fundamental architecture of the CCM has not changed, additional features are introduced in CCM 4.*x*. Therefore, this section of the quick reference sheets highlights several of the most significant enhancements that are found in version 4.*x* of the CCM.

System Administration Features

One of the most significant enhancements in CCM 4.*x* is a collection of security features. The CCM has the following two modes of security:

- **Non-secure mode**—This mode is the default mode of the CCM. In this mode, security features are disabled.
- **Mixed mode**—The newly introduced secure mode uses digital certificates to authenticate phones with the CCM. However, when CCM 4.*x* was introduced, only the Cisco 7970 IP phone included a factory-installed certificate. The 7940 and 7960 phones can use the Certificate Authority Proxy Function (CAPF) service for certificates. In addition to RTP voice packets, call control packets between a Cisco IP phone and the CCM can be encrypted. An IP phone can operate in the non-secure, authenticated, or encrypted mode. Therefore, an IP phone can use the authentication feature without necessarily encrypting voice packets. Even TFTP configuration files can be signed digitally for authentication purposes.

Video endpoints also are supported in CCM 4.*x*. Also, to preserve a customer's existing investment, CCM 4.*x* can interoperate with existing H.323-based video systems.

Whereas previous CCM versions functioned in H.323 and MGCP call control environments, CCM 4.*x* adds Session Initiation Protocol (SIP) functionality. Specifically, CCM 4.*x* supports SIP trunks, which allow the CCM environment to communicate with SIP networks.

For troubleshooting, the Dialed Number Analyzer (DNA) utility makes its debut in CCM 4.*x*. The DNA utility allows administrators to view detailed call setup information. For example, an administrator can see which route pattern matches and which transformation mask is applied to a dialed number.

Cisco also enhanced many of its existing features, such as hunt groups, the Cisco TSP, H.323, Trace features, network management, RTMT, and BAT. For a more comprehensive listing of new CCM 4.*x* features, visit http://www.cisco.com/en/US/products/sw/voicesw/ps556/products_qanda_item 09186a00801f8e18.shtml.

User Features

CCM users who need multiple speed-dial buttons might have been restricted by the limited number of speed-dial buttons that were found on phones such as 7940 (with a maximum of one speed-dial button) and the Cisco 7960 (with up to five speed-dial buttons). However, CCM 4.*x* introduces *abbreviated dialing*, which allows a user to dial a number by pressing only three buttons. Specifically, the user presses the AbbrDial button, followed by two digits. A total of 99 abbreviated dialing entries are supported. A user can configure his abbreviated dial settings through http:// CCM_*IP_address*/CCMUser/speeddial.asp.

CCM 4.*x* also enhances a user's privacy. Consider that your extension number also appears as a shared-line appearance on your manager's phone. Perhaps you do not want your manager reviewing the name and number for a particular call that you received, or you do not want your manager to use the barge feature to join the call. You can now prevent such an occurrence by pressing a Privacy button (that is, a line button that is configured as a Privacy button) when you receive an incoming call. Alternatively, you can already be engrossed in your conversation and then decide to enable the privacy feature for that call.

Malicious calls (for example, harassing or threatening calls) also can be flagged quickly by users who have the Malicious Call ID (MCID) softkey enabled on their phones. This feature can mark a call as malicious in the CCM call detail records, send a network management trap, and even notify the local central office of the malicious call. Such a feature can expedite dramatically the apprehension of an offender.

Finally, consider a situation in which you are in an important meeting and your phone rings. Instead of waiting for the phone to continue ringing for a predetermined number of rings before being forwarded to voice mail, you can use the Immediate Divert feature to send the incoming call directly to voice mail, by pressing the iDivert softkey. The Immediate Divert feature is not limited to incoming calls, however. You also have the ability to divert active calls, or calls that you currently have on hold, to voice mail. A logical question would be "Can you divert calls to a number other than voice mail (for example, your cell phone number)?" With the initial release of CCM 4.*x*, diverting calls to a nonvoice number is not supported.

For a comprehensive data sheet, including new and existing CCM 4.*x* features, visit http:// www.cisco.com/en/US/products/sw/voicesw/ps556/products_data_sheet 09186a00801f8e2e.html.

NOTES

NOTES

NOTES